Ethical Reflections

Ethical Reflections

Essays on Moral Themes

by

Henry Stob

William B. Eerdmans Publishing Company

255 Jefferson Ave. S.E., Grand Rapids, Mich. 49503

Printed in the United States of America

Library of Congress Cataloging in Publication Data

Stob, Henry, 1908–
Ethical reflections.

1. Christian ethics—Reformed authors—Addresses, essays, lectures. I. Title.
BJ1251.S86 241'.04'57 77-16258
ISBN 0-8028-1708-4

To Hilda
Wes and Ellen
Dick and Nancy
Amy and Elizabeth

Grateful acknowledgment is due for permission to reprint the following articles:

"Ethics: A Preliminary Characterization," from "Social Ethics" in BAKER'S DICTIONARY OF CHRISTIAN ETHICS, edited by Carl F. H. Henry. Copyright 1973 by Baker Book House and used by permission.

"Ethics: An Account of its Subject Matter," from "Ethics: With What Does it Deal?" in the *Calvin Theological Journal* XI, 1 (1976) and used by permission.

"God and Man," from "Justification and Sanctification: Liturgy and Ethics" in MARBURG REVISITED, edited by J. I. McCord. Copyright © 1966 by Augsburg Publishing House and used by permission.

"The Ethics of Jonathan Edwards," from FAITH AND PHILOSOPHY, edited by Alvin Plantinga. Copyright © 1964 by Wm. B. Eerdmans Publishing Co. and used by permission.

"The Concept of Justice," from "Observations on the Concept of Justice" in the *Calvin Theological Journal* IX, 2 (1974) and used by permission.

"Nuclear Warfare," from "Is Nuclear War Justifiable? An Ethics Professor's View" in *Christianity Today*, June 21, 1963. Copyright 1963 by *Christianity Today* and used by permission.

"Social Strategy: Christian Power Organizations," from "Christian Organizations" in *The Reformed Journal,* October, 1963. Copyright © 1963 by the Wm. B. Eerdmans Publishing Co. and used by permission.

"Christian Ethics and Scientific Control," from THE SCIENTIST AND ETHICAL DECISION, edited by Charles Hatfield. © 1973 by Inter-Varsity Christian Fellowship and used by permission of InterVarsity Press.

"Abortion," from *The Banner,* June 4, 1971 and *The Reformed Journal,* March, 1976 and used by permission.

"Judgment: Divine and Human," from "Judging, Judgment," in THE ZONDERVAN PICTORIAL ENCYCLOPEDIA OF THE BIBLE by Merrill C. Tenney. Copyright © 1975 by The Zondervan Corporation. Used by permission.

Foreword

IN JUNE, 1975, Henry Stob completed an enviable career of thirty-six years on the faculty of Calvin College and Seminary. It was a happy providence that placed me under his tutelage for seven of those years and a fortunate coincidence that in the year of his retirement I was able to invite him to present the lectures in the annual *Detroit Lectureship in Contemporary Thought*. It was the timely stimulus of those lectures that led to this book.

Dr. Stob is the most provocative and profound teacher in my experience. The clarity, relevance, and scope of the essays in this book are adequate evidence of that. To make permanently and generally available what has previously been enjoyed so much by so few of those who will now find stimulation and growth in becoming students of Henry Stob is ample apology for this work.

Henry Stob did not come by accident into his destiny as a teacher, philosopher, and Christian mentor. He rose to that stature by wise forethought, a gracious providence, and diligent work. His forethought is evident in his decision in 1925, at the age of seventeen, to leave his two-year employment with the Chicago Machine and Washer Company for further education at Chicago Christian High School, in preparation for degrees in Philosophy and Theology at Calvin College and Seminary. At the College he studied under William Harry Jellema. At the Seminary he was a student of Clarence Bouma and Louis Berkhof.

A scholarship to Hartford Theological Seminary led to a ThM in 1936 and an exchange scholarship led him to the University of Göttingen for a PhD in 1938. Stob's dissertation was *Eine Untersuchung zu Max Webers Religionssociologie* and was published in German by Dietrich Verlag in 1938. During his stay in Europe, Stob also studied under Vollenhoven and Dooyeweerd at the Vrije Universiteit te Amsterdam. In 1939 Dr. Stob accepted an appointment to the faculty of philosophy at Calvin College. From 1939 to 1943, when he began a three-year stint as a naval officer, he was the sole Professor of Philosophy at Calvin, teaching the full curriculum of courses for the entire department. In 1946 he returned to the position, and in

1952 was appointed Professor of Ethics and Apologetics at Calvin Seminary, a position in which he remained until he retired.

This publication deals with three facets of the discipline of ethics: theological underpinnings, theoretical principles, and practical application in moral Christian life. Dr. Stob has organized these matters in his typically lucid and logical fashion, dividing the twenty-four essays into seven parts, ranging from definitions in ethics to treatment of such concepts as love, justice, and freedom, and such currently relevant issues as nuclear warfare and abortion.

The book is directed to the Christian reader. It is essentially explicative of the Christian way, not apologetic. It requires a thoughtful, motivated reader and, for such, will be found pleasant, profound, and illuminating. Such a series in ethics could not come at a more crucial moment in our cultural and spiritual history as American Christians. Though it is the distillation of years of reflection and formulation, the book is fresh and lively in its pointed address to our current ethical dilemmas. In it all Henry Stob's erudition as a scholar, teacher, and philosopher is prominently evident.

Genuinely to understand and appreciate Henry Stob and his work, it must be clearly seen that he is a *Reformed* scholar. He knows Medieval thought thoroughly, has a substantial appreciation for Lutheranism, and holds a deep and broad scope of scholarly insight against the backdrop of the classical culture of the ancient world. But he is Reformed. He stands solidly in the tradition of John Calvin, and of the nineteenth-century Dutch theologian and statesman Abraham Kuyper. Kuyper contended nearly a century ago for the notion that Christ is Lord in every sphere of life. That is Stob's business in this book—to inquire and declare what is *God's* business in Christian life and social order, *God's* business with love, justice, and freedom among men. That is the enterprise of God's sovereign claim on every facet of human experience.

I am personally honored to provide the foreword to this valuable volume from Dr. Stob—returning to him the bread of enriched living he first cast upon my life's waters a quarter century ago. I return it with a sense of urgency driven by the warmth of love, with a sense of awe stirred by the love of wisdom, and with inexpressible gratitude because he incarnated an "abundant kind of living" I learned to share.

—J. Harold Ellens

Contents

Preface

THE FOLLOWING essays, several of which have not previously appeared in print, are here assembled through the courtesy of the publisher and sent into the world at the behest of a number of students with whom it has been my privilege to be associated in the never-ending quest for knowledge and understanding.

I release them with some hesitation. There is not much in them that has not been said before, and those who know the relevant literature will discern how deeply in debt I am to other writers in the field. To all of them, too numerous to mention, I am very grateful.

I want to give special thanks to the Rev. Dr. J. Harold Ellens, my friend and colleague, without whose promptings and initiatives these essays would have remained in limbo. I thank him for many kindnesses performed with solicitude and grace.

Three of the essays here appearing were delivered as the Morgan Lectures at Fuller Theological Seminary, and to the trustees of the Morgan Foundation I express my hearty thanks. The reception I received on the Fuller campus was very generous, and I retain the most pleasant memories of the Christian hospitality afforded me by faculty and students alike.

One of the essays commemorates my involvement over a number of years with the several participants in the Reformed-Lutheran Talks. From these Christian gentlemen I learned much, and I share with them the hope that the two reformational bodies may, in faithfulness to the Gospel, be someday joined in table and pulpit fellowship.

The Wm. B. Eerdmans Publishing Company has been most kind. Messrs. Eerdmans, Van Elderen, and Pott have done everything to facilitate publication, and I herewith tender them my thanks.

The dedication is to my wife who in loving partnership has for more than forty years shared my life with grace and patience, and enriched it with her wisdom; and to my children who, though they sometimes suffered under my preoccupations, have supported and strengthened me with their understanding and affection; and to my little granddaughters, in whom Hilda and I rejoice, and whom, with all God's children, we commend to the care of our heavenly Father.

—Henry Stob

Part I

THE NATURE OF ETHICS

1

Ethics: A Preliminary Characterization*

ETHICS IS conveniently defined as the science of morality, morality being understood as the set of judgments people make regarding what is right or wrong, good or bad, in the relations within or between individual or collective centers of intelligence and will.

It is sometimes said that all ethics is social, since man, the agent of morality, is by nature, and therefore inalienably, social. There is no doubt that man is social in this way; he has no ultimate privacy. It is true, accordingly, that when he acts others are unavoidably affected by what he does; his choices and decisions have social consequences. It is equally true that a man's moral behavior is significantly influenced by the community in which he is imbedded and by the social history which is his heritage and, in a sense, his destiny. It is true also that more often than not man acts not as a single individual, but as a member of a group which includes and overarches him, and of which he is ineluctably representative. But these facts, important as they are, do not make meaningless or unimportant the traditional distinctions between personal, interpersonal, and social ethics.

As already observed, men are not sheer unrelated atoms of being. But they nevertheless are individuals, unique centers of consciousness and power. And because they reside on a vertical as well as horizontal plane of existence they are able through the exercise of their God-oriented freedom to transcend the social matrix. This transcendence is indeed the reason why individuals are able to work creatively on social structures and processes. But this feature of man's existence also provides a charter for that department of ethics which has come to be called personal. Personal ethics cannot be finally isolated from social ethics, but, unlike the latter, it does not concentrate on collectivities and communities or on impersonal structures and arrangements. It concentrates instead upon the individual moral agent who lies behind and participates in these. Personal ethics contemplates man as a centered self, and

*This article appeared first in *Baker's Dictionary of Christian Ethics,* Carl F. H. Henry, ed. (Grand Rapids: Baker, 1973).

it observes and evaluates the development within him of those habits, postures, attitudes, and traits which characterize him as a person. Since in Christian perspective true personhood is unthinkable outside a man's relation to God, Christian personal ethics is as much concerned with the "supernatural graces" of man as it is with man's "socially redemptive virtues," though it never regards these as antithetical or unrelated. Personal ethics, then, may be said to be chiefly concerned with self-discipline, with character formation, and with the cultivation and development of those virtues and graces which fit him for the discharge of his religious and social responsibilities.

Since an individual or person is never merely centered on himself, but always stands in relationships, ethics cannot restrict itself to a consideration of the moral agent as such. It must also contemplate the person in his attitudes and actions toward others, and in the first instance toward those others whom he meets in individual or one-to-one encounter. These sorts of encounters take place all the time; individuals meet other individuals in a vast variety of situations, and they are required to respond to each other in morally appropriate ways. Interpersonal ethics is concerned with human behavior on this level and in these restricted contexts. Enveloping social structures cannot be ignored in this branch of ethics, for they simply exist and must be reckoned with, but critical attention is not focused on them. What is chiefly considered here is the moral response an individual makes to the neighbor who is immediately present to him—a response not mediated through the structures and agencies of society, but a response made directly and with a certain degree of intimacy. The case of the Good Samaritan may be taken as typical of those contemplated in interpersonal ethics.

Social ethics derives its special character from the explicit attention it pays to the social dimensions of human existence. One consequence of its social orientation, and one mark of its distinctiveness, is its unique awareness of and preoccupation with super-individual entities—its concern with the moral significance of more or less integrated human groups, collectivities, and communities. In this respect it is significantly unlike personal and interpersonal ethics.

It is not true, however, that in social ethics the individual falls out of purview. Social ethics is concerned with the moral behavior of individuals as well as with that of super-individual corporate realities. Its concern with the individual is, however, of a special sort; it is socially qualified. It contemplates the individual not merely as the centered self it is, nor specifically as one who responds without explicit intermediation to the neighbor who in his singleness or indeterminate plurality directly confronts him. It rather contemplates him as one who either makes an individual response to some super-individual community, or as one who, functioning communally, acts in concert with others through the agency of some group with which he is affiliated.

But since social ethics is concerned not only with the behavior of individuals in relation to or from within community, but also with the morally significant vitalities and interactions of communities as such, at least four sets of moral problems are customarily considered by those who work within it.

One important area of concern in social ethics which has already been suggested is that in which the individual is confronted by and set over against some social magnitude, such as the State, which while embracing and assisting him also limits and sometimes threatens him. The central problem here is how to harmonize the interests of the individual and the community. The problem arises because individual and collective centers of life and purpose, though interdependent, are always in tension; the freedom and spontaneity espoused by the one is balanced by the authority and order espoused by the other. The moral task here lies in establishing such social arrangements as will prevent a lapse from balance into conflict. What needs to be secured is that delicate adjustment of freedom and order which will exclude both anarchy and tyranny, that measure of harmony which will prevent either individualism or collectivism from taking root.

Another set of problems arises in social ethics because not infrequently the individual acts not singly but jointly, not on his own but in concert with others, not against but from within some organization or community by which he is embraced. The chief issues arising here concern the existence or non-existence of common ground for deliberation and action, and the reality and meaning of such things as corporate responsibility, collective guilt, exemption from the effects of majority decision by reason of conscience, and the like.

A third set of problems in social ethics arises because there are many organizations and communities in society whose relations and interactions require definition and regulation. At issue here is the exact nature of these communities, the fixity of their boundaries, the status of their claims, and the nature and extent of their possible cooperation. Typical of the problems in this area of existence and inquiry is the age-old problem of the relation of Church and State. Calling for attention here too are the economico-political issues involved in Socialism, Communism, and the Welfare State. Involved here also are such inquiries into the nature of family, state, church, and school as may provide warrant for public, private, or parochial education.

Closely related to the set of problems just referred to, but distinguishable from them, are the problems arising from the issues of plurality and unity. In social ethics one is concerned not only to determine and appraise the relative claims of the several communities existing within society, but also to discover under what conditions and by what sanctions all the particular groupings can be joined and harmonized. During the Middle Ages Occidental society achieved a kind of unity under the hegemony of the church. Since then, through the impulses set loose by the Reformation and the Renaissance, religious diversity, ethnic heterogeneity, cultural variety, and social pluralism have characterized the society of the West. The big question in social ethics is whether a society so characterized can endure, and if so, what view of man and God is calculated to make it viable. It is at this stage of its inquiry that social ethics impinges on the ultimate questions of metaphysics and theology, the answers to which relate not only to the questions here raised but to all the questions considered in the other departments of ethics.

2

Ethics: An Account of its Subject Matter*

EVERY SCIENCE has its object, or that which, by a curious turn in language, we call its subject-matter. The "object" or "subject-matter" is that with which the science *deals*. Thus arithmetic deals with numbers; geometry with space and its configurations; biology with the phenomenon of life; logic with the relation of ideas; psychology with feelings; etc. The question now arises: What is it that ethics deals with? What is the object that it contemplates? What is its subject-matter? I shall try to answer this question (for the questions are really one) by stating a series of propositions, each more complex and restrictive than the preceding one.

A. ETHICS DEALS WITH MAN

Ethics does not deal with nature on the sub-human level, at least not directly and centrally; ethics is not one of the natural sciences. Ethics is a spiritual science *(Geisteswissenschaft)* and belongs to that class of disciplines commonly called the Humanities.

It should be obvious that ethics is not directly concerned with such entities and quasi-entities as *geometrical figures*, *stones*, and *plants*. These things have no moral function and do not stand under moral obligation; they are not moral agents. They may indeed, and do, become objects of human solicitude, and in this way they do come to stand in a moral *relation*, but they are not themselves moral *subjects*, since they lack intelligence and will and have no responsibility. Except by extreme pan-psychists, this is universally acknowledged.[1]

The case is not so clear in the case of *animals*. We speak of some dogs as

1. Note that we act *as if* we were pan-psychists when we become angry with a shoestring that won't untie, or with a machine that "refuses" to function, or with a chair or table that "obstructs" our path. But we know on reflection that our anger and impatience is irrational; the "resistance" that nature offers is not moral in character.

*Appeared first in the *Calvin Theological Journal*, II, 1 (1976).

being "affectionate" and "obedient." Others we regard as ill-behaving or "vicious." We praise and blame them, and sometimes punish them. Is this an acknowledgment that they are moral beings, possessing a sense of right and wrong?

I am quite sure that the answer is No. Animals, even though there is that in them which anticipates intelligence and will, are still wholly caught up in the matrix of nature. They are not made in the image of God, and they have no apprehension of God and of his purposes and demands. They do act or "behave," i.e., they do "respond" to their environment, but such response, we have reason to believe, should be interpreted causally, in terms of motor impulses, natural drives, and antecedent events. Animal behavior is either instinctive or "conditioned"; it is not deliberate and free.

When we praise or blame our dog, therefore, we are either approving or disapproving of nature's (God's) arrangements, or of these arrangements as they are affected by the Fall of man; or we are expressing satisfaction or dissatisfaction with our work of conditioning the animal. Anything beyond this is to be accounted for by our persistent habit of thinking anthropomorphically.

We must conclude, therefore, that animals are not moral agents and do not enter into the purview of ethics, except, of course, as objects of human concern. That we have obligations to animals, that we can be guilty of cruelty to them, and the like, is generally recognized, and by the Christian certainly. "Thou shall not muzzle the ox that treadeth out the corn." But the ox itself has no moral duties and obligations, and is not a subject of ethics.

But what about the entities at the other end of the scale of being? What about *angels* and *demons?* Is ethics concerned with these? Is the science of ethics obliged to work out a system of angelic and demonic morality?

There is no doubt that angels and demons (who are also angels, though fallen and incorrigible) are part of the created cosmos, and thus so far forth legitimate objects of scientific inquiry. It is also evident that they are persons, with intelligence and will; that they stand under moral law; they they can be praised or blamed; in short, that they are moral beings.

Yet they are not the proper objects of ethical discussion. This does not mean that we cannot say anything significant about them and do this in an ethical context. We know, for example, that both angels and demons are obliged to love God with all their heart, and to be ministering spirits to man; that the angels delight in God's praise and service and are steadfast in it, while the demons hate and oppose God and attempt to frustrate his purposes by tempting and encouraging man to sin. All this and more we know about these beings, yet we do not include them in our ethical purview.

One reason why we do not do so is that we know so little about them. God has not seen fit to tell us much about them, and we ourselves are not in a position independently to investigate them, since they inhabit a realm quite other than our own.

But another, and perhaps more telling reason why we do not treat them as the subject-matter of ethics is this: They are no longer in moral tension; they stand above and below the threshold of moral struggle. The angels, by their fidelity to God at a crucial juncture, are confirmed in virtue; they can no longer sin *(non posse peccare).* The demons, because of the fateful act of rebellion, are confirmed in vice; they can no longer do any good and are irredeemable *(non posse non peccare).* In the situation of these entities, moral injunctions are in a significant sense irrelevant; what they are to achieve, they have achieved; each class of beings has reached a kind of perfection, the one a positive, the other a negative perfection. So far forth they stand outside the moral arena, where the fight takes place.

But tensions, struggles, fears, and fightings are the definitive marks of moral existence in the human situation. A science which addresses itself to this situation cannot take into its purview the other (angelic) situation. The two are too disparate. Ethics, therefore, excludes consideration of angels and demons, except, again, relatively, insofar as these entities are related to and affect the human situation.

Although *God* is a moral being, indeed the supreme moral being, he too does not constitute part of the subject-matter of ethics. If angels stand above the threshold of moral struggle, and by that token stand outside the moral arena, God does more so. He is eternally what he is; he is the Unchangeable One. Although he is involved with the moral struggles of his human creatures—setting their goals and empowering them to achieve these—and although he is engaged in a cosmic struggle against evil, he is not himself subject to temptation or in his own being striving for perfection.

Moreover, though he is a moral being, he does not stand under law. He is not subject to obligation. He subjects everything else to his holy and eternal will. He is not so much a "good" being as Goodness itself; not so much a moral subject as the one and only moral foundation.

There is another reason, too, why God is not the object of ethical science. The reason is that it is only with the cosmos that science can deal, and God is not part of the cosmos. God is not created; he is creator. This is why it is true to say, as Abraham Kuyper said, that God is not even the object of theological science. Theology deals with the revelation of God. It does not deal with God as such, and neither does ethics.

This is, of course, not to say that God is not involved in ethics, or that one may ignore him while pursuing the study of it. God is involved in everything, and we ignore him only to our hurt. But it is to say that God is not the proper object of ethics.

Again, this does not mean that God, as some philosophers have supposed, is above good and evil. Although it is only in an analogical sense, God can indeed be called Good. But his goodness does not consist in conformity to something outside himself. His goodness is an essential, absolute, and inalienable property of his being. He is thus the source and guarantor of all good. But his goodness is not of the sort with which ethics deals, except relatively, as productive of human good.

We conclude, therefore, that *man*, and only man, is the proper object of ethical study. Man is the one existentially moral being. Made in the image of God, created perfect, but fallen from his high estate, he stands in tension between the actual and the ideal, involved to the end of his days in the moral struggle between good and evil. Subject to moral law, with an ineradicable sense of obligation, he lives in the presence of God, the sway of whose imperious will he cannot escape. It is with this being that ethics is concerned.

But now a qualification must be added. The second point to be observed is that:

B. ETHICS DEALS WITH INDIVIDUAL MAN

Unlike politics, which, as Sidgwick rightly observes, "seeks to determine the proper constitution and the right public conduct of governed *societies*," ethics is concerned with existential persons in their concrete individuality. Ethics is focused upon the individual because only the individual is truly personal and therefore an authentic moral agent.

No group or society is this. It is true that a society or communion, when infused and animated by a single spirit and organized into a single institution, is more than a mere sum or aggregate of discrete entities, and has a certain "personality" and "individuality" of its own. It is also true that such an institution, as for example a state or a church, can in a sense be held accountable for its deeds and become the object of moral approval or disapproval. But only "in a sense." Strictly speaking, societies and communities, far from being true persons and individuals, do not even "exist." They are "real" enough, but they are abstract realities; they lack concreteness. Where, for example, shall we look to find "the public," or "the American people," or "the Christian Church," or "the modern man," or similar entities? They are not discoverable for the simple reason that they do not "exist." What is referred to by these terms is either an idea, or a collection, or a mean (an average), but all of these are manifestly abstract! They are universals; and universals do not exist *in rerum natura*.

For this reason they cannot be morally judged, either now or at the end of days. Those whom the Lord will call to account when he comes in judgment are not societies, or organizations, or generalities, but precisely individuals, for these alone are existing and responsible entities, and these alone can stand before his throne. It is with individual men, therefore, that ethics has to do.

What has been said must not be taken as a denial of "corporate responsibility." There is such a thing as corporate responsibility, and it is meaningful both from the side of the individual and from the side of the corporate body. When an individual joins a voluntary organization he is, as long as he remains a member of that organization, co-responsible for the actions taken by that organization. If the actions are evil, he may mitigate his guilt by entering a protest and by advocating amendment, but he cannot completely absolve himself of guilt by disassociation. In the case of non-voluntary organizations, such as the State, the possibility of disassociation does not exist, and however much one may denounce the policies and programs of the government, one is inescapably involved in the common guilt. What is to be observed, however, is that the guilt rests upon individuals. Each shall be judged according to the measure of his involvement and responsibility. It is not "the State" that will be punished, but the individuals constituting the State. In the process the State may indeed be weakened, but only in the sense that the desire or ability of the several individuals to reestablish the State has been weakened.

It should be obvious that I am not pleading for the kind of individualism which maintains that one is responsible only for that which he has done by his own hand or in his own person. I maintain that there is corporate guilt (consider our guilt in Adam, and consider also how the Lord said, "I the Lord thy God am a jealous God, visiting the iniquity of the fathers upon the children unto the third and fourth generation of them that hate me, and showing mercy unto thousands of them that love me, and keep my commandments"), but I also maintain that this guilt is distributed and, as it were, focused, upon the *individuals* constituting the corporation.[2]

What is to be observed, then, are two things. *First*, responsibility rests ultimately upon individuals, and only upon individuals, and the proper concern of ethics is with these alone. And, *second*, the individual is not a wholly discrete, unrelated, atomistic entity; he always stands in a social context with which he is morally involved. But an individual he nevertheless remains. And it is with him that ethics has to do.

A distinction is sometimes made between personal ethics and social

2. It would carry us too far afield to explore all the ramifications of corporate and individual responsibility. It is enough here to add that we should not normally impose direct penalties upon anyone for deeds he did not himself commit. So, for example, we should not imprison a son when his father alone committed the crime. We do, of course, indirectly punish the son by bringing shame upon him and perhaps by depriving him of the financial and other support his father would give him were he not in prison. This kind of social consequence is unavoidable, though it is mitigable in various degrees.

ethics, but this distinction should not be allowed to obscure the personal character and individual orientation of all ethics. Personal ethics has to do with self-culture and the development of one's own character in the way of virtue; social ethics is concerned with the proper ordering of the life of society and with the cooperative effects needed to effect such ordering; both sorts of ethics deal with the individual, either as he is turned more immediately upon himself, or as he is turned toward the social matrix in which he is imbedded.[3]

It should next be observed that:

C. ETHICS DEALS WITH THE CONDUCT OF INDIVIDUAL MAN

Man is a very complex being. He participates in and functions through every aspect of the created world. He runs the gamut of the universe, being, indeed, a micro-cosmos, exhibiting in himself all the modalities of being distinguishable in creation. He functions, for example, in the arithmetical sphere, and has a number; he functions in the geometrical sphere, and has shape and dimensions incident to space-occupancy; he functions in the physical sphere and is an electronic field of force which in relation to this planet gives him weight; he functions in the biological sphere and possesses that mysterious quality called *life*, which he shares, though not in the same way, with animals and plants; he functions in all the spheres of existence, including the psychological, the logical, the historical, and more.

Among these spheres is the moral, and it is as man functions in this realm that he becomes the object of the science called ethics. Ethics is not concerned with man's geometrical aspects as such; it ignores man's shape or size, except as it is morally induced, as through gluttony, fasting, self-mutilation, and the like. Similarly, ethics is not concerned with man's physical weight or his center of gravity; nor with his geographical location as such; nor with the color of his skin; nor even with the power of his intellect (his I.Q.) taken by itself. Ethics is concerned with a man's actions, with his conduct or behavior.

Yet it is not with the whole even of man's actions that ethics is concerned. Because man is tied in with nature (belongs to the animal kingdom) he *does* some things which do not distinguish him *as man*. He breathes, for example, and digests his food, and twitches his muscles, and performs other vital functions which are not uniquely human. This kind of action, this sort of behavior, is not of direct concern to ethics.

Hence we must make a further qualification and say that:

3. For a further account of the distinction between personal and social ethics, see the first essay in this collection.

D. ETHICS DEALS WITH THE VOLUNTARY CONDUCT OF INDIVIDUAL MAN

This is to say that ethics deals with behavior only insofar as it is uniquely human, or at least not sub-human; that is, insofar as it is an exhibition of character and rational will.

It should be observed that voluntary conduct excludes: (1) all *involuntary* acts, such as heart-beat, breathing, etc., and (2) all *non-voluntary* acts, such as are done under unwithstandable external constraint and compulsion, as moving when pulled by ropes, or not moving when tied by them, or speaking under the influence of a secretly administered drug. In the case of involuntary and non-voluntary acts man is not morally responsible, except perhaps indirectly or mediately, insofar as by previous voluntary conduct he has prepared the ground for the kind of behavior here being exempted from praise or blame.

Voluntary conduct includes: (1) all *activity* under the control of, or able to be under the control of, the will. Activity under the control of the will embraces inner as well as outer activity; it embraces thinking, feeling, aspiring, etc., as well as running, speaking, striking. Activity able to be under the control of the will embraces activity which in fact is not, or not wholly, under the control of the will. It includes, for example, activity performed under the influence of intoxicating liquors freely imbibed. Such activity, when censurable in a sober man, is censurable also in a drunken man, even though in the latter instances the will is partially paralyzed. The intoxicated man is held accountable because what he did could have been placed under the governance of his will, and would have been vetoed had the will been properly exercised. Moral judgment is tempered, however, by the circumstance that in the instance contemplated the will did not, in fact, operate under the guidance of a clear intelligence. Therefore, although we hold a man accountable for what he does when drunk, we do not hold him fully accountable. This is the respect we pay to the principle that only voluntary conduct is subject to praise or blame. This principle is similarly honored in most courts of law when the defendant is permitted to plead drunkenness as an "extenuating circumstance."

Voluntary conduct includes also: (2) all "*non-activity*" insofar as it is an exhibition of character and will. As is well known, there are sins of omission as well as of commission. A man is as responsible for the negative acts and attitudes of passivity, quietude, inertia, hesitancy, indecision, etc., as he is for the more positive acts he commits. A decision not to act is as much a decision as is a decision to act; and lassitude and apathy, when it is a habit and disposition and not the involuntary consequence of illness, comes into the purview of ethics as surely as does violence and aggression.

Although this is not the place for a full discussion of *motives* in ethics, it should be remarked that ethics is concerned not only with overt action, but also with the hidden springs of action, the motives and intents of the heart. It is concerned with these because these, too, are bound up with the will. Moral judgment takes into account not only what a man does or does not do, but also what he intends to accomplish (the proximate or ultimate end he chooses), and why he is moved to envision this end and perform this deed (the motive he adopts or permits to control him).

We may conclude, then, that *the fact of volition* is of central importance to our study. Where there is no involvement of the will, there morality is impossible and ethics is irrelevant.

But we have still not precisely defined the subject-matter of ethics. We must make a further qualification and say that:

E. ETHICS DEALS WITH THE VOLUNTARY CONDUCT OF INDIVIDUAL MAN INSOFAR AS IT IS JUDGED (APPRAISED, EVALUATED)

Here it must be observed that human conduct can be brought under scrutiny in a number of ways. It can, for example, be simply *described*, at least in its external and observable aspects. The facts about it can be set down. A close inspection may disclose that a man shot a gun, that he ran from the house, that he got into his car, that at a certain intersection his car skidded thirty feet, etc. All of these things, which we may discover, doubtless have some moral significance, but what significance they have the facts do not themselves declare; and in any case, when we are engaged in discovering the facts, we are not yet doing ethics. We are not in the realm of ethics until we make a *judgment* about the man and his acts. It is not that we can omit ascertaining the facts; it is only that while we are still on the level of fact we are below the threshold of ethics.

One may, of course, do more than describe the fact. One may *explain* the facts. That is, one may account for them scientifically, in terms of their (efficient) causes. In an age dominated by natural science, as ours is, it is common practice, not only to "explain" human conduct in this way, but to regard such (causal) explanation as the last word to be said about human conduct. This is a mistake. One can, indeed, as we shall see, give a partial explanation of human conduct by disclosing the natural causes of it, but much of it will then remain still unaccounted for, for human conduct has a moral as well as a natural dimension, and the former cannot be surveyed by the methods employed in the natural sciences and adopted by certain social scientists.

These social scientists err in failing to distinguish between the *causes of* and the *reasons for* human behavior. They assume that there is no realm other than nature and nature's forces. They fail to see that man has membership in the world of spirit, and that he has a rational will which can be engaged by the transcendent Good, attachment to which evokes behavior inexplicable in terms of natural stimuli. They think of what man does as the determinate consequence of the influences playing upon him from behind; they refuse to acknowledge that man has the freedom to set himself ideals and to aspire after them; they fail to recognize that moral values are more than psychological projections of selfish interest, and that they have objective existence in a world which, though it is not precisely like Plato's realm of ideas, nevertheless lies above and beyond the causal nexus of nature. Against these social scientists we must declare that human conduct transcends causal explanation and has a rationale which calls for a distinctively moral analysis and judgment.

Having made this declaration, we must not fall, however, into the opposite error and deny that human behavior is influenced, even though not finally and determinatively, by sub-moral forces. The moral dimension of man is unique and inviolable, but it is part of a structure which has other dimensions as well. Although each of man's aspects and functions is unique, each is tied in with every other and is affected by them. Man's moral life, though not the product of physical, biological, social, economic, and other forces, is nevertheless lived in the context of such forces, and cannot escape their influence. God has not created man as a stark unit, nor even as a pure spirit inhabiting a disposable tenement of clay, but as a highly complex being who is the center of a veritable web of interrelations with all of reality, the whole of which comes into focus in him. Man cannot, therefore, escape being conditioned in some measure by what happens in him and about him.

It is evident, for example, that our mood and temper is affected by the chemical processes that go on in the body, and that alterations in these not only raise or lower the level of our moral efficiency, but strengthen or weaken our hopes and fears.

On the biological level, too, man's conduct is influenced by the instincts, drives, and vital processes of the living organism. Although it is very true that such characteristically moral behavior as faithfulness in marriage, patience in adversity, thankfulness in prosperity, and helpfulness to those in distress cannot be understood in terms of organic life-factors such as response to stimuli and conditioned reflexes, yet the effect upon our attitudes and conduct of sickness, old age, malnutrition, brain injuries, glandular malfunctionings, and the like is very real and too significant to be ignored.

Again, although the moral life cannot be understood in terms of such psychological factors as sex-drives, oedipus-complexes, associations of ideas, fears of punishment, and expectations of reward, yet who is to deny that man's conduct is influenced by the desires and sensitivities that constitute his psyche? And is not the well-intentioned but foolish and blundering man evidence that the truly good life is importantly associated with the logical power of thought?

Moving into the economic sphere, we may well ask whether Marx was wholly wrong in declaring that our moral judgments and institutions are modified by changes in economic conditions. Is it not plain, at any rate, that the good life is dependent (at least for full actualization) on economic goods as means for the articulation of moral decision? And was not Archbishop Temple at least partly right when he said of unemployment that it "has power to corrupt the soul of any man not already far advanced in saintliness"? "Because the man has no opportunity of service," he explained, "he is turned in upon himself and becomes, according to his temperament, a contented loafer or an embittered self-seeker."[4]

When all of this is acknowledged, however, and genuinely taken to heart, it remains true that man's moral life is not the mere product of his psychological nature, nor the mere effect of environmental forces. What John Bennett says about the latter is true also of the former: "Christians cannot . . . admit that man's nature is entirely determined by the environment in which he lives. They know that the mature soul can transcend cramping and destructive circumstances. . . . They know that men often are at their best, that men may become heroes and saints, when external conditions are at their worst."[5] This is very true, and the reason for it is that man is not a mere child of nature but by creation nature's king under God, able by grace since the Fall to transcend nature's conditioning and to fit his life into a moral framework that exceeds the causal nexus.

Ethics, as the science of the moral life, is satisfied, therefore, neither with the mere *description* nor with the scientific *explanation* of human conduct. It is oriented centrally to an aspect of human conduct which is neither open to sensible observation nor amenable to causal explanation. It is oriented to that aspect of conduct by which conduct is related to a transcendent norm or demand, in terms of which it is required to be and is in fact *judged, appraised, evaluated.*

This *appraising* or *weighing* of conduct is a typically and uniquely personal and spiritual activity, which God does supremely, but which we, his image-bearers, do in imitation of him; for none, not even the most depraved, is without some apprehension of the norm constituted by God's demand, and none fails to pass judgment on conduct in terms of his apprehension of it.

4. *Christianity and the Social Order*, London: SCM Press, 1950, p. 12.
5. *The Christian as Citizen*, New York: Association Press, 1955, pp. 18–19.

Ethics is basically oriented to this fact; it centers its interest on this point. Ethics deals centrally with the voluntary conduct of individual man *insofar as it is judged.*

But this needs further elucidation. We must qualify our statement and say:

F. ETHICS DEALS WITH THE VOLUNTARY CONDUCT OF INDIVIDUAL MAN INSOFAR AS IT IS JUDGED TO BE GOOD OR BAD (RIGHT OR WRONG)

It is necessary to make this qualification because conduct may be judged in many different ways and in a variety of perspectives. Conduct may be judged from the point of view of biology, as wholesome or unwholesome, healthful or unhealthful; from the point of view of psychology, as pleasant or painful; from the point of view of logic, as consistent or inconsistent; from the point of view of social intercourse, as polite or impolite, refined or vulgar; from the point of view of economics, as valuable or not valuable, precious or common; from the point of view of esthetics, as harmonious or disharmonious; from the point of view of the juridical, as legal or illegal; and so on.

It is obvious that all of these predications reflect judgments or appraisals. It is equally obvious that none of the appraisals is specifically moral in character. All of the judgments appeal to norms, but none of the norms is of the sort that is of central interest to ethics. Also these norms are for the most part relative and contingent, as those of ethics are not.

Take, for example, the biological norm of "wholesomeness" or "healthfulness." It quite evidently lacks all absoluteness and universality, for whether a given mode of conduct is healthful or not, depends upon a host of variable factors. In the limited area of what goes into the body (as through the mouth), what is healthful or not healthful depends, within the more or less fixed limits of the human organism's tolerance for solids and liquids, upon the variable and accidental condition of the body in question.

It is in the area of what happens to the body from the outside that the stark relativity of this norm is perhaps most clearly seen. Whether the perpetration of robbery, deceit, murder, rape, etc., is *healthful* or not depends, in a relatively ordered society, upon one's cunning in escaping detection, and in a relatively disordered society upon the arbitrary and accidental application of sanctions by the constituted authorities.

But, waiving the question whether this biological norm is relative and contingent or not, it certainly is not *ethical.* It not only provides no moral guidance; it subverts morality. For it is clear that I am not always required to do the biologically healthful thing: The path of moral duty may lead to the gibbet or the pyre. Not health, not even life is an ultimate value. I may have to sacrifice both in the interest of being good; virtue has more than once led to martyrdom. It is plain, therefore, that to call a course of conduct "healthful" is not to pass a moral judgment upon it.

This does not mean, of course, that the virtuous man may ignore his health; it is ordinarily his duty to preserve and foster it. It simply means that doing one's duty and keeping one's health are not to be identified; to be good and to be healthy are not the same.

What has just been said holds, *mutatis mutandis*, for all the other judgments listed above. That a course of conduct yields pleasure or pain indicates nothing about its moral quality. While it is ordinarily my duty not to inflict pain upon others, and always my duty not to inflict it unnecessarily; and although I ordinarily regard the absence of pain in myself as a blessing and a good, yet there is no strict correlation between moral value and psychological feeling. The virtuous man, in pursuit of his duty, may sometimes be required both to cause and to suffer pain, and the evil man may often afford and receive pleasure in the performance of his nefarious deeds. It is therefore not ethically illuminating to know that this or that act is attended by pleasure or pain.

Logical appraisals likewise are quite different from ethical judgments. Consistency is a logical excellence, but it is not necessarily a moral virtue. Like logic itself, consistency is purely formal, and it may be put into the service of evil as well as good. Satan is doubtless consistent in his behavior; he is absorbed since his rebellion in one single integrated effort to thwart the designs of God. On the other hand, there is inconsistency, even contradiction, in the total conduct-pattern of the man who in his middle years passes by grace from darkness into light.

When within an historical perspective one declares that a person or policy is progressive or reactionary, conservative or liberal, traditional or modern, one is saying little or nothing of ethical significance, because the norms employed are purely historical in character; the judgment is made in reference to a period which itself is in flux and which, like many ages the world has known, may be generally evil. To be told that a man is conservative or progressive does not help us to decide whether he is good or bad.

To be polite is to observe the forms of etiquette prevailing in a given cultural situation. Even apart from the fact that such observance may be purely formal and external, the norms governing social intercourse in the supposed situation may, from a moral point of view, be unacceptable. Thus, though politeness is ordinarily a requirement of virtuous living, it may be incumbent upon us in the interest of moral rectitude to be impolite on the purely social level of existence. The saying, "When in Rome, do as the Romans do," is ethically dubious.

A pattern of conduct may be economically fruitful without being good. One has only to consider the great barons of capitalism who in the nineteenth century amassed great sums of money at the expense of others to recognize the truth of this. It is obvious, too, that the good man, whether because of his meekness, his generosity, his other-worldliness, or simply his meticulous honesty, is often economically "unsuccessful." It is evident that an economic appraisal is something quite different from a moral one.

It should be observed, finally, that to be legal is not necessarily to be virtuous. Legal behavior is behavior that conforms to statute or common law. But the law itself may be evil or wrong, in which case it may be one's duty to break it, on the principle that it is better to obey God than man. A juridical judgment, therefore, is far from being an ethical judgment. Even though it is ordinarily our duty to obey the law, law-observance may on occasion be morally objectionable.

In the light of this discussion it should be clear that ethics, as the science of morality, is not concerned with every kind of judgment upon the voluntary conduct of individual man, but only with a very special kind of judgment—the *moral* judgment, a judgment about the rightness or wrongness, the goodness or badness, of conduct.

What does this mean?

It means that ethics is oriented to the fact that conduct is judged, indeed should be judged, from a *unique* point of view, with reference to a *peculiar* or singular *norm* or *ideal*, the norm or ideal of the *right* or the *good*. Just what the norm (or standard, or law) demands, and what the ideal (or goal) involves, and just what the *meaning* is of right and good, are matters of central concern to ethics, and we shall soon have to take them under consideration. At the moment, however, what is to be observed is that the terms right and good are *different* from the terms we have just passed in review, and that by means of them we make a *unique* judgment of behavior. The moral judgment is not to be confused with any other. Because it is interested in the *moral* aspect of behavior, and because the moral aspect is *sui generis,* ethics does not care, immediately, whether a course of conduct is pleasurable or not, or healthful, or consistent, or progressive, or polite, or profitable, or legal, or anything else, but only whether it is good or bad, i.e., whether it conforms to moral law or embodies the moral ideal. This is why it was necessary to qualify our statement F (above) and say that ethics deals with the voluntary conduct of individual man *insofar as it is judged to be good or bad, right or wrong.*

It is one thing to say that the terms good and bad are unique; it is another thing to indicate in what their uniqueness consists, to what singular feature of reality they refer, what it is that they peculiarly *intend* or *mean.* The difficulty of indicating the meaning of "good" and "bad" is, however, more formal than real, and the necessity of doing so is more apparent than real, because the notions of good and bad are *intuitive;* their meaning is directly known. This is why it is difficult, if not impossible, to define them in any formal way. They are what is known in Logic as "simple" or "primitive" ideas. As such they do not lend themselves to definition. This is not serious, since all people possess an innate awareness of their meaning, and do not require a definition. These words or their equivalents appear in all languages. All people say, in their own way and in their own tongue, "This is good" and "That is bad." Of course, not all people apply these expressions in the same way, but that is another matter. What is here of interest and importance is that all people possess the category of "the Good," and use it. Ethics takes its departure from this fact.

It is also to be observed that, whatever other qualities the good and the right may have, they have this quality, that they lay men under obligation. The good and the right are imperious *oughts,* and they are this intrinsically, essentially. What is right *ought* to be done; what is good *ought* to be actualized. This ought is not hypothetical; it is categorical. The requirement to be good is not a conditional requirement, a mere precondition for the attainment of this or that end. It is an absolute requirement. The injunction to do right and to be good is an unqualified imperative which rests on every man in every situation at all times, regardless of his wishes or desires.

One can hardly avoid making reference in this connection to *conscience,* for it is by conscience that men both become aware of the existence of the good and feel its constraining power. Conscience naturally apprehends the distinction between good and bad, is necessarily charged with a sense of obligation, and unavoidably makes judgments of approval and disapproval.

Conscience can never die. It can be (and is) corrupted, but it can never be extinguished. The reason for this is that moral awareness is indelibly impressed upon the soul. As Calvin says, the soul exists "to hold the supremacy in the government of human life; and that not only in the concerns of the terrestrial life, but likewise to excite to the worship of God. Though this last point is not so evident in the state of corruption, yet there remain some relics of it impressed even on our very vices. For whence proceeds the great concern of men about their reputation, but from shame?, but whence proceeds shame, unless from a respect for virtue? The principle and cause of which is, that they understand themselves to have been born for the cultivation of righteousness; and in which are included the seeds of religion. But as, without controversy, man was created to aspire to a heavenly life, so it is certain that the knowledge of it was impressed on his soul. And, indeed, man would be deprived of the principal use of his understanding, if he were ignorant of his felicity, the perfection of which consists in being united to God."[6]

6. *Institutes,* Bk. 1, Ch. 15, Par. 6.

After one has acknowledged the truth of all that has been said under this head (F), two very important questions still remain. The first is: What is the *content* of the good, of the existence of which everyone is intuitively aware? The second is: What is the *basis* of that good? Granted that, as conscience tells me, I am under obligation, there remains to ask: *To* what course of conduct am I obliged? and *By* what or by whom am I obliged? After admitting that I am in duty bound to act in certain ways, I must still inquire: *What* precisely is my duty? and Who or what ultimately *imposes* this duty?

G. ETHICS DEALS WITH THE VOLUNTARY CONDUCT OF INDIVIDUAL MAN INSOFAR AS IT IS JUDGED TO BE GOOD OR BAD IN REFERENCE TO A SINGLE, INCLUSIVE, AND DETERMINATIVE PRINCIPLE OF MORAL VALUE

All people act, i.e., they *behave* in certain ways. All people, too, pass moral *judgment* upon their acts, i.e., they appraise their conduct (and that of others) in terms of good and bad. This is significant enough. More significant than this, however, is the fact that when they *act*, and especially when they *judge*, they have in mind a certain notion of *what* the good life substantially is, of how the terms good and bad are to be *materially* understood, of what the essential *content* is of sound morality, of what it is that ultimately *constitutes* true virtue. In other words, they operate, more or less consciously, with a specific *theory* of morality; they appeal to a particular *definition* of the good; they act and judge in the name of some accepted and contentful *principle* of moral value.

This principle may be, as in Christianity, the principle of obedient love; it may be, as in Hedonism, the principle of pleasure; it may be, as in Kantian Formalism, the principle of respect for law; it may be, as in Platonism, the principle of justice; it may be, as in Aristotelianism, the principle of eudaemonistic self-development; it may be any one of a number of things. But the point is that, *underlying* both behavior and judgment, there is a principle or theory by which both are supported and directed, the judgment more directly and usually more strictly than the behavior.

Now ethics is pre-eminently *the systematic elaboration of principle:* the Christian ethic being the systematic elaboration of the principle of obedient love; other ethics being the systematic elaboration of other and rival principles. It is by this articulation and elaboration of principle that any given ethics discloses and sets forth what it regards as man's supreme duty, in the discharge of which lies his chief good. It is by this that it sets forth that *general* thing, like loving, which is always and in every circumstance to be done.

It is by this articulation and elaboration of principle, too, that any given ethics *interprets* and *accounts* for the conduct and morals of man. It is in this sense that ethics "explains" morality, that it "justifies" a particular set of judgments. This justification, to a reflective person, is necessary and inevitable, which is but to say that a reflective person cannot fail to develop an ethic.

What is now particularly to be observed, however, is that the justification is always made by an appeal to a supporting or validating principle, which is believed to *dictate* the judgment under scrutiny.

So, for example, the reflective Christian will justify the judgment that hospitality is good by showing that it is an implication of the deeper principle of brotherly love. Of course a Hedonist may also commend hospitality; but he will do so for a different *reason*. Although he may advocate hospitality no less than the Christian, he will give a different answer to the question: *Why* be hospitable? That is, he will provide, not a Christian, but a Hedonistic "justification" for moral judgments. And so it will be with every other kind of ethics. The various existing ethics differ among themselves according as they differently define the good, differently conceive of the highest duty, differently justify the more particular moral judgments.

Men differ among themselves in the same way, although it must be admitted that none of us consciously justifies *every* judgment that we make. Even the trained moralist finds it difficult if not impossible to trace every judgment back to its source in principle. Yet every judgment ought to be so traceable, and every judgment *requires* the justification that only basic principle can provide.

It is on the level of principle and theory (theory being nothing more than an extended and orderly presentation of principle) that significant differences appear among men. It is true, differences appear on the level of behavior and judgment as well, as everyone can easily observe. The existence of such differences is what one would expect if it be true, as it is, that "principles make a difference," that "ideas have consequences." Yet the differences on the level of behavior and judgment do not disclose their own true depth until one observes them from the deeper level of principle. On this level the fact of *the antithesis*, taught in Scripture (cf. Gen. 3:15), begins to come into focus, revealing more sharply than before the basic cleft that divides the man in Christ from the man outside of Christ.

In the Occident, within that great spirituo-cultural magnitude called "Christendom," one frequently finds people who, though alienated from the Church and making no profession of Christ, nevertheless *behave* in ways that are not easily distinguishable from the ways of Christians. This similarity in walk is due in part, no doubt, to the fact that the non-Christian in western lands is living on inherited Christian capital. But even in non-Christian lands one finds people who on the level of behavior are so distinguished for virtue that they frequently put the ordinary Christian to shame. The reason for this is that, on the one hand, God restrains the power of sin in unregenerate men through his common grace, and imparts moral power to them through the general operation of his Spirit; and that, on the other hand, Christians have to fight until the end of their days the evil nature that remains in them even after their regeneration. Because of this double fact non-Christians frequently appear in their works to be better than they are at bottom, and Christians appear to be worse. The result is often (though not always and not necessarily) an appearance of sameness or similarity that obscures the basic difference that exists between them.

This difference discloses itself on the level of *judgment*. Here, on the level of morality as distinct from behavior, one can more easily observe the divergence; the Christian and the non-Christian are seen frequently to distribute their approbations and disapprobations in importantly different ways. Yet even here it is not crystal clear that a deep and unbridgeable gulf divides them. For the reasons already mentioned, and because underlying the antithetical powers of sin and grace there is the shared humanity fashioned in creation, non-Christians and Christians frequently make similar moral judgments, i.e., they approve and disapprove of the same things, a fact which makes cooperation with non-Christians in certain kinds of social programs both possible and obligatory for the Christian.

It is on the level of *principle* that the antithesis becomes quite clear. Existing on every level, it comes here to open manifestation. A Christian and a non-Christian may frequently *do* the same things; they may also frequently *approve* of the same things; but they are not likely to act and to judge as they do *for the same reason*, with reference to the same ideal, in obedience to a command understood in the same way. Here, in their deep-level orientation to duty, they are set apart from each other. And here, where one is close to the center of ethics, the reality of the distinction between a Christian and a non-Christian ethics discloses itself. Here one must choose between ethical schools; here eschewing all syncretism, one must select a single ethical theory to the exclusion of all others. This does not mean, of course, that all Christians will agree in the details of the Christian theory, but it does mean, if the term "Christian" is taken seriously, that all will fashion the theory in the light of God's revelation in the incarnate and inscriptured Word, a circumstance which is bound to distinguish the resultant theory from all others in a very fundamental way, in so fundamental a way, indeed, that one cannot embrace both it and some other theory fashioned in independence of the Word.

We have now seen that ethics is concerned with the *principle* of morality which, while defining and giving content to the otherwise vague and abstract idea of the "good," supports, accounts for, and justifies our moral judgments and practical behavior. We have also seen that, within the moral context, it is on the level of principle that Christians most significantly distinguish themselves from non-Christians. We have seen that a distinctively Christian ethics, as well as various sorts of non-Christian ethics, emerge as rival and incompatible structures precisely on this level.

But something more must be said. Ethics not only sets forth the content of the good, by positing and elaborating a determinate moral principle. It also lays bare the *ground* on which this principle, and by that token the whole of the moral life, is believed to rest. The principle was appealed to for the justification of behavior and judgment; but the principle itself stands in need of justification; it requires the support of nothing less than Ultimate Reality. Lacking this it is an aery nothing, without ultimate meaning because without anchorage in the universe.

Now it is the Christian contention that its moral principle has such anchorage. The Christian believes that love is rooted in the very nature and will of God. Christian ethics, therefore, claims as ground the very bedrock on which the cosmos rests.

But in making this claim, Christian ethics—and in making a comparable claim, every ethics—goes beyond what we have thus far considered. In its farthest reaches ethics, every ethics, deals with the very nature of the real and impinges upon and merges with metaphysics and theology.

We must, therefore, make a final qualification of our statement concerning the subject matter of ethics, and say:

H. ETHICS DEALS WITH THE VOLUNTARY CONDUCT OF INDIVIDUAL MAN INSOFAR AS IT IS JUDGED TO BE GOOD OR BAD IN REFERENCE TO A SINGLE, INCLUSIVE, AND DETERMINATIVE PRINCIPLE OF MORAL VALUE GROUNDED IN AND VALIDATED BY ULTIMATE REALITY

A great many modern philosophers are contemptuous of metaphysics. They are not sure that the term "ultimate reality" is meaningful at all, and in any case they are sure that nothing can be discovered about the thing the term may possibly signify. They deny, therefore, that ethics is or needs to be established upon it. Indeed, the more radical among them hold that moral values, with which ethics deals, are not "real" in any objective sense at all, and thus not the proper objects of philosophical knowledge. Values are for them purely subjective entities, with no other basis than human thought or feeling. In their opinion, our patterns of behavior, our judgments, and our theories are "validated," if the term is to be used at all, by nothing more than our unstable and changing selves.

Thus Bertrand Russell says: "Questions as to values lie wholly outside the domain of knowledge. That is to say, when we assert that this or that has value we are giving expression to an emotion, not to a fact which would still be true if our personal feelings were different."[7]

W. D. Lamont, the Positivist, speaks in a similar vein. "I regard philosophy," he says, "as a theoretic inquiry in pursuit of truth. Valuations are not theoretical assertions claiming to express truth. The question whether a thing has value is not to be determined by any criterion independent of actual valuations."[8]

And for Analytical Empiricists like A. J. Ayer, ethical statements are not statements at all; they are merely "expressions and stimulants of feeling, or exhortation to action."

It is evident, however, that if this be true, then morality and ethics have no justification at all. Then there are no binding oughts. Then nothing and no one legislates for us. Then conscience is a delusion and a snare. Then each man may do what seems good in his own eyes or what he considers to be to his own personal advantage. Then Whirl is king, and nothing matters any more.

But things do matter, as even they must admit who in theory relativize and subjectivize morality into nothingness. For they think, in spite of themselves, that people *ought* to be subjectivistic in ethics, and *ought not* any longer to believe in the objective reality of moral distinctions. Their theory to the contrary notwithstanding, they do believe that men are *obliged* to think and act in certain ways and not in others.

This being so, they are inescapably confronted with the inevitable *Why?* They must answer the question: Why act and think in this way and not in that? And they must answer the question: Who or what obliges me? Who or what legislates for me, and lays me under obligation? The only possible answer to these questions, in the final analysis, is: It is the nature of things that legislates for me; the universe lays me under obligation; reality dictates what I should do and what I should avoid. But this answer assumes that we know what reality is and what it requires of us. It refers the *ought* for justification to the *is*, thus positing the *is* as the *ground* for morality. It presupposes metaphysics.

Russell, Lamont, and Ayer are, therefore, metaphysicians in spite of themselves. All men are. If they think they are not, this is because they have not thought their position through to the end.

The Pragmatists are a case in point. Pragmatism is an antimetaphysical movement which arose as a protest against Idealistic metaphysics (against which particular kind of metaphysics, incidentally, the Christian must also

7. *Religion and Science*, New York: H. Holt and Company, 1935, p. 230.
8. *Proceedings*, Aristotelian Society, Vol. 15, p. 226.

protest). Pragmatism is oriented not to being but to becoming, and with this orientation it set out to construct what it believed to be a quite unmetaphysical ethic. But surely the affirmation that the universe is plural, fluid, and ever in the process of becoming is no less a theory of reality than the rejected Idealistic theory according to which the universe is fixed, stable, and eternal. Ethical realism is no less metaphysically determined than ethical idealism. The controversy between empiricism, positivism, or phenomenalism on the one hand, and idealism on the other, is not a controversy between science and unscientific philosophy. It is a controversy between divergent metaphysics. In rejecting the block universe, the Pragmatists are substituting one metaphysics for another, and the substitution reflects itself in their ethics. Truth and goodness are inseparable, and our view of the one determines our view of the other.

In illustration of this principle we find Pragmatism contending for the relativity of ethical principles. Since truth itself is in the making, so is goodness. Apriorism, according to the Pragmatist, is the bane of morals, and value judgments are possible only after the event. Goodness is predicable of anything not because it conforms to an external standard, but because it produces wholesome results. Good and evil are not existences; they are merely distinctions that help us to get on. Ethics is not a way of conforming; it is a way of creating. Virtue is not fidelity to eternal and immutable laws; it is an adaptation of personal capacities to environing forces. Thus on the basis of a pluralistic and evolutionistic metaphysics the Pragmatist builds a fluid and positivistic ethics.

From this interdependence of ethics and metaphysics there is no escaping. All ethics assume that men ought to be good, but this assumption commits the ethicist to two important admissions. He admits membership in a world which legislates for him, and he admits residence in a world of freedom. Both admissions advance him beyond the strictly ethical sphere. Both are judgments concerning the nature of the world in which he resides and the place he occupies within it. Both are metaphysical. Ethics simply cannot resist this inner compulsion to advance beyond itself. Every obligation demands ultimate validation. There is no genuine "ought" that does not need the whole universe to back it.

The study of ethics is, therefore, inseparable from the study of that underlying *system* of truth—called variously philosophy, theology, or metaphysics—which delineates the Ultimately Real and sets forth the basic structure of the cosmos in which the moral life is lived. At its center ethics is chiefly concerned with these competing systems of reality; deep down its interest is focused on the rival definitions of what is the ultimate justifier of moral principle, moral judgment, and moral behavior. At its center the prime question of ethics is: Who or what legislates for me? Who or what gives meaning to my moral struggles and aspirations? Who or what guarantees morality? Who or what justifies me in living by the principle I have adopted?

It is obvious that the answer to these questions is not provided by ethics itself. Our ethics presupposes an answer to these questions; it is the result or outcome of our metaphysics or theology, and not the determiner of it. What kind of ethic we have will depend upon what kind of all-encompassing world and life view we embrace. The decision in favor of this or that "system" is prior to the construction of the ethic. As Professor Harry Jellema says: "Ethics may clarify the decision; show me something of what is involved in it; contribute to the intelligence of the decision; but it cannot furnish the last ground for the decision." For that is a religious, and not a merely moral act.

A *Christian ethic* is, or should be, rooted in and fashioned in conformity to a Christian world-view—a Spirit-inspired, biblically-determined world-view—commitment to which requires a religious decision of faith, as indeed does commitment to any other world-view. Underneath ethics is *faith*, and since faith can in the end be in only one of two objects—the Creator or the creature, God or the cosmos—and since God is truly and fully known only in Christ, there are only two kinds of ethics, deep down—Christian and non-Christian.

Part II

THEOLOGICAL FOUNDATIONS FOR CHRISTIAN ETHICS

3

Principle and Practice

A. INTRODUCTION

When one considers ethics there is, I think, no topic which lies closer to its center than that of principle and practice. Principle and practice is what the whole of ethics is about, and no topic seems better fitted to afford a survey of the entire field.

But the topic has another advantage as well. It enables one to exhibit the relation that exists between ethics and dogmatics, the two positive and coordinate disciplines embraced by systematic theology. It is commonly said that dogmatics is concerned with truth and that ethics is concerned with goodness, that one deals with doctrine and the other with life, that one elaborates the faith of Christians and the other considers their works, that one deals with the principles of godliness and charity and the other with the practice of them. It may be questioned whether this is actually so, but there is enough truth in the suggested distinction to justify the expectation that a discussion of principle and practice will illumine not merely the field of ethics as such, but also its interconnections with dogmatics, its companion discipline.

In any case, this essay, under this title, will move not only circularly within the field of ethics, but also horizontally between the two disciplines which lie together in the larger field of systematic theology. A certain oneness or mutuality may in this way come to light, a oneness reminiscent of the nature and function of our Lord, who once said: "I am the Way, i.e., the Truth and the Life."

It should be remarked that I shall be using the term "principle" in the broadest possible sense. I shall use it to denote not merely ethical, but also dogmatical and indeed even ontological realities, on which account it will appear variously as a synonym for truth, fact, norm, doctrine, dogma, and the like. I shall allow myself a similar latitude in using the word "practice." It will be employed in general as a synonym for existence, life, process, and for conduct or behavior in any field or under any aspect, though its connotations will tend to be predominantly moral. It is hoped that this elasticity will not obscure the sense of the words in any given context.

B. PROBLEM AND THESIS

Ethics, it is clear, is a *practical* science. It is concerned to understand and structure human conduct, to grasp and form the patterns of good behavior. What it seeks to apprehend and urge is the deepest rationale of sound practice. But ethics is also a practical *science*. As such it is concerned with principle and truth. It must, through the insights of faith and by the power of reason, penetrate to and disclose the last ground—and above this, the cosmic structures—which underlie, define, and direct good behavior. Ethics, therefore, represents a combination of principle and practice, a set of things which it contemplates as existing in indissoluble union.

Being a *normative*, and not a merely descriptive, science, ethics is concerned not merely or primarily with the variable actualities of practice, but with the persistent norms of practice. What it centrally addresses itself to are the abiding structures and values which define approved behavior. On the other hand, being a practical and not a merely theoretical science, it is concerned not with abstract truth, static structures, and exclusively transcendent principles, but only with dynamic and relevant principles, i.e., with such truths and structures as make a difference, or are able to make a difference, in practice.

In ethics a practice that is not structured by and interpretable in terms of principle or truth is of little interest. And conversely, a principle or truth which is not related to, and which is not able to direct practice, falls outside its purview. Ethics deals only with practice that is or can be structured by principle, and it deals only with principle able dynamically to shape and regulate practice. Ethics—at least Christian ethics—knows nothing of unprincipled practice or of impracticable principles. From the point of view of ethics, principles and practice are inseparable; they do not and cannot exist, or at least worthily exist, in isolation. A principle that does not issue into practice is empty; a practice that does not flow from principle is blind. A theory or doctrine is worthless that is not calculated to influence the conduct of the person who assents to it; and a course of action is worthless that does not ultimately root in a principle able finally to validate it.

Now, what the ethicist discovers to appertain to ethics, he universalizes. Instructed by his analyses in his own field, he hazards the judgment that every meaningful practice is principled, i.e., roots in theory or dogma; and that every meaningful principle or dogma is practicable, i.e., is amenable to and demands incarnation on the level of behavior. What has become apparent to him in his own field is recognized by him as having general validity and application. The togetherness of principle and practice has for him universal or philosophical import, and he apprehends that no one in any field of inquiry is entitled to separate the two. Everyone, from the ontologist and the dogmatician on the one hand, to the practical schemer on the other hand, is obliged to recognize and preserve the indissoluble unity of principle and practice. No one, anywhere, may say: "This is good practice, though it is merely whimsical and arbitrary"; and no one, anywhere, may say: "This is a good principle or doctrine, though it has no bearing on behavior, and will in fact not work." The sign of sound principle is always its power to transform personal and social existence; the sign of responsible action is always its accord with right principle and true doctrine.

He who says this has, however, a battle to fight on two fronts.

In the first place, there are those who think the ethicist has, or need have, no concern with fixed and abiding principles. Admitting that ethics deals with practice, the objectors think it unnecessary and perhaps impossible for the ethicist to settle practice upon dogma, to found it on truth, to root it in basic principle. Those who think this way either repudiate ontology and theology outright, or consider that ethics has nothing to do with these. They are afraid of a theological or dogmatic ethics, and they shun an ethics with metaphysical dimensions. Occupying this position are the positivists, many pragmatists, and, on another level, all those who think of themselves as hardheaded practical men.

In opposing these people the Christian ethicist can, fortunately, count on the support of the metaphysician and the dogmatician. These are always ready to declare, with the Christian moralist, that the *ought* is founded upon the *is*, that good conduct rests on true beliefs, that underlying all commands is a fact or a set of facts, that imperatives are based on indicatives, that dogma undergirds injunctions, that only ontological and cosmological descriptions justify behavioral prescriptions, that only the truly real has the right and the power to move to action, that, in short, to found, illumine, and estimate practice recourse must be had to fact, principle, and dogma, and ultimately to being as such or God.

If there be those who think practice can be divorced from principle, there are those, on the other hand, who think principle can be divorced from practice; or they think, at any rate, that there is only a unilateral connection between the two. These people deny or obscure the mutuality of principle and practice. They think principle affects practice, but they do not think that practice affects principle. Those who think this way give to principle not only a certain priority over practice; they conceive of principle as a detached a priori. They place truth, dogma, theory beyond the reach of process. They are quite willing to explain and structure process in terms of theory, but refuse to alter theory or to deepen it in the light of process. Occupying this position are many metaphysicians and, one suspects, not a few dogmaticians. For them a pure reason or a fixed immobile faith is sufficient to disclose the structures of the real. In their view practice or living can do little or nothing to disclose otherwise unrecognized aspects of reality. They think that understanding or belief should remain unaffected by developing experience, by the course of daily conduct, and by the quality of practical decisions.

In opposing these people the Christian ethicist can count on the support of the best elements in the Christian tradition and in the contemporary Christian community, and he can count also on the support of some pragmatists and existentialists in the secular world. With the best of these the Christian ethicist is able to declare that truth and principle is not disclosed to those who sit in ivory towers raised high above the stream and flow of life, but only to those who are set in life's arena and who there grasp truth not through static contemplation but through dynamic decision in direct and immediate relation to the existential situation. Truth, he can declare, at least such truth as men can possibly take interest in, is always truth connected with the human situation, and never something divorced from it. Profound truth, religious truth, is emphatically not relative, but it is related. Itself not born of process, it neither exists nor is conceivable apart from process. Truth is always living truth, which justifies itself in practice and in life. It is essentially dynamic, because ultimately personal, and this is why it always escapes the grasp of one whose faith and reason is untutored by experience and undisciplined by the immediacies of historical existence.

The fight on two fronts is therefore a fight in the first place against an ill-conceived practice, and in the second place against an ill-conceived principle or dogma. It is evident that the nature both of conduct and of truth can be misunderstood. Behavior can be mistakenly reduced to mere blind process, and doctrine can mistakenly be reduced to mere empty formulas. Biblical Christianity is, however, proof against both of these errors. It is satisfied neither with intellectual abstractions nor with practical expedients. It repudiates both rationalism and pragmatism. Yet it recognizes the element of truth in each, and is idealistic and realistic, transcendent and immanent at once. It insists on principles, but is conscious of the need of an expanding experience both to illustrate and to sharpen them.

In what follows I shall attempt a further elaboration of these points. I shall consider first the fact that significant practice is undergirded with principle, and shall consider in the second place the need both of incarnating principle in practice and of enriching principle with the insights of expanding experience.

In the first place, then, it must be observed that, in the Christian view, practice is and should be principled.

C. PRACTICE AND PRINCIPLE

When one moves on the upper surface of life, all that presents itself to view is overt action or outward behavior. Like the waves of the sea or the cap of an iceberg, these do not immediately suggest a dimension of depth.

Yet there is more to behavior and practice than what immediately meets the eye. All actions have their under side, upon which, hidden from superficial view, various generating and conditioning forces play. This is true even of those apparently accidental actions or whimsical happenstances which seem to dance like flotsam on the waves of life, and which appear to be as shallow as a line in mathematics. Even these do not stand alone.

What immediately underlies all actions is, of course, the actor, a human being who in these actions reveals himself. When the question is asked, however, who this man is, and why he acts the way he does, two sets of answers are forthcoming.

One set of answers moves exclusively on the horizontal plane, and presumes to "explain" man and his behavior in terms of "conditioning" factors. Implied in these answers is the assumption that while behavior has a dimension of depth in man, man himself is without a similar dimension and resides wholly on the horizontal plane of history and nature. Upon the basis of this assumption the natural sciences set out to account for him in terms of matter and energy; and the biological, psychological, and social sciences set out to do the same in terms of heredity and environment.

Because man does in fact have a horizontal dimension, and because he is in fact tied in with nature, the presence of "conditioning" factors cannot be denied. There is that in man which is amenable to "causal explanation." Accordingly, the effect upon him, and upon his conduct, of chemical processes, biological instincts, psychological drives and complexes, economic determinants, and social pressures may never be ignored. It would be a mistake, however, to suppose that the natural sciences, or those social sciences which proceed by way of the quantitative analysis of empirical givens, are able really to interpret man and his behavior. The methods employed within these sciences, fashioned as they are for use on the horizontal plane, are simply not fitted to plumb the depths of man.

Attention must be given, therefore, to another set of answers to the question about man and his behavior. These answers, proclaimed by Christian ethics, arise out of theology and metaphysics, and reflect an apprehension of man's vertical dimension. Integral to them is the recognition that, though man is undoubtedly tied in with nature, he is even more certainly tied in with God. This being tied to God, it is recognized, is precisely what accounts for man's humanity. It is this which raises man above mere animality and constitutes him a moral person. It is this, moreover, which enables him to break through the causal nexus and transcend merely natural determinants. Being tied in with God, having a dimension of depth, oriented to some object of ultimate concern, he can rise above the influences playing upon him from the side and exercise a genuine freedom—the freedom to set himself ideals and to aspire after them.

To the question, what is man, and why does he behave the way he does, we can give no proper answer, therefore, until we have recognized that, being tied to God, man is inextricably religious and consequently theological. Of the God to whom he is ontologically related, he forms some conception, and to the God thus conceived he makes determinate response. Man is what he is *coram deo,* and it is before the face of God that he learns just what his duties are, and therefore what his choices and decisions ought to be. Man, the actor, is a being who, supporting his own behavior, is himself supported by the ultimate ground of all existence. Himself residing on the plane of history, where he is affected by a variety of influences, he can shape his life and the history of himself and his society by grasping the nature and structure of the real which undergirds and challenges him.

It is through this grasping of the real, or of what is taken as such, that man does in fact always patternize his overt behavior. It is ultimately by apprehending and applying real or presumed ontological principles that he shapes his practice. This is true of all men, Christian or not. There is no intelligible and responsible moral practice which does not look for validation to a set of moral principles embraced in some elaborated or incipient ethics, and there is no ethics which does not articulate some embryonic or full-blown ontology; which is to say that there is no ethics which does not set forth, implicitly at least, some view of God or of ultimate reality. All practice rests on principles which in their depths are metaphysical or theological.

There is a disposition in some quarters to deny this. There are contemporary ethicists who will have nothing at all to do with theology and who equate ontology with meaningless speculation. They attempt accordingly to construct what they like to call a "scientific" ethics, which distils its norms and ideals from social existence as this is illumined by controlled experience. What seems to escape these men, however, is that there is implicit in their Positivism a vast ontological denial, which is no less ontological for being a denial. They aver that underlying human life and experience is neither God nor a stable and determinate cosmic structure, and therewith they have ventured into metaphysics. Conversely, they have therewith made obeisance to the god of Heraclitus. This sort of thing is quite inevitable; to be ontological or theological is man's fate.

Those, accordingly, who disclaim ontology and discredit dogma are not really freeing themselves from these; they are merely substituting their own ultimate affirmations for certain others which they do not like; they are proposing that new absolutes replace the old. So, for example, when Immanuel Kant declared, "There are those who argue that we must first have God and then morality," and when he himself replied to this by saying "but Ethics and Theology are neither of them a principle of the other," he was not really removing the theological support of ethics; he was merely altering the underlying theology by unseating the Christian God and placing Rational Law upon the empty throne. God was made subject to Law; and in that instant Law itself became a god and began to determine the Kantian ethic. The case is similar when the modern man reproaches dogma and its divisiveness and cries out for unity and love. A call for authentic love is surely always warranted, but the contention that love is basic is itself a dogma, which may be good or bad depending on what love is conceived to be, it being evident that there are several kinds of love, each qualified by its context, i.e., by the specific kind of all-embracing faith in which it lies.

It appears, therefore, that old and new protests against a theologically determined morality need not be heeded. Those who make the protest do not themselves heed it, for they cannot; a dogmatic ethics is inescapable; men are theologians in spite of themselves. Because God exists and cannot be evaded, men cannot help proclaiming God—the true God or some spurious one—and they cannot help placing him (or it) beneath their lives as a foundation. Implicit in their practice and prescriptions is an ontological principle or *arche*, and attending it are derivative principles which in accordance with the way in which they are held determine ethical judgment and shape moral conduct.

At this juncture, however, a difficulty arises, and a short excursus must be made to meet it. If what has been said be true, we are bound to declare that all practice is principled; but then we are prevented from stigmatizing any behavior as "unprincipled," which seems a pity, for we are accustomed to distinguish a man of principle from one who acts out of mere expediency. Is there a way out of this? I think there is.

We have only to remember that the person who seeks the depth of his existence in order to find reality, or God, or an object of ultimate concern, may in fact impinge on that which is not ultimate at all. He may take for absolute what is only relative, he may take for God what is not God, and undertake to regulate his life by *that*. He will then be acting formally on principle, but since the principle is spurious, he will be acting materially on what in fact is not a principle or *arche*, and thus perhaps be following the prudential path of mere expedience. Take the man, for example, who in living his life does nothing but follow the crowd. Is he a man of principle? From the *formal* point of view he is, for he has taken the "Crowd" as god, and he is determined to follow the dictates of the crowd. Yet from the *material* point of view we should declare him quite "unprincipled," for his god is wholly caught up in process, and his loyalty to it drives him from one expedient to another; he changes his behavior in continuous adjustment to the variable moods of the ever-surging crowd.

This is not to suggest, however, that all those who misconceive reality or mistake God are in some sense "unprincipled." It is possible, even on the basis of a faulty ontology or theology, to rise above a merely prudential ethics. Plato and Kant, among others, illustrate this. They were able to circumvent expediency because they located their principles at a point below the level of process—the one in timeless ideas, and the other in immutable law. On the basis of these stable principles each constructed a rigoristic ethics calculated to produce men of principle who could chart a tolerably straight course through life. The only trouble was that these principles were not in fact ultimate—not really real and therefore not really true—in consequence of which their ethics was defective and the practice it engendered was in significant areas inauthentic.

If, after this excursus, we recall and assent to what has been the general thesis of this section—that practice rests on principles which in their depths are theological, and that there is no ethics which does not set forth some view of God or of ultimate reality—then we are in a position to draw a number of inferences for the Christian ethicist.

1. It is apparent, first, that a crucial question in ethics—no doubt the most crucial—concerns the character and quality of the ultimate principle to which conscious or unconscious appeal is made by men when they undertake to regulate their lives. That men do orient their lives to one principle or another is, I think, incontrovertible. It seems equally clear that they do this in a religious way; their deepest principle is an object of ultimate concern, a "god." It is also evident that when an account is given of this principle, it is a theological account that is given; all significant practical prescriptions rest finally on theological assertions.

When all this is declared and assented to, however, one has to ask the further question: But are these theological assertions true? and are the objects of them appropriately real? For though men be ever so religious and theological, this does not mean that they have really embraced *God.* In the case of the crowd-pleaser it was not God but process that was served; in the case of Plato it was Eidos; and in the case of Kant it was Moral Law. Things of this sort can indeed be taken as "gods," but if they are not truly God they cannot possibly make absolute demands, and if no absolute demands are made nothing can prevent the structure of morality from collapsing into utter relativity. To insure that on the level of behavior Whirl shall not be king, it is necessary at the deepest level of the universe to lay hold on what is really and truly God. To be ultimate, and thus be able really to control behavior, a principle must be actually and exclusively divine. Because this is so the question about God is the central question in ethics, and the apprehension of him is or should be the ethicist's chief concern.

It is impossible to discuss in this brief space the several ramifications of the question as to how the ethicist's interest in apprehending God can best be satisfied. It must suffice to indicate what the ethicist who is a Christian says when questioned on this matter. He will say: "It is not I who apprehended him; he apprehended me." In this short reply the Christian ethicist has done two things: by designating himself as the apprehended one he has expressed implicitly an entire epistemology; and by characterizing the ultimate as the apprehender he has pointed to the only "principle" which can properly be called God. God, as Christians know him, is many things; his attributes are numerous, and each of them is infinite. But what distinguishes him from the gods of the philosophers is precisely this, that he is a person who apprehends, rather than a thing which is apprehended. He is the living God. He is not an object that is searched out, but a subject who invades. He is preeminently a person who wills community and is actively engaged in establishing a spirituo-moral kingdom of men made perfect under his tutelage and lordship. He is a person who does not wait to be courted, but who in love and grace always seizes the initiative, being the first in every saving encounter with the race of men. He is, in short, not the God who has been discovered, but the God who has *revealed* himself.

It is the God revealed in many saving acts among his ancient people Israel, in many words spoken to and through the prophets and apostles, in one great sacrifice made in and through his well-beloved Son our Lord—it is this God who is the true and only principle of all good behavior. It is only as it is placed in relation to this God—the only God there is—that practice can be determined unto good and fashioned into virtue. All morality is grounded in the character, the acts, the purposes, and the instructions of the God of revelation. It is upon this God, the God spoken of in the Bible and professed in the Christian Church, that the Christian ethicist attempts to build his ethics and establish all practice. This is his *ultimate principle.*

2. As has already been indicated, but must now, and in the second place, be emphatically affirmed, this God meets the children of this age primarily in *the Bible.* The personal God, active throughout history in creative, sustaining, and redemptive work, informs us of himself and of his acts through the pages of a book, a book which the Christian ethicist accordingly lays down as the veritable platform for his work. He does this because he apprehends that this book discloses God not only in his being and person, but also in his will for our lives. He has discovered that in it, and in our behalf, God publishes the nature of true values, depicts the norms of good behavior, and sets the goals for moral striving—proclaiming his will to his children less as imperious demands than as gracious prescriptions for enjoying the fellowship which he

mercifully proffers and freely imparts in Christ. Without this authoritative book the Christian ethicist would not only not know the ultimate *arche* as he may and should be known, but he would remain ignorant or uncertain about the divinely established maxims, laws, and ordinances which constitute the indispensable *secondary principles* in ethics and in life.

3. In the third place, since in the biblical view virtue is the doing of *the truth*, it will surprise no one that the Christian ethicist bends every effort to appropriate the theological truth stored up in the Church. Illumined, purified, and enriched through ever new addresses to the Word of God by the active theological community, this funded knowledge is the very stuff of ethical reflection and the designated tool for the moralist's reforming work. The truth grasped in the creeds, in the classical treatises on dogmatics, and in the responsible conclusions of contemporary theologians, is all that the ethicist has with which to transform personal and social life. In the last analysis, the good life is the life patterned after God in Christ, the Truth; or alternately, it is the life patterned after what God has done, the fact. And since God and Christ, and what they have done for men, are systematically portrayed in dogmatics, the latter is indispensable to ethics.

The relation of dependence that ethics sustains to dogmatics is similar to that which the second half of most Pauline epistles sustains to the first. The *kerygma* first proclaimed is connected by a "therefore" with the *didache* which follows. An exposition of God's *Gabe* issues into an account of man's *Aufgabe*. The almost invariable formula is: This is true, therefore this must be done. From this we may conclude that we cannot love as Christians unless we believe as Christians. Good conduct rests on the solid ground of fact. Good practice rests on good principle.

This brings me to the second thesis of this discussion: That principle must be apprehended through, incarnated in, and enriched by, practice.

D. PRINCIPLE AND PRACTICE

We have seen that principle underlies practice, upholds it, and is calculated to shape and control it. From this it is evident that principle has a certain priority over practice. It is obviously more basic and more stable, and it is probably earlier, than practice. If the living God is thought of as a principle, as he was at one point in the foregoing, then one principle at least is surely earlier than practice, and in every other way prior to it.

We are not to conclude, however, that nothing can be said about practice except that it rests upon principle and suffers its invasions. There is a certain priority and independence in practice as well as in principle. This priority and independence is not of the sort that would require us to retract what has already been said, but it is of a sort that is both real and important, and it may not be ignored. In what follows I shall seek to point out this priority, and to delineate some of the ways in which practice puts principle in its debt.

In order to place this part of the discussion in focus it should be remarked that the term "principle" is here employed in its proper sense. As has already been observed, it is proper to use the term as a synonym for knowledge, truth, fact, doctrine, theory, conception, and the like. In the foregoing it was generally used in this sense. But, for what I trust were sufficient reasons, it was used in other senses as well. It was used once to designate the living and personal God in his real concreteness. This was an extraordinary and analogical use of the term for the purpose of indicating that God is *arche*, beginning, or *princeps*—the source and ground of all being and all good, the ultimate principle of the universe. Once, too, the Bible was called a "principle." The concern in that instance was to indicate that God's inscriptured Word underlies, or ought to underlie and thus determine, Christian practice. During most of the discussion, however, "principle" was used in the sense of "theory" or "doctrine," as it properly should be, and in what follows I wish the term to be taken in this common and familiar sense.

This being settled, it may be observed that principles—i.e., theories or doctrines—are normally not "given"; they are made. They are constructs. They are intellectual products fashioned in the mind. They are not found ready to hand; they are hewn out by the thinker. Of course, if they are proper principles they are not constructed out of mind-stuff, spun out of the head. Though made by the mind, they are not made out of mind. They are fashioned by the mind out of "givens." So, for example, sound theological principles, or dogmas, are made out of the "givens" presented by revelation. But these "givens" are prior to the principles, and are in fact the test and monitor of them. The "givens" are both there and in some way apprehended prior to and independently of their being fashioned by the power of thought into principles.

With these facts and distinctions in mind, we shall be prepared to recognize that practice underlies principle quite as much as principle underlies practice; we shall be able to see that behavior influences dogma quite as much as dogma influences behavior; we shall, in short, be able to accord to practice a significance which rivals that enjoyed by principle.

To recognize the importance of practice, and to appreciate the active role it plays in forming principle, one could profitably look in several directions, but it is perhaps most helpful to begin by attending to the central doctrine or principle of Christianity, and indeed of all religion, the doctrine of God.

If we consider not the living God in his dynamic concreteness, not the infinite and incomprehensible *arche* or *princeps* of the cosmos who lies beyond the reach of all our theoretical formulas; if we consider rather our human doctrine of God, our theory or conception of him, our rationalized knowledge concerning him; if we consider, that is, our construct of God, our dogma concerning God, the "principle" of God enunciated in our theologies; if we consider this, what is prior: dogma or behavior? knowledge or conduct? principle or practice?

By the terms of our problem, behind both principle and practice stands the living God. He is for both principle and practice, for both our dogmatic constructions and our spiritual attitudes and acts, the concrete "given," giving or disclosing himself in Christ, or in nature, or in history, or in the human consciousness, or in this or that event or pronouncement recorded in the Bible. What then, in our encounter with him, is first: principle or practice? our notion of him or our response to him? In the divine-human encounter does knowledge precede action or does action precede knowledge? does principle determine practice or does practice determine principle? Standing before the personal and dynamic presence which is God, do we know him first and then make obeisance to him? or do we first bow down before him and therein get to know him? Is our moral and spiritual posture before God a consequence of our knowledge of him? or is it the precondition of such knowledge? Do we surrender to God after we have identified him? or do we discover him only after or in the act of surrender? Questions such as these suggest that something can be said, if not for the strict and exclusive priority of practice, then at least for the simultaneity of practice and principle.

The fact is, I think, that God cannot be known—as God—except in and with a surrender to him. The surrender is not prior to the knowledge, but neither is the knowledge prior to the surrender. They are simultaneous. Here practice is as significant as principle; here conduct claims equality with knowledge. Love is here as much the ground of truth, as truth is of love.

One is tempted to say, indeed, that this interdependence of behavior and cognition is universal, not restricted to man's relation to the deity. As is well known, knowledge of finite persons, as distinct from finite things, requires certain attitudes and acts in the knower before the object can be known. This is because a finite personal object is only partially an "object" available to disinterested technical reason; he is partially, and at the core, a free "subject," who can and does lay down conditions for being known. He will allow himself to be known only by those who approach him with empathy; he will be understood only by those who in his presence dispose themselves in appropriate ways. It is perhaps not too much to say that even impersonal entities—proper "objects"—lay down practical conditions for being known; even these are cognitively impenetrable when patience and humility, and modes of conduct dictated by these virtues, are completely lacking in the knower.

But if this be so, it is a fortiori so when knowledge concerning the living God is in question. God is not centrally an "object." He is infinite person, in the most radical sense a "subject." He cannot be hunted down, stalked, taken unawares, and detachedly observed. If he is to be known at all, he must reveal himself freely, and in that revelation be embraced. It is only in and through this embracement that he is existentially disclosed and really "known." Only as he is loved is he truly apprehended.

Of course, it is true: God *has* revealed himself objectively, and thus in a sense he is exposed to observation even by those who do not love him; but the knowledge that is born in this relation is meager. It appears to be just enough to justify our calling it an "ignorant awareness." To really know God—to know him as he is in both his awful majesty and his loving tenderness—one must lie prostrate before him. There must here, as in all knowledge at its depth, be a dynamic union of subject and object, knower and known, a union in which love and knowledge meet. There must be this, for in relation to God all indicatives are imperatives. To say that God *exists* is to say that what exists is *God,* i.e., he who by definition has a claim on our whole existence and who requires and deserves our total obedience. There can be no recognition of a fact here except in a posture of commitment; there can be no awareness of truth here except through a religious decision of the will to submit unconditionally.

The Bible and classical Christian theology is of course well aware of this state of affairs. Both witness to the fact that moral sensitivity is the precondition of religious insight, that God does not disclose himself to the proud and disobedient, that knowledge of divine things is not vouchsafed to the unjust and the selfish, that only a surrendered life attains to final certainty, and that theological conviction comes only to him whose will is turned to God in pious fear and to men in selfless love. Both recognize that truth can be discerned and principles framed only through moral and spiritual "involvement"; both teach that only he who stands in the valley of decision can be said really to "understand."

This is the import of Solomon's words: "The fear of Jehovah is the beginning of knowledge" (Prov. 1:7), and of John's words: "He that loveth not, knoweth not God" (I John 4:8). It is what Jesus was concerned to say when he declared: "If any man willeth to do his will, he shall know of the teaching, whether it is of God, or whether I speak from myself" (John 7:17), and it is what Paul had in view when he discovered in the natural man's moral perversity the reason for his failure to keep the knowledge of God in his mind (Rom. 1:21). It is what Calvin taught when he said: "the knowledge of God does not rest in cold speculation, but carries with it the honoring of him." It is what Pascal meant by the words: "To love man you must know him; to know God you must love him," and it is what Herman Bavinck knew when he declared: "God is known in proportion to the extent that he is loved." John Baillie put it this way: "Part of the reason why I could not find God was that there is that in God which I did not wish to find. Part of the reason why I could not hear him speak was that he was saying some things to me which I did not wish to hear. . . . It is futile to expect God's reality to become any clearer to us so long as we continue to shut our eyes to those aspects of His reality which make difficult demands upon our lives."

The sum of all this seems to be that when it comes to God, and when it comes to religious and spiritual matters generally, the path to knowledge leads through the valley of obedience. Here, quite plainly, practice is indispensable to principle. Here it is as true to say that there can be no correct belief without correct behavior, as it is to say that there can be no correct behavior without correct belief. Life and theory, existence and conviction, love and understanding here stand and fall together.

Relative to God and to religious truth generally, practice undoubtedly influences principle. The movement of the will stimulates and guides theological insight, and obedience trains the eyes to behold the truth. Our non-cognitive attitudes and acts on the level of moral and religious existence affect our understanding and influence the formation of our principles. This gives to practice its significance; it indicates that, though practice does significantly follow principle, it also invades and directs it.

That practice plays formatively upon principle may be seen from another angle if we attend, not now to God or to the principles and constructs pertaining to him, but to the nature and function of principles generally, i.e., to the essence of principle as such. A principle ought to impinge upon and regulate practice. Whatever other function it may perform, it cannot, without ceasing to be an authentic principle, fail to interpret and patternize practice. But this means that no true principle can be fashioned in isolation from practice, without knowledge about it, or without accommodation to it. In order to be practicable, i.e., relevant to life and capable of transforming it, principles must from the outset take into account, and actually incorporate within themselves, the enduring structures and impulses of human practice.

It is necessary to point this out because the existential dimension of principle is a *second* dimension, and it often lies concealed in the shadow of the first or ontological dimension. Principles do not in the first instance point upward and outward toward behavior. Their *first* movement is downward and inward toward the deeper levels of reality. A principle represents a man's attempt to catch in a responsible formula the basic structure of the real. A good principle is therefore a transcript of what is so, presumably forever so. No doubt the object or purpose of framing a principle is to grasp in it a basic pattern of the cosmos in order later to form the inchoate upper levels of existence into conformity with this pattern; but the "grasping" is first, and precedes the "forming." So, for example, the Christian statesman *first* grasps in a principle what he considers to be the divinely ordained and cosmically validated structure of human relations within society, and *then*, in accordance with that principle, he seeks to get certain pieces of legislation passed, or policies adopted, or programs started, which are calculated to bring into existence a state or a society resembling the ideal pattern his principle embodies.

But now it can happen that a man, who in order to frame a principle is obliged to look down into the depths of revelation or of the cosmos, never comes to the point where he looks up towards the life the principle was meant eventually to serve; or else, he comes up with a principle which, because it was not fashioned in existential awareness, is quite inapplicable to life, and can only be regarded as utopian. Such a man has failed, for a principle—if it is to deserve that name at all—must always face or point in two directions. It must face the static structures of the cosmos and describe them, and it must face the flowing life at the surface of existence and prescribe for it. It must depict being and challenge becoming. It must reflect the deeper layers of reality and appertain to the shallower layers awaiting structuration. A principle which fails in either one of these functions is attenuated. It is in fact a pseudo-principle.

Of concern at this moment, however, is not that principles should comport with reality and adequately depict it (as they certainly should), but that they should be practicable, i.e., that they should be so fitted to experience as to be able to transform it. If they are not thus suited to existence, and if, in consequence, they are not effectual, they do not deserve the name they bear. Being practically impotent, they lack an essential quality of principle: practicality. Let a man say that he has a principle, but that it will not work, and he should be told that its unworkability proves that it is no principle, but at best a policy. Perhaps it is a great deal worse. Perhaps it is a figment, something he has spun out of his own head. It is quite possible in a given instance that this is the case, for the mind is a curious thing. It has the ability not only to read and transcribe objective reality and thus construct genuine principles, but to excogitate in the blue and spawn intellectual abstractions able to parade as principles. Unoriented either to basic reality or to the processes of life, these spinnings-out of the mind's own substance are without practical relevance, and are existentially meaningless.

But no true principle can be this. It always intends both the real and the actual, and its "actualness" is as great a test of its authenticity as its "correspondence" to reality. It is in fact the integral combination of actualness and correspondence which constitutes its "truth." In the area of theology this means that Christian doctrines can be recommended as true only as they can be presented as also practically efficacious. John Calvin is himself a classical witness to this. The only principles he recognizes are those which are pregnant with practical meaning; all the doctrines he fashions, he does so with practical intent. He is a Christian pragmatist who, however deeply he may probe into God's revelation, never allows his attention to be abstracted from the plane of behavior where the "meaning" of truth is disclosed. He is a Christian pragmatist who habitually characterizes as speculative any doctrine which lacks "cash value." Truth, he maintains, is always a "power" producing "profit."

In commenting on Philippians 1:10, Calvin says: "Here we have a definition of Christian wisdom—to know what is advantageous or expedient—not to torture the mind with empty subtleties and speculations. For the Lord does not wish that his believing people should employ themselves fruitlessly in learning what is of no profit." What Calvin here deprecates is the scholasticism (not limited to the Middle Ages or to Roman theologians) which by isolating principle from practice produces nothing but arid logisms destitute of life and power. He therefore continues: "From this you may gather in what estimation the Sorbonnic theology ought to be held, in which you may spend your whole life, and yet not derive more of edification from it in connection with the hope of a heavenly life, or more of spiritual advantage, than from the demonstrations of Euclid. Unquestionably, though it taught nothing false, it well deserves to be execrable, on the ground that it is a pernicious profanation of spiritual doctrine. For Scripture is useful. . . ." In commenting on Titus 1:9 Calvin once more requires of principle that it subserve the interests of practice: "But what is meant by 'according to instruction or doctrine'? The meaning is, that it is useful for the edification of the Church; for Paul is not wont to give the name of 'doctrine' to anything that is learned and known without promoting any advancement of godliness; but, on the contrary, he condemns as vain and unprofitable all speculations which yield no advantage, however ingenious they may be in other respects." Practice, thinks Calvin, is the very test of principle. Commenting on what Paul writes in I Timothy 1:4, he says: "He judges of doctrine by the fruit: for everything that does not edify ought to be rejected, although it has no other fault; and everything that is of no avail but for raising contentions, ought to be doubly condemned. . . . Let us, therefore, remember that all doctrines must be tried by this rule . . . ." Consider as a final example of Calvin's characteristic emphasis, his observations on I Timothy 6:4: "The 'doctrine' will not be consistent with 'godliness' if it do not instruct us in the fear and worship of God, if it do not edify our faith, if it do not train us to patience, humility, and all the duties of that love which we owe to our fellow-men.

Whoever, therefore, does not strive to teach usefully, does not teach as he ought to do; and not only so, but that doctrine is neither godly nor sound, whatever may be the brilliancy of its display, that does not tend to the profit of the hearers."

Calvin is not in these and similar remarks abetting the later Ritschlianism which held that moral and spiritual "value" is the whole meaning of doctrine. Calvin believed that all genuinely Christian doctrines have moral import because they are true, and because truth is inextricably bound up with goodness. For him, unlike the Ritschlians, the power of principle to influence practice originated on a level deeper than practice. Yet he was convinced that the way to this deeper level led through practice, and he never supposed that he understood that which undergirded practice as long as he did not understand that practice which was thus undergirded. He never supposed that he could ever either know or fashion a principle without knowing and expressing its practical import too. For him the "meaning" of principle included practice.

And so indeed it does. A "bare" principle, unmounted, undirected, untriggered, is without significance. To be significant a principle must be practical, and since principles are "made," they must be *made* practical by fashioning them in conformity to the structures of existence. Since this can be done only through obedience to the actual, it is clear that so far as this obedience goes principle depends on practice.

There is still another sense in which principle depends on practice. Not only does religious existence influence the formation of our theological principles; not only are principles obliged to undergo a focussing calculated to direct them outward, and to make them practically effective; principles must be sensitively responsive to historical changes on the level of existence.

There is no doubt that principles are in the first instance transcripts of the enduringly real and not tracings of the merely actual. Rooted in ontology they are more the shapers of historical existence than the products of it. Yet, however deeply they are anchored in abiding truth, and however faithfully they may depict the changeless structure of being, they can never be entirely free of time-conditioned contingencies which, with changing times, must be removed and substituted for. There is in every sound principle a timelessness which makes it relevant to all times, and there is in every one of them a universality which enables them to cope not merely with this or that particular situation, but with the human situation generally. Yet no principle is absolute and therefore beyond amendment, for every principle is a construct fashioned at a particular time, by a particular person or community, with reference to a particular complex of problems and concerns. This means that there is no principle in which a note of relativity has not entered. Built into every principle is something of the "situation"; a part of "practice" has been incorporated into it. This is by no means all loss, for this note of particularity helps the principle, in its time, to achieve relevancy; it assists it to interpret and direct the contemporary behaviors and concerns of men.

But times change, and with the changing times the principle tends to lose the sharp edge of its practical reference. If it is a genuine principle it will never lose its essential truth; it will remain permanently and universally true, and on that account be basically relevant always. But it will, if nothing is done to avert the consequence, lose some of its creative import and become in that degree more formal and less existential than it ought to be. This will happen because there is that in it which is historically conditioned and thus subject to the ravages of time.

What is required, therefore, is that the principle be kept under practical surveillance. What is demanded is not constant tampering; a principle has a status and dignity of its own, which must be respected. But required, relative to principle, is, in addition to insight into the eternal verities, concrete good sense disciplined in life's processes. This is required for keeping a principle fresh and timely, and for preserving its relevance and power. We have no call, indeed, to substitute one principle for another in chameleon-like response to changing situations; principles are not the pawns of circumstance. But such principles as we have we should be constantly enriching with the accumulating wisdom of practical experience, and when occasion demands we should not be afraid to alter them to fit the dimensions of our growing world and of our expanding intelligence. We should, moreover, be always ready to refocus them in order to make them impinge with maximum sharpness on the concrete problems of the day. If we do not do these things, if we treat our principles as literally timeless, if we worshipfully conserve them in some ivory tower, if we carefully insulate them against every alteration, then we will perhaps not kill them, since their inner truth is imperishable; but we will stultify them and effectively prevent them from fructifying life and regulating practice.

That in doing the work here recommended we will be involved in tensions is undeniable. But the polarities of reality and existence, truth and life, are simply there, and they tolerate no selective absolutisms. A Christian is here obliged to take pains to stand firmly on the center line of truth, between formalism on the one hand and relativism on the other. He is required to regard principles neither as the mere projections of the situation nor as, in their concreteness, totally sacrosanct ultimates. And he is required to regard practice neither as unprincipled and unformed nor as unfree and uncreative. To stand on this center line is difficult and precarious, and we need not suppose that we shall be able always to maintain our balance; but balance is what is required, and this is what the Christian strives and prays for.

E. CONCLUSION

The conclusion of the matter can be quickly stated: principle and practice are interrelated and mutually dependent. For the total theological enterprise this has many implications which cannot here be recited. With reference to theological disciplines it means that the ethicist is thrown back, for the formulation of his prescriptions, upon the descriptions of divine fact made by the dogmatician. By the same token it means that the dogmatician is obliged to construct and manipulate principles with moral sensitivity, and to realize that new insight into the givens of revelation are possible if the light of growing experience, and the light that is kindled in moral decision, is allowed to shine both into his mind and onto the pages of the sacred Scriptures.

A certain tension between principle and practice, dogmatics and ethics, there will doubtless always be. The confidence that these tensions need never erupt into unbrotherly strife or pernicious heresy is based on the conviction that when head and heart, intellect and will, are both surrendered to the Lord, principle and practice, truth and love, will rise up to embrace each other.

4

God and Man*

WHEN St. Augustine considered what it was that he ought to know, he concluded that it was two things only: God and the soul, and nothing more. It is true that this conclusion and the consequent dual concern was not peculiar to him. It grew out of the turning that Socrates had made in the history of philosophy, and it was shared by most hellenistic thinkers, notably by the Neo-Platonists. But the concern was in accord with the Christian Scriptures, and it both dominated medieval thought and gave shape to Reformation doctrine. Calvin, at any rate, allowed it to control his systematic exposition of Christian truth. The very opening statements of the *Institutes* are these: "Nearly all the wisdom we possess, that is to say, true and sound wisdom, consists of two parts: the knowledge of God and of ourselves. But, while joined by many bonds, which one precedes and brings forth the other is not easy to discern. . . . Yet, however the knowledge of God and of ourselves may be mutually connected, the order of right teaching requires that we discuss the former first, then proceed afterward to treat the latter."[1] This essay is organized in accordance with this scheme.

A. GOD

It is sometimes charged that in his doctrine of God Calvin was more speculative than Luther. The charge sometimes takes the form of the assertion that Calvin, unlike Luther, recognizes a God prior to and beyond the Christ, a God other than the one active in the drama of man's salvation, a God resplendent in his self-contained holiness and concerned with nothing so much as his exclusive glory, a God who exists not *pro nobis* but in and for

1. John Calvin, *Institutes of the Christian Religion*, John T. McNeill, ed., Philadelphia: Westminster Press, 1960, Bk. 1, Ch. 1, Par, 1, 3.

*Originally appeared as "Justification and Sanctification: Liturgy and Ethics," in J.I. McCord, ed., *Marburg Revisited* (Minneapolis: Augsburg, 1966).

himself. This charge is sometimes summarized by saying that, whereas Luther's theology is Christocentric, Calvin's is theocentric. What must be said to this?

I hazard no opinion about Lutheran theology, but as respects the theology of Calvin, the charge, I suggest, is both true and false. Calvin's theology is neither merely theocentric nor merely Christocentric, but both of these at once, though in differing perspectives. These perspectives are formed by making a distinction between God in his being and God in his act, between the God who inhabits eternity and the God who has entered into a covenant with man in time, between the God who in his aseity is wholly independent of the world and the God who, having created the world, is ineluctably involved with it and ceaselessly concerned about it. This distinction is perhaps not dissimilar to that which the philosopher makes between the static structures and the dynamic operations of God.

When Calvin contemplates God in his dynamic operations *ad extra*, particularly in redemption, he knows no other name than Jesus; he is then as Christocentric as is Luther—perhaps more so. He finds that, though Scripture is the word of and about God, it speaks of no one but the Christ, and, what is equally important, that, though Scripture comes in many parts, no part fails to articulate the Savior. Calvin, accordingly, finds Christ no less in the book of James than in the book of Romans, no less in the Old Testament than in the New, no less in the law than in the gospel. Christ is what the Bible is about from first to last. What to some may appear, therefore, to be Calvin's undue orientation to Old Testament motifs or his sub-Christian legalism, is in fact his Christocentrism, his conviction that it is the whole of Scripture and the entire fabric of revelation *was Christum treibet*.

But Calvin does know, I suggest, a God "beyond" and "prior" to Jesus Christ, a God who is more than the revelation he has given, a God who in the infinite fulness of his trinitarian being cannot be contained in anything finite, a God mysterious, incomprehensible, highly exalted, and "wholly other." This God is the *Deus absconditus*, the hidden God, whose ways are past finding out. He is the sovereign God whose providential rule is over all, the absolute God of the fixed and eternal decrees whose inexorable sway none can withstand. This is the God who is man's destiny. It is, I suspect, insofar as Calvin has confessed this God that his theology has come to be called theocentric, rather than Christocentric.

(1) God in and for Himself

There is nothing in Calvin or in Calvinism which suggests that there is that in God which is at variance with the Christ who stoops to save. Yet there is the recognition of a God who is wholly self-sufficient and self-contained, who needs no world at all to be himself and therein perfectly blessed, and who even when he acts, as in creation and redemption, is his own final end. Also, there is in Calvin and Calvinism a sense of God's greatness, independence, power, and transcendence, which has imparted to the tradition its undeniable "theocentrism," its characteristic "God-consciousness," and its own consequent "style." The lofty God of Calvinism is not a God into whose presence one enters boldly or with whom one associates on easy and intimate terms; mysticism can hardly grow on Calvinist soil. Nor is the God of Calvinism a God whose worship can be framed and fashioned in accordance with man's sense of fitness and propriety; God is the sole determiner of how he is to be acknowledged, praised, and served; church order and church liturgy are therefore fitted closely to the scriptural pattern. Nor is the God of Calvinism a God whose commands can be taken lightly; he is the imperious law-giver whose will must be unconditionally obeyed; he is not a God before whom it is possible to "sin boldly." Nor is the God of Calvinism a God before whom one vaunts himself; he is a God who veritably abases men.

But this abasement had a curious effect upon the Calvinist; it stood him erect among his fellows. Having become a slave of God he lost the capacity to act slavishly toward any creature. Having bowed at one point he could do so at no other. Having given his allegiance to the King of kings, he could count no man his master. The Calvinist in history became therefore two men: one all self-abasement, the other "proud, calm, inflexible"; one all meek and worshipful, and other set like flint against all tyranny. The Puritan, in Macaulay's view, was of this sort: "He prostrated himself in the dust before his Maker; but he set his foot on the neck of his king."[2]

(2) God in and for Man

Although the Scriptures do not allow us to ignore the existence of the *mysterium tremendum*, and although all their representations of God are made against the background of his distant and awe-ful holiness, yet the God they announce is centrally not one who exists in splendid isolation in and for himself, but one who moves outward in creating, preserving, and redeeming love. This Calvin knew well.

(a) *Creation*—Although the central function of the Christian doctrine of *creatio ex nihilo* is to cut off any thought of the continuity between God and man, i.e., to assert God's absolute transcendence and man's radical contingence, the doctrine also serves to express God's gratuitous benevolence. God, we learn from the apostle John, is *agape*, self-giving love, and while this

2. T. B. Macaulay, *Essay on Milton*, Margaret A. Eaton, ed., Boston: Educational Publishing Company, 1899, p. 97.

love is centrally displayed in God's redeeming work through Christ, it is by no means absent from creation. In a sense, indeed, it is there exhibited in its purest form. If to love is to impart, and to impart without regard to any foundation in the beloved, then the giving of existence (and essence) to a creature who before was not at all, is the most basic sort of giving or loving that there possibly can be.

Ever since Augustine the Church has accordingly ascribed creation to God's love, and has discerned in God's creative work the gracious divine determination to share with others his inexhaustible perfections. God, who is all glorious and cannot be enriched by anything outside himself, was not in creation seeking himself, but only man, and man's beatitude. Calvin is not slow to acknowledge this; when he considers the end God had in view in creating the world, he declares that this end lies in man: "God has destined all things for our good and salvation. . . . God himself has shown by the order of creation that he created all things for men's sake."[3] If, as Calvin acknowledges, "God's glory" is also an end, this can only mean that the God of love is glorified precisely herein that a community of men should possess, enjoy, and mirror forth the excellencies he freely confers.

The basic continuity between creation and redemption is thereby indicated. The God who created a world designed to share in his goodness is the same God who is active in redeeming a world that has turned aside from its true beatitude. And the name of Christ appears in both contexts of operation: the personal Word through whom God saves the world is also he through whom God made the world.

(b) *Providence*—There is no call to enter here into all the knotty problems that inhere in the Christian doctrine of divine providence. It is enough to say that the Reformers did not surrender the created world to the ultimate direction of the creature, but kept the governance of it in the hands of the loving creator, whose concern for the establishment of a "kingdom of life" never suffers abatement, and whose determination to effect it cannot be thwarted. Calvin, as is well known, everywhere stresses God's ceaseless activity in the world. God is active directly in "the order of nature," where no so-called "natural laws" exist to obstruct the free exercise of his power. He is directly active in "the order of history," where, through general and special providences, he sets up and puts down men and nations in his determination to secure the ends of love and justice. And he governs "the hearts and lives of his children" through the power of the Holy Spirit, living and reigning within them to the end that, being justified and sanctified, they may eventually be glorified.

Indeed, all God's providential ministrations are centrally directed to this

3. *Institutes,* I, 14, 22.

end. This is why Christ stands, in Calvin's view, in the center of providence as well as in the center of creation and redemption. The movements of the stars and planets, and the rise and fall of nations subserve Christ's kingdom. Understanding this, Jonathan Edwards could say of the members of this kingdom, the saints: "The wheels of the chariot of the universe move for them; and the progress that God makes therein on his throne above the firmament, the pavement of his chariot, is for them; and every event in the universe is in subserviency to their help and benefit."[4]

(k) *Redemption*—Clearly, the culminating act of God on behalf of a race of men estranged from him—on behalf of men in flight from him or in rebellion against him—took place in Palestine, A.D. 1–30. In the incarnation, crucifixion, resurrection, and ascension of Jesus Christ redemption was once-for-all accomplished: God was in Christ reconciling the world unto himself.

It is, of course, not the purpose of this essay to exposit the Calvinist Christology and soteriology, nor to expound in depth the nature and meaning of those key events by which salvation was obtained for men. It is enough here to declare that in the view of the Reformers all that God means or can mean for men who are lost and undone is contained in Christ: he and he alone is our salvation; there is no other name given under heaven by which we can be saved.

It may be said, however, that in Calvin's view it was not what Christ *was*—God and man—so much as what Christ the God-man *did* that matters. The incarnation was the precondition for the work of redemption, but it did not in and by itself redeem. The incarnation did not humanize God, nor did it deify man, as some in the history of Christian thought have tended to suppose. Even the unique conjunction of two natures in one person, as in Christ, could not be considered by Calvin as forming an exception to the absolute transcendence of divinity or the ineluctable finitude of man. It is at this point, it will be remembered, that a difference arose with Luther about the *communicatio idiomata*.

Although Calvin regarded the biblical language used concerning what Christ *did* as not altogether "appropriate," he does not hesitate to say, in accommodation to such language, that Christ's task in offering atonement was to "interpose between us and God's anger and [to] satisfy his righteous judgment." He represents Christ as "beaten and struck by the hand of God," thereby appeasing the wrath of God and giving God satisfaction. What this comes down to is that Christ was and is our substitute, the propitiation for our sins. What Christ *did*—in dying, rising, and ascending—was to pay the debt of sin man owed to God, thus laying the foundation for that forgiveness

4. *The Works of Jonathan Edwards* (2 vols.), Henry Rogers and Edward Hickman, eds., London: Ball, Arnold and Company, 1840, I, 100.

which God grants to his elect; and what he did was to bring that life and immortality to light which was to make new creatures of all who believed in his name. In short, through what he did Christ became man's justification and sanctification; he became the remedy both for man's guilt and for his depravity. In and through his substitutionary atonement Christ made available to men the righteousness and life of God.

He who takes Christ's name upon his lips says many things, but among the things he says—and this is central—is that the way of salvation leads from God to man, and not vice versa. There being no way from man to God, every form of autosoterism must be cut off at the root. There is no word or work or attitude of man that can move him one step toward heaven. Neither obedience nor aspiration, neither *nomos* nor *eros*, neither circumcision nor uncircumcision—nothing human at all—can extricate man from his predicament. It is only Christ who is the lost world's hope.

B. MAN

(1) Man in and for Himself

Since man does not and cannot exist in and for himself, the heading of this section is basically inappropriate. If it is nevertheless set down, this is to draw a parallel between it and the corresponding section under God, and to strike a contrast between it and the section yet to follow. Having made these concessions to formality and artificiality, it is now to be observed that man, in the biblical view, most certainly does not exist in and for himself. This may be expressed by saying that man, unlike the self-contained and uncreating God, does not so much exist as *co-exist*. He is always *in relation*, and this essentially; he is by definition relative. What defines him is his relation to the world in which he is caught up, especially the social world of men, and, most basically, his relation to his Maker.

Unlike the angels who presumably exist discretely, man exists as a member of a race. He is born in relation to a mother, is normally fixed and nurtured in a family, is united by ties of law and consanguinity to many others with whom he forms a clan or tribe, and is enclosed by other ever-widening circles of human association. He is by nature a "political animal," as Aristotle already knew, and he is by creation set "in company," as Moses teaches: "male and female created he them." This is mentioned here, not for its own sake, but in order that it may serve as a point of reference when we consider that unique community, the Church, a type of association and organization which, though effected by grace, is founded on nature, i.e., on the necessity men are under to *co*-exist.

If man is a social being, he is even more definitively a *religious* being; if he is tied in with men and things, he is even more securely tied in with *God.* The one all-determinative fact of human existence is that God cannot be escaped. There is no way that can circumvent him; there is no maneuver that can evade him. Man cannot flee God, for as Augustine already pointed out, to flee him is but to go *from* him pleased *to* him displeased. All men both know God and are haunted by him. Perhaps no one stressed this more than Calvin. There is in all men, he insisted, a *sensus divinitatus*, a sense of God that never can be lost. All men are therefore "religious." Without exception they make response to him whom they cannot but perceive. The religions of the world are just such responses, but even when a man disdains the cultic and throws himself into what are called "secular" pursuits, he is articulating an unavoidable, even though mistaken, "ultimate concern." Man cannot but have a "god," either the true God or a spurious one. It is man's fate to be "religious," to commit himself to something, and to have that commitment govern at the bottom all of life's expressions.

(2) Man in and for God

Grace does not destroy nature, but perfects it. Redemption does not negate the creation, but restores it. Christ does not make a literally new man of us; he inwardly renews the old man that we were. This means that the Christian Church is made up of people who were social before they entered the fellowship, were religious before they were confronted by the Christ, and were liturgically and morally expressive before they were made right with God. This is not said, however, to minimize the change that does take place when a man becomes a Christian. The change that takes place is radical. From being enemies of God we are made his friends; from being afar off we are brought near; from being under judgment we are made at peace. The outer darkness that awaited us at the end of our flight from God, and the consuming fire that awaited us at the end of our hostile ascent up the holy mountain of the Lord—this has been averted. The God of grace arrested us in our flight, and the God of peace halted us in our assault, and he set us before his face. What is involved here can, I think, be put down under three heads: incorporation, involvement, and articulation.

(a) *Incorporation*—Christ is the repository of all grace. In him are contained all the blessings and benefits that can possibly accrue to man. He is the true "blessed possessor." In him resides righteousness and truth and life, and every other perfection which God is willing, and even concerned, to share with men. Christ is in particular the justified one, and the sanctified one, the very foundation of salvation.

The question now is, as Calvin poses it, "How do we receive those benefits which the Father bestowed on his only begotten Son—not for

Christ's own private use, but that he might enrich poor and needy men?"[5] The answer to that question is simple and direct: we must be joined to Christ, a spiritual union between himself and us must be effected, for "we must understand that as long as Christ remains outside of us, and we are separated from him, all that he has suffered and done for the salvation of the human race remains useless and of no value for us."[6]

The union that is necessary, and which is never merely external or adventitious but always inward and spiritual, can be described in either of two ways: Christ dwelling in us, or we dwelling in Christ. In either case what is required is a vital connection, by which the merits of Christ are transferred to ourselves. An ontological identification between Christ and the sinner there cannot be, but a living union is indispensable. As Calvin conceives of it, this union is not a *unio mystica* in the technical sense, but it is an *insitio in Christum*, a veritable participation in the Savior's life.

This union cannot be effected by man; no one can insinuate himself into Christ and thus tap the divine resources resident in him. The author of this union can only be God himself. It is in fact the Holy Spirit; it is "the secret energy of the Spirit by which we come to enjoy Christ and all his benefits."[7]

But how, it may be asked, does the Holy Spirit effect the union? The answer is: by creating in us a true and living *faith*. This faith is of course something in us (it is we who believe, not God), but it is not a human property, quality, or virtue. It is a bond. It may be likened to an umbilical cord, made and maintained by the Holy Spirit himself. It is never a basis upon which Christ's benefits are conferred; it is ever only an instrument by which the divinely directed transference of Christ's graces is effected. It is therefore not anything valuable in itself; whatever value it has lies in its content, which is Jesus Christ.

And how by the power of the Holy Spirit is this faith brought into being? The answer is: through the preaching and the hearing of the word, more particularly of the word of promise, the gospel or good news, for "man's heart is not aroused to faith at every word of God."[8] Accordingly, "we need the promise of grace, which can testify to us that the Father is merciful, since . . . upon grace alone the heart of man can rest."[9] Calvin comes then to define faith as "a firm and certain knowledge of God's benevolence toward us, founded upon the truth of the freely given promise in Christ, both revealed to our minds and sealed upon our hearts through the Holy Spirit."[10]

If we ask what, in Calvin's view, are the benefits that Christ imparts to

5. *Institutes*, III, 1, 1.
6. *Ibid.*
7. *Ibid.*
8. *Ibid.*, III, 2, 7.
9. *Ibid.*
10. *Ibid.*

us when we partake of him through faith, the answer is succinct and unmistakable. What he imparts to us is justification and sanctification. "By partaking of him, we principally receive a double grace: namely, that being reconciled to God through Christ's blamelessness, we may have in heaven instead of a judge a gracious Father; and, secondly, that sanctified by Christ's Spirit we may cultivate blamelessness and purity of life."[11]

What is especially to be noted here is that, though Calvin makes a conceptual distinction between justification and sanctification, he never allows a real separation between them. The two are indeed logically distinct and mutually independent; sanctification is not the basis of justification, and justification is not the basis of sanctification. But one never appears without the other. If a man is justified, if his sins are forgiven him, if Christ's righteousness is imputed to him, if he is declared innocent, then he is also set upon the way of sanctification; a new life-giving power has entered into him; he has become in principle a new man, and he will do works of repentance. The faith that justifies is also the faith that regenerates. Calvin here is wholly on the side of James, as indeed James is on the side of Paul. Faith without works is dead; such faith does not justify. To be forgiven is to be moved to forgive. There is only one way to be justified, namely, to be incorporated into Christ. But to be incorporated into Christ is to have his regenerating life pulsate through our being; a branch engrafted on the vine *must* bear fruit.

(b) *Involvement*—The first fruit that faith bears is social in nature. When through a living faith one is joined to Christ one is at once ushered into a fellowship. To be incorporated into Christ is to be set in the company of others who are similarly incorporated. To be a member of Christ is to be a member of Christ's body. The vertical dimension when pluralized generates the horizontal. It is not possible to be in Christ without being in the Church, for the Church is nothing more nor less than the company of those who are in Christ.

The Church needs an organization; it must become institutionalized, but it is not on its institutional side that its true character is revealed. What the Church truly is, is not an organization but an organism, not an institution but a fellowship, not a cult but a *koinonia.* It is in that fellowship that the word of promise is heard and repeated, that the common faith is confessed, nourished, and exercised, that brotherly affection is developed and displayed, and that the mission to the world is announced and implemented. The Church is not the company of the perfected, but the company of the justified embarked on the way to perfection. Of that company Christ is the head and the Spirit is the life.

Although the Church must be centrally defined as the fellowship of

11. *Ibid.*, III, 11, 1.

Christians, i.e., as the fellowship of those who by grace exist in and for God, it may also be defined as an *ecclesia*, i.e., as the community of those who have been called out from the world. The Church is inherently separatistic. It exists not to express and body forth the values and ideals of the world or the changing forms of culture, but it exists to lay these under judgment and to witness to a higher reality. But the withdrawal which is of the very essence of the Church is not a withdrawal that has its end in itself. It is a withdrawal and consequent *koinonial* involvement which has as its purpose another and subsequent involvement, an involvement with the world designed to "save" it or at any rate to illumine and preserve it in accordance with our Lord's description: "Ye are the light of the world," "ye are the salt of the earth." Such an involvement may also be regarded as a fulfillment of the apostle Peter's injunction: "supplement *philadelphia* with *agape*" (II Peter 1:7).

(c) *Articulation*—The Christian, joined to Christ in faith and joined to his Christian fellows in brotherly affection, must live out his life in obedience to the command: Thou shalt love the Lord thy God with all thy heart, and thy neighbor as thyself. There is, it could be said, no other law than this. But the question may be asked: Is this two laws or one? A brief answer to this question will conclude this discussion.

When one considers that there is ultimately only one who can lay man under obligation, that there is only one who can claim man's unconditional allegiance, one is driven to conclude that man is in the last analysis responsible to no one else but God. When it is asked with what or with whom the creature has ultimately to do, the answer can only be: with God. This can only mean that however many and diverse his responses may turn out to be, they articulate at bottom but one response: the response to God. But this is just another way of saying that man is ceaselessly religious, that every thought and word and deed of man is religiously qualified and determined.

It is one of the glories of the Reformation that it put God back into the common life and into the work-a-day world of man. It was recognized by the Reformers—certainly by Calvin—that religion is not merely one area of existence, but the whole of it; that God is to be met not merely on Sunday or in church, but on every day and in every honorable vocation in which one labors. The Reformers knew—and their children know—that a Christian lives always before the face of God, and that in everything he does and says and thinks he is bound to reckon with his Lord and to pay him homage. It is the glory of true Protestantism to have bridged the gap between the secular and the sacred, and to have left no section of life godless or profane.

Theologians such as Rudolph Otto, Paul Tillich, Dietrich Bonhoeffer, and John Robinson therefore speak to our condition when they deprecate a periodic "flight" from a supposedly "profane" domain into some "holy" place in which alone God can be met. Whatever Calvinists and Lutherans may think of John Robinson's *Honest to God*, they are natively conditioned to appreciate the author's remark that "this is the essence of religious perversion, when worship becomes a realm into which to withdraw from the ['godless'] world [in order] to 'be with God.'" The Calvinist certainly knows of no "religious" life discontinuous with that which he lives during every waking hour of every working day. He recognizes nothing as legitimately secular or profane; he allows no moment undedicated to God's praise, no realm unsanctified by God's presence. With Robinson he is ever prepared to find the "beyond" in the midst of life, the "holy" in the common, the "divine" in the mundane. He is prepared to repudiate a Christianity which reserves for God a mere "sphere" of religion, a "last secret place" in the "private" world of the individual's need. If "religion" is to be thought of as a separate and sacred garden plot in the much wider field of the world, then with Bonhoeffer the Calvinist is prepared to advocate a "religionless" Christianity. What he wants is nothing less than to love God with all his heart and soul and mind, everywhere and always, on every road, in every task, and at every hour.

But a perceptive Calvinist who claims all of life for God, and who recognizes religion as embracing every area of existence, does not on this account fail to distinguish, *within religion*, between worship and work, prayer and service, communion and accomplishment. Religion, like all of life, is, he knows, a matter of inhaling and exhaling. He knows that the "quiet hour," the "retreat," the resort to the "inner room" is not to be identified or confused with the "outward thrust" and the "worldly activity" of the dedicated Christian. Religion is an ellipse with two foci. There is in it a certain alternation in which its nature is displayed. Prayer and service, which are *not* the same, are both embraced within it. As the institution of the Sabbath amply indicates, worship and work support and complement each other. It is, however, not only to the "holy day," as contrasted with the other six, that a special kind of sacredness attaches, but also to those special times on every day in which, through prayer and scriptural meditation, we hold communion with our God and find new strength for daily tasks.

C. CONCLUSION: LITURGY AND ETHICS

Although *leitourgia* is an inclusive word which can mean both worship and work, and which can therefore stand for that centered and unified response which I have called "religious," I use it in this section to stand more narrowly for worship, or for that which goes on in church. By the same token, the term ethics is here taken to designate the moral relations that persons or groups of persons sustain to each other. What needs to be considered, I suppose, is the bearing within Christian existence that liturgy and ethics have or should have upon each other.

That the Scriptures establish a close relation between the two is evident. Our Lord's summary of the law, already cited, joins our duties toward God most closely with our duties toward our fellow men. It has therefore become a commonplace of Christian teaching that only as we love God can we truly love our fellows, and only as we love our fellows are we fit to enter into God's presence. It is also generally recognized that only as we are spiritually attuned to God will we find and exploit areas of service to men, and only as we are morally sensitive will we discern spiritual truth: "if any man's will is to do his will, he shall know whether the teaching is from God . . ." (John 7:17).

As far as I am able to judge, the Reformed churches have always sought to keep worship and service, piety and love, cultus and ethos in a mutually fruitful relationship. Of course, as many ethicists have observed, it is difficult to move at once in a vertical and horizontal direction. It frequently happens therefore that, as was the case with the priest and the Levite, one is too much involved with the affairs of the temple to pause at the side of the road to bind a neighbor's wounds. By the same token, one can become so much concerned with programs of social reform as not to lay them or oneself either upon God's altar or under his judgment.

However that may be, there has been in the Reformed tradition—as no doubt in the Lutheran—a steady attempt to fit the liturgy of worship to the demands of everyday existence, and infuse the common relationships of life with the sense of God's presence. In the Reformed churches the Lord's table has usually been strictly guarded; an untoward walk of life has usually earned for the offender banishment from the Supper and in extreme cases other forms of discipline. The preaching has usually been both declarative and didactic; the gospel has been proclaimed, but in imitation of Paul the *kerygma* has usually been attended by the *didache*. The reading of the ten commandments is a feature of most Reformed worship services, though it is not always plain to the worshipper precisely what function it serves; it is meant to serve both as a mirror of sin, thus inducing repentance and stimulating prayer for pardon, and as a rule for a holy life. The regular offering not only supports the work of the church but also effectually symbolizes for the worshipper the Christian necessity he is under to make his whole life a sacrifice.

Whether or not the Reformed churches or any other churches are succeeding in keeping the two together, it would seem right that Christians should combine adoration with resolution, pardon with effort, the mystic with the moral, the passive with the active. It seems indisputable that every *Gabe* is an *Aufgabe*, that justification must be attended by sanctification, and liturgy should be in alliance with ethics.

5

The Kingdom and the Church

MOSES, AS the representative of Israel, with whom the Covenant was made, sees the redemptive activity of God in the context of the Creation and the Fall, and against the background of God's cosmic and historical design. I think we can do no better than follow him here. I propose therefore to begin by setting our discussion of church and Kingdom in the context of the three great movements of the biblio-historical drama (A). I shall then undertake to say some further things about the Kingdom (B) and the church (C).

A. THE CONTEXT OF THE KINGDOM

(1) Creation

I conceive that in the beginning, as he emerged from an eternal trinitarian council, God the Father said: "I (we) will not be alone. I do therefore now decide to create a world and to people it with beings, resembling me, whom I will introduce into my fellowship, and upon whom I will confer divine graces and virtues. I determine to include in the divine life those whom, presently having no being at all, I will call into being in order that they, finite though they be, may share in the blessed fellowship which I have with my Son and Spirit. I purpose and intend a Kingdom, a divine-human fellowship, a living and holy communion, which will include myself and those upon whom I will confer being and existence." Having so spoken, and moved by *agape*, the essential divine will to impart and to enrich, God uttered the creative words: "Let there be man, male and female, made in my image and fit and furnished for my fellowship. And to house him, let there be a world, rich, variegated, and adapted and adaptable to the Kingdom of love that I envision."

These creative words inaugurated the first stage of the world's history. This first stage was an age of innocence, unfinished at the start, but yet set straightly on its course, and capable, by linear development under the joint stewardship of God and man, of attaining the goal of creation: the *civitas dei.* Although time waited to be filled and fulfilled, the purposed goal, the intended city or kingdom, was in a meaningful sense already present at the outset. Man and God were at peace, and all the other creatures were united under their beneficent and effective rule. The world was as God, its Creator and Lord, willed and intended it to be, and contemplating it God called it good. He saw that it conformed in every part to his grand design.

In the foregoing account I have several times used the word "Kingdom" or one of its cognates. This was deliberate. I mean by such language to suggest that in the first stage of man's existence we have a paradigm and promise of man's latter end, when God shall be supreme in an abiding fellowship of free spirits, contextualized by a controlled environment. I also mean to suggest by such language that paying attention to the doctrine of creation will enable us to see that questions concerning the Kingdom's time and extent need not be as puzzling as they are sometimes taken to be. Whoever takes creation, and therefore history, seriously will immediately see that the Kingdom must be both present and future; it must as long as history endures be both actual and eschatological. And whoever takes creation, and therefore totality, seriously will know that the Kingdom must include the cosmic environment of persons as well as these persons themselves; it must in its final form be both realm and reign.

My reference to the Creator's will for fellowship and my acceptance of Eden as paradigmatic of the Kingdom must not, however, be misunderstood. I do not conceive the Kingdom hoped for in the Old Testament and introduced in the New as identical with the Paradise that was lost. History is too real in Scripture to allow us to think of returning someday to a primeval state. I am also aware that the Kingdom which is depicted in the Bible is a redemptive rather than a creational magnitude and that theology can go seriously astray when it mixes redemptive and creational categories. I do nevertheless suggest that the Kingdom idea is primordial and that the whole of God's engagements with men, from first to last, is understandable in terms of his will for fellowship and communion. His will to create is identical with his will to establish a kingdom.

(2) The Fall

After creation came the Fall. It is not my purpose to consider all of its entailments. It is sufficient here to note that in and through the Fall man fell away from God into the grip of anti-God, known in the Scriptures as Satan. To God's thesis (the Kingdom of Heaven) this figure posed an anti-thesis (the Kingdom of the World), and he managed by flattery and half-truths to entice the entire human race to come over to his side. Adam and Eve, the father and mother of us all, forsook the God who made them, abandoned his design for their lives, and adhered with religious devotion to the adversary. In the moment that they did so God lost his earthly Kingdom, and Satan became a prince—the ruler of this world. God's reign upon the earth was at an end, his cosmic realm was occupied by alien forces, and the still young embodiment of his grand creational design lay fractured and attenuated.

I say "fractured and attenuated," and not "lost," for if Augustine is right (as I think he is) in holding that the holy angels are also members of the Kingdom, then it would be inaccurate to say that in the Fall God's Kingdom vanished completely. His regency in the hearts of his loyal heavenly subjects and his use of their ministry upon the earth, kept God in the lists against the adversary even on the kingdom level. This being the case we may, in some sense at least, speak of two kingdoms—God's and Satan's—even at the moment of the Fall and "prior" to God's redemptive counter action. Yet, as I have already observed, the Kingdom is in the Scriptures a predominantly redemptive concept, and it receives its deepest meaning from the contest between God and Satan that rages in the world for the hearts of men once free and innocent but now captive and despoiled. And from this point of view it may be said that when God lost the allegiance of the man and woman he had created he lost the reign he once possessed, and if there were ever to be a Kingdom of God it would have to *come*. And when it came it would have to come, not through linear development, but through a radically new manifestation and exercise of that Divine Love from which the world issued in the beginning. And it would have to come in and through a crucial engagement with those demonic powers which since the Fall have claimed title to the world and held oppressive sway over the lives of men.

I cannot well leave the topic of the Fall without remarking that the biblical characterization of Satan as the prince and ruler of this world obliges us to draw a distinction between God's sovereignty and God's Kingdom. Sovereignty is an inalienable property of God. It is not affected by anything that happens, and it is secure if nothing happens. It follows from this that since God did not cease to be God, he did not cease to be sovereign when the Fall occurred. His right and his might remained intact, and he could have exercised his authority and employed his invincible power to contain his rebellious creatures in hell or (*in extremis*) to annihilate the cosmos. But this was not his will. His will was not simply to be the Sovereign which he always was and will be, but to be for others. He willed not merely to be God but to be God in fellowship with men. In short, he willed a Kingdom, and this required of him not merely action, but creative, and since the Fall, redemptive and re-creative action. His sovereignty he possesses; his Kingdom he must achieve. The divine sovereignty is; the divine Kingdom comes. The divine sovereignty is given in and with God's being; the divine Kingdom comes at an incalculably high price. There is no cheap grace.

(3) Redemption: Christ

Grace, the Scriptures tell us, came with Jesus Christ. In and through him God was freeing the world from the grip of Satan and reconciling it to himself. This is to say that in Christ, his incarnate Son, God was establishing or re-establishing his Kingdom, doing so on grander lines than before had been envisioned, and securing it by a final and decisive victory against all future threats. Jesus Christ accordingly stands at the very center of that Kingdom. In the biblical representations he appears first as its proclaimer or announcer, then as its inaugurator, and finally as its Lord.

(a) *Proclamation*—According to the Gospel of Mark, "after John was arrested, Jesus came into Galilee, preaching the gospel of God, and saying, 'The time is fulfilled, and the kingdom of God is at hand; repent, and believe in the gospel' " (Mark 1:14,15). Repentance and belief are the two sides of one coin. One turns *from* one thing *towards* another, in this case from sin to grace, from Satan's hold to God's embrace, from the kingdom of the world to the Kingdom of God. And the call to do this is in Jesus' preaching urgent and insistent, for the Kingdom is at hand and in its forward movement it brooks no delay.

When Jesus said that the Kingdom was at hand or imminent, he meant, we may believe, that it was even now—in his own person—breaking in upon the world and establishing itself there. But two questions arise at this point. First, was the Kingdom, according to Jesus' teaching, about to arrive, or was it arriving, or had it arrived? And second, was there no authentic Kingdom of God before the Christian era? The answer to the first question is, I believe, that the Kingdom decisively broke in only in and with the death and resurrection of our Lord. Before that time—in the period of his ministry of preaching, teaching, and healing—it was approaching, on the threshold as it were, though the power of it (as attested in the miracles) was already present and manifest. The answer to the second question is, of course, that Jesus is the center of history as well as of the Kingdom, and that his significance and power extends backward and forward through all time. By this token all those who accepted the *promise* of God that he would one day by a crucial redemptive enactment establish the Kingdom became proleptically members, beneficiaries, and exponents of it.

When Jesus said that "the time is fulfilled," that the long-expected *Kairos* had arrived, he was vindicating the eschatological hope of God's ancient people, and giving the Kingdom its proper and enduring eschatological, and even apocalyptic, reference.

All this, according to Christ the Proclaimer, is the "gospel *of* God," which is basically the gospel, or "good news" *about* God. What men are here being told is that God is not for himself only, but also for others, or better: for *himself with others*, i.e., a God of a Kingdom, a God of a people, the God of the covenant. In the situation of men's rebellion and alienation it is the announcement that God pities his perverse and recalcitrant creatures, takes no delight in the death of sinners, and has made provision for their entrance into life and happiness. It is his will that in preaching this be universally communicated, that all men be invited, indeed implored, to believe that God is for them, so that in believing they may join his blessed fellowship and enter his eternal Kingdom.

(b) *Inauguration*—As has already been indicated, the Kingdom may be said to have been inaugurated, made actual, presented, by Christ. This actualization took place, specifically, in the crucifixion and resurrection of our Lord. When he died on the cross he was not merely passive; he acted. And he acted in two directions. Satanward, he entered the house of the strong man and plundered him; he dethroned the god of this world (II Cor. 4:4) and destroyed every (foreign) rule and power (II Cor. 15:24). Through him God the Father disarmed the principalities and powers, and made a public example of them, triumphing over them in him (Col. 2:15). Godward, Christ satisfied the divine justice, thereby freeing God to forgive. In this way men were in principle freed, freed from the captivity of sin, death, and hell, freed for fellowship with God, and freed for joyous and triumphant participation in the course and work of the world now no longer subject to alien thrones and authorities.

(c) *Lordship*—When Jesus was raised by the power of God, he was elevated by the faith of the believing community to the status of *Kyrios* (Lord) and worshipped as such. But more importantly he was by God himself, by virtue of his selfless sacrifice, made in fact and deed the Lord of the entire world.

Christians are therefore bound to believe that the Son of God, who in lowliness and self-denial gave his life for them, is the same one who by his resurrection and ascension has been given "all authority in heaven and on earth" (Matt. 28:18). God, we Christians may and do believe, is now in the ascendency, not by the power of sheer omnipotence, but—in Christ—through the redeeming might of his love and grace. The Kingdom has been made real. God reigns in Christ, the firstborn of the dead, who in everything is preeminent; for in him all the fulness of God was pleased to dwell, and through him God has reconciled all things to himself, making peace by the blood of the cross (Col. 1:18–20).

This being the case, Christians can and need be anything but timid and pessimistic. Knowing that Christ is Lord they may move confidently into the world, being assured that Christ holds title to it and will in it most surely accomplish his beneficent purposes.

And so it happens that members of the Kingdom do in fact enter the world, there by warnings to expose to men their lost condition, by proclamation to witness to Christ's love, by persuasion to allure men into his presence, and by service and action to establish righteousness and peace in every department of life.

B. THE KINGDOM

When now we come to consider the Kingdom itself, it is easier to grasp what it is than to find words to express it. It is obviously nothing physical. It cannot be reached or discerned by the senses. It is also not an organization or institution, although it can come to expression in these. It is also not a realm, although it is operative in all actual realms. It is, it appears, essentially a "reign" or "rule." It is the active and effective rule of God in Jesus Christ over all things in all places toward the gracious ends that he has set. What God intends, the Bible indicates, is a community of persons animated by a single spirit, the spirit of God, and set down in an environment completely serviceable to righteousness, peace, truth, and every other value. His present kingdom or reign is his faithful and invisible ordering of things toward the fulfillment of that fixed and gracious intention. His future Kingdom will be that state, situation, or condition in which that intention is actualized, and when he in the company of his children will be all in all.

If this, or something close to this, be what the Kingdom is, how are we to answer the questions that are most often put concerning it? And how are we to judge among the various interpretations put upon it?

It seems evident, to begin with, that if the Kingdom is God's rule—in the existential sense of a fixed divine determination to do good—there is nothing we can do to evoke or hinder it. All we can do is recognize it as a fact and thankfully accept it as a gift—or remain blind and unbelieving and fall under its judgment. It is certainly not by our moral efforts that God is enticed to be gracious or by our enmity that he is deterred therefrom; his love and mercy flow unprovoked and invincibly from his free and sovereign will.

If in a related question it is asked whether the Kingdom can be participated in, not only in the sense of submitting to it and thereby reaping its benefits, but also in the sense of witnessing to it, reflecting it, and even embodying it, then the answer would seem to be that indeed we can. We cannot put a finger on God's reign and say, "lo here, lo there," but we can experience, absorb, and exert its power and so act redemptively in imitation of and in cooperation with our Lord. This, in fact, is the Christian's calling. Having been renewed by having been placed under God's gracious and re-creative rule, he is called on to preach the Gospel of the Kingdom in order that others may also fall under its beneficent sway. And this means, not only to do missionary work, though this is central, but also to go out into the public arena in order with disciplined vision and balanced judgment to work upon socio-political structures and institutions. The Kingdom will not be established that way, but signs and tokens of its presence will thereby be set up and its end will be thereby served.

If, in another question, it is asked where the Kingdom is operative, the answer must be: wherever the Spirit blows, wherever the Word is taught or preached, and wherever Christ's healing ministry is undertaken—and in the latter case whether it is done in his name or not. God demands and expects the service of his own children, but he is not bound to this, and those who do not know him, or do not know him yet, are often made serviceable, beyond their willing or knowing, to the ends of his Kingdom. When such people are discovered by Christians they must be joined and helped, or alternatively recruited, whatever their open or hidden profession.

I shall conclude this discussion of the Kingdom by remarking on its universal or worldwide character. The Kingdom is worldwide, first, in that it embraces in its membership men of every epoch, tongue, race, color, and condition. The Old Testament theocracy was exclusive. It was for the most part the rule of God over men of a single race. The Kingdom of Christ is not so. It is universal in its spread. It overleaps all natural boundaries. The conditions for membership are not historical or biological, but exclusively supernatural, namely, grace and faith. One need but believe to get in.

The Kingdom of God is worldwide, secondly, in the sense that it calls into exercise all the faculties of men. It uses as instruments every single gift and talent man possesses. The Kingdom takes control of the entire being. This makes the Kingdom worldwide because man participates in and functions in every aspect of creation. When a man is incorporated into the Kingdom, therefore, he takes the whole creation with him, not indeed that which is sinful, but yet everything that is human, and allows it there to be sanctified.

The Kingdom of God is worldwide, finally, in the sense that it embraces the whole of human society. There are, as we all know, two kingdoms, two commonwealths, two cities—the City of God, and the City of the World. As Augustine said, two loves have built these cities. The earthly city, the city of the world, is built by a self-love that despises God. The heavenly city is built by a love of God that despises self. Now the existence of these two cities or kingdoms recurrently tempts us to think that the world is mathematically divided between them in such a way that a line can be drawn separating the

Kingdom of God on the right from the kingdom of the world on the left. According to this representation the Kingdom of God is not worldwide, but only half a world wide; or, since the other kingdom seems in this age to be in the ascendency, a good deal less than half a world wide.

Against this it must be pointed out, first, that neither kingdom is satisfied with half a world. Both want and intend the whole. And what is more, both do in fact penetrate and influence the whole. The kingdom of the world is in the Church. It is there making its influence felt. And, conversely, the Kingdom of God is and ought to be entering as a conquering force into the bastions of the enemy. The two kingdoms are founded on antithetical principles; the one will ultimately destroy the other; but for the present, in this age before the judgment, they struggle for supremacy, and in the conflict the lines of battle are not so clearly drawn that one can always with precision fix the boundaries of the rival cities. Each interpenetrates the other. In this interpenetration they do not indeed lose their identity and character, but the ground they are struggling for can seldom be assigned with clear and full title to either contender. It is precisely this which makes the moral life as difficult as it is. Were the situation different than in fact it is, one could replace the fluid and spiritual line that distinguishes the kingdoms with a definite empirical line that separates them into two halves, one could erect a wall upon that line and, taking refuge behind it, keep oneself from every contact with the world. This, however, from the nature of the case is impossible, and this it is that makes Christian living dangerous indeed, but also the constant challenge that it is.

C. THE CHURCH

The Church is, quite simply, the body of believers. It is variously represented in the Scriptures. It is first of all the new Israel, the extension and continuation of the Old Testament people of God. It is also the body of Christ, made up of those who, being joined to Christ in a living grace-induced faith, are subject to him as their head. It is also the new community of the Holy Spirit, the Spirit of Love and Fellowship, by whose inspiration we cry "Abba, Father" and by whose instrumentality we are enriched with all the graces of Christ.

In relation to the Kingdom the Church may be defined as the totality of those who at any time have been delivered by the power of God's reign in Christ from the toils of sin and death and have been reconciled to God. As such the Church is the living, burning center of the Kingdom, a witness to its presence and power, and a harbinger of its final coming. It is not the Kingdom, it is narrower than the Kingdom, but it is its central exponent.

This church may be called an organism, but it is an organism organized and institutionalized by Christ himself. The form of its organization may vary with time and circumstances, but its institutional character is not an accident or proprium but an essential attribute. The New Testament knows no church that is not thus instituted, and no other Christian organization can, if one abides by Scriptural usage, be properly called Church.

The Church—like everything else—stands in the God-world setting, but it uniquely reflects the ambiguity of existence in its ambivalent attitude to the world, in its complex attitude to that created being which is qualified by sin on the one hand and by redemptive grace on the other. Because the world is sinful the Church condemns the world and calls its members out of it; because the world proceeded from the hands of a benevolent creator and was reaffirmed by him in redemptive grace, the Church affirms the world and settles its members in it.

Like its Lord, who was both God and man, both divine and human, the Church is both sacred and secular, both holy and profane. It is the congregation of those who have been "separated" from the world and "drawn up" into sainthood, the community of those who have been "called out" (the *ecclesia*); it is the congregation of those who have not been taken out of the world but simply "met" and "visited" and "addressed" within the world which, with them, has, in the very act of being addressed, been justified and affirmed.

If this is the nature of the Church, this is also its mission, the character of its ministry. Its mission is to alienate people from the world and from the saeculum, and to orient them to God and to eternity, to the realm of the holy and the sacred. And its mission is to resettle people in a world that came perfect from the Creator's hands and that is now, after being fractured though not destroyed by sin, in the process of being renewed through the power of redemptive grace. Its duty is to be both God-oriented and world-oriented, both God-affirming and world-affirming. Its duty is to endorse both what God is and what he has made, while yet retaining its clear perception of sin and passing its negative judgment on worldliness.

This complex duty it has not always fulfilled, and because it has not, the Church itself has frequently been censured—at one time for being too sacred, at another time for being too secular; at one time for being too world-denying, at another time for losing the celestial vision.

The current criticism is directed against the Church's world-denying tendencies. A resurgent and very vocal secularism finds the Church much too sacred and otherworldly. I myself do not think that the Church is all that bad, and more of us should start filing disclaimers with the Church's detractors both within and without its walls, but it must be acknowledged that the Church has seldom held its double orientation—to God and to the world—in strict equilibrium. It has sometimes—as in culture

Protestantism—minimized its vertical reference altogether. But more often it has been the other way around; the Church, when it erred, has usually erred in minimizing and undervaluing the saeculum. It has tended to deny the world in and through its affirmation of God, and thus tempted the world, and even some members of the Church, to deny God in deference to the values of the saeculum.

The Church, in whom Christ the incarnate Word was meant to be historically embodied, has too often been docetic. It unduly spiritualized existence. It plucked its members as brands out of the fire, immersed them behind high walls, set them to kneeling and chanting behind stained glass windows, enlisted them for exercises in heavenly contemplations, induced them to adopt ascetic practices, dressed them in drab clothing, killed in them the taste for food and drink and for the chaste delights of lawful sex, weaned them away from any participation in worldly affairs, stifled their impulses toward social involvement, muted their laughter while they blunted their compassion, and generally unfitted them for earthly existence. This picture, of course, is overdrawn, but it bears a certain resemblance to the church we know, at least to the world-deniers within it.

This is the docetic error, and it is a massive error that must be stoutly disapproved. But as Chalcedon has taught us, there is another and opposite error as serious as the first, the error of minimizing or denying the sacred and the divine, the error of absolutizing the historical and the horizontal dimension. This error has many advocates today—within as well as outside the Church. Outside the Church it takes the form of naturalism, positivism, secularism, atheism. It expresses itself in the so-called "new morality" that knows no laws or any supernatural sanctions. Within the Church it takes the form of a demand for a religionless Christianity, for an incarnational theology reflecting an absolute *kenosis*, for a form of the Church that dispenses with liturgy and worship and exercises itself incognito on the streets in the service of the underprivileged and dispossessed.

The Church in this situation must hear and proclaim the authentic Gospel, move steadily in both a vertical and horizontal direction, and be at pains to combine liturgy with ethics.

Part III

STUDIES IN THE HISTORY OF CHRISTIAN ETHICS

6

The Heidelberg Catechism in Moral Perspective

It is among the many virtues of the Heidelberg Catechism that it takes account of moral existence and lays down a pattern for the good life. In doing this it faithfully echoes the Scriptures, which everywhere declare that grace effects renewal and that faith without works is dead. One could perhaps argue that in spite of this biblical and creedal insistence on Christian virtue and obedience the Reformed community has sometimes lacked a sensitive social conscience and its theologians have in their concern for dogmatics done less than justice to ethics. It can be fairly countered, however, that historic Calvinism has been among the strongest moral forces operating in western Europe, and that the Catechism has not allowed Reformed theologians and pastors to neglect for long the pressing concerns of ethics.

However these things may be, the Catechism has witnessed for four centuries to the indispensability of love and obedience, and to the inescapable necessity Christians are under to disclose in their lives the reality of redemption. And, it must be added, the Catechism has done this with remarkable fullness and power. In the short space of eight pages Ursinus and Olevianus have presented an account of the moral life that leaves almost no important question unanswered and no relevant biblical teaching unrecorded. In this brief essay I wish to call attention to salient features of their account.

The first thing to be observed is that in the formal structure of the Catechism the ordering of the Christian life is placed on a par with the Fall and with Redemption. Three things are considered necessary to be known by a Christian who would live and die happily: first, how great his sins and misery are; second, how he may be delivered from all his sins and misery; and third, how he is to be thankful to God for such deliverance.

According to the Catechism, God's revelation, and by that token the Christian religion, is centrally concerned not with two things only—sin and salvation, guilt and grace—but also with a third: a life of gratitude in which the renewing power of redemption is manifest and in which human depravity and perverseness, though not indeed overcome, are yet negated and disowned. Starting with man's existential predicament, the Catechism treats the divine remedy for sin in unbreakable connection with the new life of devotion evoked by God's re-creating action. A divine action is described in which God both destroys evil and calls forth goodness; a human life is described in which, through the work of Christ, the flesh is mortified and the spirit renewed; a circle is drawn in which faith and love shine forth in equal splendor against the dark background of sin. Good works are thereby linked inseparably to grace, and morality is made integral to Christianity.

The exact position of good works in the scheme of things ought next to be observed. Although good works are integral to Christianity, they are not placed by the Catechism at the entrance to it. It is in the view of the Catechism, as in the view of the Bible, not the righteous but sinners who are called; it is the sick and not the whole that Jesus came to save. There is no entrance into heaven *without* good works (Question 87), but also there is no entrance into heaven *by* good works. Salvation does not follow service, but precedes it; grace is first, and gratitude follows after. It is neither by religion (prayer) nor by morality (law) that a man enters the Kingdom, but only by the inscrutable election and mercy of God.

This clear teaching of the Catechism cuts off at the root every false doctrine of merit, and every brand of autosoterism. For all its insistence on the good life, it is for God and not for man that it reserves the center of the stage. God in Christ is in its representation the alpha and the omega of Christian existence. This is why gratitude, though it *must* characterize Christian existence, must always bear the nature of a *response*. Good works are not a cause but an effect. Morality unlocks no treasure chests; it sets forth and proclaims treasures freely bestowed. Gratitude is not the first, but the third of the things the Christian must know in order to live and die happily.

Closely related to the foregoing is the question concerning the source or fountain of virtue. Where must a man stand who would do well; in what must he be rooted to bring forth good fruits? The first Lord's Day of the Catechism answers this question in the clearest possible way: one must stand on, be rooted in, and belong to Jesus Christ. There is no life productive of good available to mankind save the life that Christ imparts. To share that life and thus to entertain the prospect of virtue we must be united with him, incorporated into him. We must be animated by his Spirit, shaped by his mind, conformed to his image, and set in his embrace. The first thing a Christian who aspires to goodness therefore knows is "that I, with body and soul, both in life and death, am not my own, but belong to my faithful Savior Jesus Christ."

The Christian, called to perfection, is a transplanted being, an engrafted thing. He has been uprooted, and placed in a soil and a context foreign to his erstwhile existence. He is no longer his old self. Indeed, he is no longer his own self. He is now Christ's, upon whom he must wait for everything. Of course, in another sense he is now for the first time his real self. Having lost himself, he has found himself. Having been wrenched free from that with which he formerly identified himself, he has been made free indeed—free in the only sense a man can be free, made a captive of God, placed in the context of the divine, made a member of the body of Christ.

Being so placed, the Christian is free "from all the power of the devil," released from the bondage of sin. The process of disengagement goes on through all the years of his existence and is terminated only when in the twinkling of an eye he is ushered into glory; but the tie that fastened him to evil has been unloosed and disengagement is really possible. The process is therefore carried on in hope, and in hope he already now lives victoriously with Christ the victor.

The Christian's mystical union with Christ issues of necessity into good works, as the Catechism plainly teaches. Question 86 reads: "Since, then, we are delivered from our misery by grace alone, through Christ, without any merit of ours, why must we yet do good works?" The use of the word "must" here is interesting. It is not used in the sense of "obliged," though obligation most certainly rests on us. It is used to express the "inevitability" of the new life. Why *must* I be virtuous, why can't I escape doing good works, why is it impossible for me to avoid showing forth God's glory, why is morality inseparably linked with redemption, why does gratitude necessarily follow upon grace? The answer is: "Because Christ, having redeemed us by His blood, also renews us by His Holy Spirit after His own image."

This answer proclaims that redemption is not partial, but complete. Christ saves from guilt and redeems from bondage, but he also stops the wells of our depravity and makes us pure. He not merely rescues us from destruction, but he inwardly renews us. He not only shatters the grotesque pattern of our former existence, but he reshapes us into his own image and forms us into replicas of himself. Simply to *be* a Christian, therefore, is to show forth Christ's visage, to disclose his mind, to breathe out his Spirit, and to articulate his will. This is why he was able to say in the days of his flesh, "By their fruits ye shall know them." Whoever has been with Jesus will evince it; it is inevitable. It is impossible to be in Christ and not sooner or later betray the fact. To be a Christian one *must* do good works.

Since the function of good works is not to open the gates of heaven, what is their function? The Catechism gives three answers to this question in Answer 86. First and foremost, the good works of men are to the praise of God. By them he is glorified. This means that in human virtue, in the forms of human goodness, the nature and purposes of God are disclosed. God is not in need of glory; he is all glorious. But in the patterns of morality his glory becomes manifest. His excellence is reflected. His true and exclusive divinity is imaged forth. Man's good behavior reveals God, and in this revelation God delights, for he wills neither to be alone nor to be hidden, but to be manifest and shared. By being good, men therefore both mirror God and serve his redemptive purposes.

A second and related function of good works is "missionary." We must do good works, according to the Catechism, not only so that God "may be praised by us" but also that "by our godly walk our neighbors may be won for Christ." This reflects the Catechism's awareness that one cannot reasonably recommend a power that is unable to transform, or a person to whose influence one is himself impervious, or a pattern of life that one himself has not adopted. Actions speak louder than words; where there is no love, even prophecy will fail.

A third function of good works is one which is biblical enough, but which taken out of biblical context can prove to be mischievous. According to the Catechism we must do good works in order that "each of us may be assured in himself of his faith by the fruits thereof." It must be acknowledged that a lively sense of the Spirit's stirring in us can indeed serve to confirm us in our hope of sonship, but we must not be tempted by this fact to find in our "moral excellence" the foundation of our hope or the ground of our assurance. This foundation and ground is always only *Christ*, and never our experience or accomplishments. If this be remembered, we will be able both to endorse the statement of the Catechism and to give the lie to the thesis of Max Weber that in Reformed circles "success" is the proof of election.

If the function of good works is to glorify God, win the neighbor for Christ, and strengthen our own assurance of faith, the motive of good works is simple *gratitude*. The Catechism is very clear about that. What drives the Christian to love and obedience is thankfulness. This gives to the moral life a characteristic note of joy. Appreciative of God's mercy, thankful for his unspeakable gift, happy in his gracious conferments, the Christian seeks with might and main to show forth his praises and to do his will. Living in the context of grace, he no longer strives to reach a heaven that is in any case beyond his reach; resting from his labors in Christ's embrace, he seeks in all things to please him. He is always inquiring, "What wilt thou have me do," not in order thereby to coerce his love, but in order to celebrate and praise the love he freely gave and still imparts.

In this frame of reference morality loses all its hardness and harshness. Duties are no longer onerous. The Law is certainly still there, but it is no longer contemplated as a code of perfection that no mortal can ever satisfy; it is contemplated as a gracious prescription supplying a happy and thankful man with helpful directives concerning how to satisfy someone whom it is his deepest desire to please.

If gratitude is the motive of the good life, love is its content. The Law prescribes one thing only, for there is only one thing that God desires both in reference to himself and in reference to men. What he wishes to be manifest everywhere in the universe and to be exercised in all relationships is one thing only: Love. What is not love, or what does not comport with it, or does not flow from it, he negates. It is a community of love he is concerned to build, a community of self-giving love, the kind of love that he himself manifested in the giving of his Son, and the kind he wishes us to exemplify not only in the Church but in all our relations, even with our enemies.

It is interesting to observe how quickly the Catechism gets to this theme of love. In Lord's Day II, Question 3, the teacher asks, "Whence do you know your misery?" The question is, In comparison to what do you find yourself deficient, perverse, miserable? The answer is, In comparison to the standard of perfection, the norm of rectitude, the "law of God." And so in Question 4 the teacher asks, "What does the law of God require of us?" In the answer given there is no recital of the Ten Commandments. There is given instead the summary of the Law which Jesus formulated: "Thou shalt love." This we must do, and this only we may do. Nothing else. By nature, the Catechism goes on, in Question and Answer 5, we do something else: we hate. But hatred of God and neighbor is nothing but the measure of our deviation from the Law. In Christ, in obedience, in love that excludes all hate, we fulfil the Law.

Love must shape our life, but how must it shape it? The answer in the Catechism is twofold: according to the Ten Commandments and according to the provisions of the Lord's Prayer. In this the Catechism follows a venerable Christian tradition, and in this we who follow the Catechism distance ourselves from a number of ancient and contemporary thinkers who think that love is its own guide and that the Christian is exempt from law. It is supposed by these people that the Christian life is entirely inner, that the believer is driven only by the Spirit, and that all external regulation has collapsed under the weight of the Gospel. But that this is not so Paul himself, to whom appeal is made, is witness. To him the Law is good and perfect. In it God gives to love its general pattern and direction, and the same can be said of the Lord's Prayer. In the petitions we there make, we ask that our life be shaped in definable ways. The Law, whether in the Decalogue or in the petitions we are taught to utter, is not for us, of course, a means to heaven, and because of grace it can no longer condemn. It is and remains an expression of God's will, and this will we are to follow, if in the power of the Holy Spirit we are to please our heavenly Father and his well-beloved Son, our Lord.

Ethics is not the whole of Christianity, and the good life is not the entire Gospel, but they are integral to Christianity and inseparable from the Gospel. Grace and gratitude belong together, and the Catechism is there to keep us from dissevering these two.

7

The Ethics of Jonathan Edwards*

When Jonathan Edwards was fourteen years old and a junior at Yale College,[1] John Locke's *Essay on the Human Understanding* fell into his hands and exerted a powerful influence on him. He says of the book that he found greater enjoyment in it "than the most greedy miser finds when gathering up handfuls of silver and gold, from some newly discovered treasure."[2] Stimulated by the volume to more or less systematic thinking on philosophical themes, he began about this time a series of what he called "Notes on the Mind,"[3] a collection of observations which reveal at once his indebtedness to Locke and the strength and originality of his own thinking.[4] The scattered notes are little more than philosophical fragments jotted down "at the happy moment a thought opened spontaneously on his mind,"[5] but it cannot be doubted that he seriously contemplated a systematic treatise of considerable scope on the themes here commented on. This is evident from the broad title he prefixed to his observations: "The Natural History of the Mental World, or of the Internal World, being a Particular Enquiry into the nature of the Human Mind, with respect to both its Faculties—the Understanding and the Will—and its various Instincts, and Active and Passive powers."[6] He pro-

1. Yale College was founded at New Haven, Connecticut, in 1701, two years before Edwards' birth, with the purpose of providing training in the liberal arts and languages, and preparing young men for the Congregational ministry.

2. Sereno E. Dwight, *The Life of President Edwards*, in *The Works of President Edwards* (8 vols.), Leeds, England: Edward Baines, 1806–1811, I, 30.

3. *Works*, I, 664–702. It "was commenced either during, or soon after, his perusal of Locke's *Essay*. It contains nine leaves of foolscap, folded separately, and a few more, obviously written at a later period. . . ." Dwight, *Life*, in *Works*, I, 34.

4. "Even when a boy, he began to study *with his pen in his hand:* not for the purpose of copying off the thoughts of others, but for the purpose of writing down and preserving the thoughts suggested to his own mind, from the course of study which he was pursuing." *Ibid.*, p. 33.

5. *Ibid.*, p. 33.

6. *Works*, I, 664. There also appears as an appendix to the "Notes" a list of "Subjects to be handled in the Treatise on the Mind."

*From *Faith and Philosophy*, Alvin Plantinga, ed. (Grand Rapids: Eerdmans, 1964).

posed to distinguish in the introductory chapter between two worlds—"the external and the internal: the external, the subject of Natural Philosophy; the Internal, our own minds"—and above all to show "how the Knowledge of the latter is, in many respects, the most important."[7]

The choice of subject and statement of purpose clearly reveal where Edwards' interest lay. It was spirit, not nature, that intrigued him. What is especially to be observed is that his preoccupation with the spiritual and invisible world was as much due to a profound conviction of its superiority as to any aptitude and consequent inclination he may have had for abstract thinking. He did not lack scientific talent. At the age of 12 he wrote an essay on the habits of spiders, based on his own observations, which reveals an inductive and empirical genius of the first rank. Dr. McCook, the author of a monograph on American spiders and their spinningwork, tells of his chagrin upon learning that "Master Jonathan Edwards" had one hundred and sixty years before described spinning processes of which he (Dr. McCook) had thought himself the discoverer,[8] and Professor Benjamin Silliman, in speaking of Edwards, expresses the opinion that "had he devoted himself to physical science, he might have added another Newton to the extraordinary age in which he commenced his career."[9] However that may be, it can hardly be doubted that he refused to devote himself to physical science less from a sense of incapacity for such studies than from a profound conviction that the physical and external is of little weight as compared with the inner and spiritual. On this conviction, expressed in the proposition that "the things which are seen are temporal and the things which are not seen are eternal," he built his imposing philosophy of inwardness.

It is largely on the series of remarks entitled "The Mind" that Edwards' fame as a philosopher rests. They contain materials for a type of Idealism which, in the history of thought, has usually been associated with Berkeley. This fact, combined with the circumstance that the English Bishop was an older contemporary of Edwards and a resident for a time of Rhode Island, caused the question to be long agitated whether Edwards was in any way dependent on him.[10] Sereno Dwight had affirmed as early as 1830 that "each wrote independently of the other,"[11] but grounds were supposed to exist

7. *Ibid.*

8. Henry C. McCook, D.D., "Jonathan Edwards as a Naturalist," *Presbyterian and Reformed Review*, I, 393.

9. *Ibid.* Sereno Dwight, in commenting on Edwards' *Notes on Natural Science*, observes: "Had his life been devoted to these pursuits, in a country where he could at once have availed himself of the discoveries of others, and the necessary instruments, he would have met with no ordinary success, in extending the bounds of human knowledge in the most important and interesting fields of Physical Science." *Works*, I, 54.

10. For the discussion, see: A. Allen, *Jonathan Edwards*, New York, 1889, pp. 141ff., 309; G. Lyon, *L'idealisme en Angleterre au XVIIIe Siecle*, Paris, 1888, pp. 431ff.

11. *Works*, I, 40.

which entitled one to call the truth of this remark in question. The investigations of Egbert C. Smyth seem, however, to vindicate Dwight's judgment completely and decisively,[12] and Prof. Schneider sums up the controversy by saying, "It has been proved beyond doubt that Edwards could not have known Berkeley's writings."[13] The philosophies of the two men bear, indeed, a merely superficial resemblance to each other.

Like Berkeley, however, Edwards takes his departure from Locke. Locke, building on the Cartesian dualism between spirit and matter, had added solidity to extension as the primary qualities of matter, but had recognized with Descartes the subjective character of secondary qualities, such as heat, color, and taste. He supposed that the secondary qualities arise within us by the impact of the primary qualities upon our sense organs, and had relegated the latter qualities to some external substance in which in some manner they inhered. This substance he held to be independent of mind and coordinate with it. This view Edwards now rejects. Agreeing that secondary qualities exist only in mind, he proves that the same is true of the material substance that had been called in to account for them. The universe, he insists, is qualitatively one. Not mind *and* matter, but mind *alone* is ultimately real. Matter, substance, and body are seen on a closer view to be in no other case than heat, taste, and color. All are merely mental. All turn out in strict analysis to be no more than ideas, objects of mind. As such they enjoy a merely derivative reality. They presuppose a thinker.

That, he points out, which we call by the name of body is clearly "nothing but Colour and Figure, which is the termination of this Colour, together with some powers, such as the power of resisting, and motion, etc."[14] But "it is now agreed upon by every knowing philosopher that Colours are not really in the things, no more than Pain is in a needle; but strictly nowhere else but in the mind." Hence, "if Colours exist not out of the mind, then nothing belonging to Body exists out of the mind but Resistance, which is Solidity; and the termination of this Resistance, with its relations, which is Figure; and the communication of this Resistance from space to space, which is Motion; though the latter are nothing but modes of the former. Therefore there is nothing out of the mind but Resistance." But even resistance does not exist out of the mind. "Let us suppose two globes only existing, and no mind. There is nothing there, *ex confesso*, but Resistance. That is, there is such a Law, that the space within the globular figure shall resist. Therefore there is nothing there but a power, or an establishment." If resistance, however, be only a power or establishment, it cannot really exist out of mind, for in such

12. Egbert C. Smyth, "Some Early Writings of Jonathan Edwards," in *American Antiquarian Society Proceedings*, New Series, Vol. X.

13. H. W. Schneider, *The Puritan Mind*, New York, 1930, p. 137.

14. *Works*, I, 668–669.

case "one power and establishment must resist another establishment and law of resistance, which is exceedingly ridiculous." It can only be conceived, therefore, as existing "in some mind, in idea." From the phrase "in some mind," however, one is not to infer that mind is a place, or that it can properly be spoken of as having an inside and an outside. "Place itself is mental, and Within and Without are mere mental conceptions." What is meant when the material universe is said to exist only in mind is "that it is absolutely dependent on the mind for its existence, and does not exist as spirits do, whose existence does not consist in, nor in dependence on, the conception of other minds."[15]

But on whose mind is the material universe dependent for its existence? Not, Edwards answers, on the mind of man. Man is not the measure of things. There are things actually existing of which no created mind is conscious. Such are, for example, the chairs in a locked room, which nobody sees. "The existence of these things is in God's supposing them."[16] That on which the physical world ultimately depends is the eternally existing, all-comprehending, divine mind. "That which truly is the Substance of all bodies, is the infinitely exact, and precise, and perfectly stable Idea, in God's mind, together with his stable Will that the same shall gradually be communicated to us and to other minds according to certain fixed and exact established Methods and Laws."[17] All nature points, thus, beyond itself to God, in whom and through whom alone it exists. "God, in the beginning, created such a certain number of atoms, of such a determinate bulk and figure, which they yet maintain and always will, and gave them such a motion, of such a direction, and of such a degree of velocity; from whence arise all the natural changes in the Universe, forever, in a continued series."[18] True, all these bodies and movements are properly and finally only ideas, and hence do not exist anywhere perfectly but in the divine mind; yet, they exist there after such a fashion that "his determination, his care, and his design" insures "that Ideas shall be united forever, just so, and in such a manner, as is agreeable to such a series." Corresponding to this series of ideas which go to make up the things which are vulgarly supposed to be non-ideal, is another series of ideas which God arouses in finite minds; and this correspondence of ideas constitutes human knowledge. "All the ideas that ever were, or ever shall be to all eternity, in any created mind, are answerable to the existence of such a peculiar atom in the beginning of the Creation, of such a determinative figure and size and motion.... God causes all changes to arise, as if all these things had actually existed in such a series, in some

15. *Ibid.*, p. 671.
16. *Ibid.*
17. *Ibid.*, p. 674.
18. *Ibid.*, p. 670.

created mind, and as if created minds had comprehended all things perfectly. And, although created minds do not; yet, the Divine Mind doth; and he orders all things according to his mind, and his ideas."[19]

Edwards is eager to point out that these representations do not involve an emptying of natures, an invalidation of science, or a denial of the real and objective existence of physical objects. "We would not therefore be understood to deny that things are where they seem to be. For the principles we lay down, if they are narrowly looked into, do not infer that. Nor will it be found that they at all make void Natural Philosophy, or the science of the causes or reasons of corporeal changes."[20] The question at issue concerns the nature of ultimate reality, and this Edwards describes as spiritual, intelligent, voluntary, and personal Being. Being, he points out, far from implying the nonexistence of physical things, is precisely that which constitutes their reality and validates their existence. The worth and meaning of things is guaranteed by God himself. Edwards insists, therefore, that "though we suppose the existence of the whole material universe [to be] absolutely dependent on Idea, yet we may speak in the old way, and as properly, and truly as ever. . . . For to find out the reasons of things in Natural Philosophy is only to find out the proportion of God's acting. And the case is the same, as to such proportions, whether we suppose the world only mental in our sense, or no."[21]

Edwards does not wish to deny solidity any more than does Locke. He wants merely to understand and account for it. Locke supposed it to be a mode of substance. Edwards holds it to be an action of an agent. Locke appeals for its explanation to a something. Edwards appeals to a someone. Of bodies, he says, "Their falling is the action we call Gravity: their stopping upon the surface of the earth, the action whence we gain the idea of solidity. . . . We get the idea and apprehension of solidity, only and entirely, from the observation we make of the ceasing of motion at the limits of some parts of space."[22] But "there is no reason in the nature of the things itself, why a body, when set in motion, should stop at such limits more than at any other. It must therefore be some arbitrary, active, and voluntary Being that determines it."[23] Solidity is interpretable, therefore, only in terms of an intelligent and voluntary agent. Locke had defined solidity in terms of substance. Edwards has no objection to the word. He, too, will use it, provided it is understood to designate spirit and not matter. He, too, believes in substance, but for him it is personal, not physical. "The reason why it is so exceedingly natural to men to suppose that there is some latent Substance, or

19. *Ibid.*
20. *Ibid.*, p. 669.
21. *Ibid.*
22. *Ibid.*, p. 674.
23. *Ibid.*, p. 675.

something that is altogether hid, that upholds the properties of bodies, is, because all see at first sight that the properties of bodies are such as need some Cause, that shall every moment have influence to their continuance, as well as a cause of their first existence. All therefore agree that there is something that is there, and upholds these properties. And it is most true, there undoubtedly is; but men are wont to content themselves in saying merely, that it is something; but that Something is He 'by whom all things consist.'"[24]

This, that there is someone "by whom all things consist," is the primary faith of Edwards. It not only controls his view of nature; it is the foundation of his ethics. Beneath the immediate appearance of things he discerned a personal and eternal reality. The world, in his view, was spiritually constituted. Of much that is immature and passing in his "school-boy compositions," this is permanent. He never came to write the treatise he so early projected, less, it would seem, from lack of time and opportunity than from lack of inclination, his maturer thought operating with an entirely different set of categories. Yet he always held fast to the centrality of God. As a Calvinist, born in a Calvinist home, the idea was not strange to him. It had, indeed, troubled him at first. "From my childhood up," he says, "my mind has been full of objections against the doctrine of God's sovereignty. It used to appear like a horrible doctrine to me."[25] But later, before he wrote down his observations on the mind, he had attained another insight. It was mediated through the ringing words of I Timothy 1:17, "Now unto the King eternal, immortal, invisible, the only wise God, be honour and glory forever and ever, Amen"; and in commenting on the experience, he says: "As I read the words there came into my soul, and was as it were diffused through it, a sense of the glory of the Divine Being; a new sense quite different from anything I ever experienced before . . . and there has been a wonderful alteration in my mind, with respect to the doctrine of God's sovereignty, from that day to this . . . . I have often since had not only a conviction, but a delightful conviction. The doctrine has very often appeared exceedingly pleasant, bright, and sweet. Absolute sovereignty is what I love to ascribe to God."[26]

His "Notes" reflect his deep interest in this truth, and his early Idealism is a real but ill-conceived application of it to the world of nature. One's philosophy is never divorced from one's faith, and this finds particular illustration in Edwards. His belief in the sovereignty of God was not a mere religious sentiment; it was, as well, a determinative intellectual conviction. God's sovereignty he regarded as an undeniable and all-important cosmic fact. Behind the changing appearances of the world, he believed, is the

24. *Ibid.*, p. 676.
25. *Ibid.*, p. 60.
26. *Ibid.*

eternal and omnipresent life of God, in whom all things exist and from whom alone they get their meaning. The stars owe their structure to him, the planets their orbits, and the flakes of snow their crystalline beauty. What is particularly significant is that Edwards invariably defines this sovereignty in ethical terms. Sovereignty, in his view, is not an abstract quality existing in splendid isolation. By so much less is it the hypostatization of some soulless force or arbitrary fate. It designates a moral quality, and reveals God as in the strictest sense good. It is, indeed, but another word for God's infinite excellence. It is because God is truly sovereign, because the harmonious system of things finds its highest term in him, that there is beauty and excellence in the world at all. Morality owes its very existence to him, and the moral life its objectivity and worth. As God stands behind the world of nature, so he stands behind and validates the life of spirit. God is not merely the substance of "things" or the cause of physical changes; he is pre-eminently the ultimate and absolute moral reality, the supreme ground of moral obligation, and the final guarantor of virtue. He is the real that makes our ideals significant, the "is" that gives meaning to our "oughts."

It is this faith in the essentially moral nature of the universe that underlies all Edwards' utterances on ethics. He regarded it as the one fact of infinite importance for human conduct. We are not surprised, therefore, to find him, in his earliest reflections, attempting to render an intelligible account of it to himself and others. In the "Notes on Mind" he devotes a number of paragraphs to a consideration of the meaning of "Excellence," and in these he lays bare the grounds of his faith and indicates at the same time the source of his own moral energy. Excellence, he says, is "what we are more concerned with than anything else whatsoever: yea, we are concerned with nothing else. But what is this excellency?"[27] What is its nature and ground? In what does it consist, and what is its validity?

In answering his own question, Edwards chooses first to consider that in which the excellence of figures and motions consists. It consists by common consent in a certain equality or proportion among parts. This means that excellence has to do with relations. If the relation is one of "similarness or identity,"[28] of agreement and correspondence, then the thing standing in that relation partakes of excellence. "So the beauty of figures and motions is when one part has such consonant proportion with the rest, as represents a general agreeing and consenting together."[29] If, however, the relation is one of disagreement, discord, and disproportion, the result is imperfection and want of beauty. "So if there are two bodies of different shapes, having no similarness

27. *Ibid.*, p. 693.
28. *Ibid.*, p. 695.
29. *Ibid.*, p. 697.

of relation between the parts of the extremities; this, considered by itself, is a deformity."[30] What we mean, therefore, when we say a thing is inexcellent or deformed, is that its relations are awry. It does not occupy the right place in the totality of things. It disrupts the harmony of existence. It does not conform to the whole. It is out of step and off balance. It disagrees with and is contrary to being-in-general. It is in collision with reality. This means, however, that reality or being-in-general is the very opposite of inexcellence, and this is precisely what Edwards holds. "Entity," he says, "is the greatest and only good."[31] It is that because it is, "if we examine narrowly, nothing else but Proportion."[32] It is a universal order, an infinite harmony of parts, a whole that constitutes a perfectly proportioned one; and by that token it is the very seat and archetype of excellence. Being and excellence are one. The obverse is just as true. Inexcellency is contrariety to being. It is "an approach to Nothing, or a degree of Nothing;... and the greatest and only evil."[33] This does not mean that inexcellence or evil does not exist; it means that they have a merely negative existence. Sin is not a positive entity; it is a lack and want. It has no ontological validity and is not metaphysically real. Goodness and excellence alone are ultimate.

The identity of being with excellence leads Edwards to correlate degrees of excellence with degrees of being or existence. The notion that when a thing *is* it simply *is*, was not that of Edwards. Existence, like excellence, consists in relations. It is, therefore, greater or less, depending on the number and intensity of those relations. "An Archangel must be supposed to have more existence, and to be every way further removed from nonentity, than a worm."[34] It is but the obverse of this fact to say that the degree of excellence anything possesses is in direct proportion to the degree of its being, considered simply as such. Excellence is measured not only by the number of equalities (which in complex beauty may be legion), but also by "intenseness, according to the quantity of being"; for "by how much more perfect Entity is, that is without mixture of Nothing, by so much the more Excellency."[35] Implicit in these assertions is Edwards' belief in the merely external and secondary excellence of figures and motions, the relative excellence of finite spirits, and the absolute excellence of God.

That figures and motions are beautiful and possess a kind of excellency Edwards nowhere denies. He recognizes that subtle balancing of part with part that makes for beauty in architecture, and that complex symmetry

30. *Ibid.*, p. 695.
31. *Ibid.*
32. *Ibid.*, p. 696.
33. *Ibid.*, p. 695.
34. *Ibid.*, III, 98.
35. *Ibid.*, I, 695.

which constitutes the excellence of a rose. There is a similar beauty in that vast complex of cause and effect which gives regularity and order to the physical universe, and which in Edwards' day deistic Newtonians loved to contemplate. But this is an inferior kind of excellence. It is as nothing compared to that spiritual beauty which consists in the consent of minds to minds. It is, indeed, only a shadow of that. He who, enthralled by the excellencies of nature, does not see beyond it to that superior excellence which explains it, understands neither nature nor beauty. "As nothing else has a proper being but Spirits, and as bodies are but the shadow of being, therefore the consent of bodies one to another and the harmony that is among them is but the shadow of excellence. The highest excellence must be the consent of Spirits one to another."[36]

There is, therefore, beyond the physical world, in which it is faintly mirrored, another and spiritual world. Behind the natural is the moral order. Here, too, there is a consent of part to part, a harmonious togetherness in the unity of excellence. But the cohesive force that binds mind to mind is not the physical law of cause and effect. It is the spiritual law of love. "When we spoke of Excellence in Bodies, we were obliged to borrow the word, *Consent*, from spiritual things; but Excellence in and among spirits is in its prime and proper sense, Being's consent to Being. There is no other proper consent but that of *Minds*, even of their Will; which, when it is of Minds towards Minds, it is *Love*, and when of Minds toward other things, it is *choice*. Wherefore all the Primary and Original beauty or excellence, that is among Minds, is love; and into this may all be resolved that is found among them."[37] But even this finite kingdom of love is not self-sufficient or self-explanatory. Behind the moral world lies the religious; behind man is God. Moral excellence or the excellence of finite spirits is therefore merely relative. It is relative because the existence of moral agents is merely relative, being dependent upon that of the Creator; and it is relative because their excellence is definable only in terms of Being-in-general, or God.

It follows that God alone is absolutely excellent. "He is . . . infinitely excellent and all excellence and beauty is derived from him."[38] This is inextricably bound up with his being. In God goodness and excellence become truly ontological. God is the prime and original Being, the first and the last, and the pattern of all. He is infinite, universal, and all-comprehending existence, and as such the sum of all perfection. "God has infinitely the greatest share of existence, so that all other being, even the whole universe, is as nothing in comparison with the Divine Being . . . and as God is infinitely the greatest Being, so he is allowed to be infinitely the most beautiful and excel-

36. *Ibid.*, p. 697.
37. *Ibid.*, p. 699.
38. *Ibid.*, p. 700.

lent; and all the beauty to be found throughout the whole creation is but the reflection of the diffused beams of that Being who hath an infinite fulness of brightness and glory. . . . God is not only infinitely greater or more excellent than all other beings, but he is the head of the universal system of existence; the foundation and fountain of all being and all beauty; from whom all is perfectly derived, and on whom all is most absolutely and perfectly dependent; of whom, and through whom, and to whom is all being and all perfection; and whose being and beauty are, as it were, the sum and comprehension of all existence and all excellence."[39] In God, therefore, ethics and metaphysics meet. He is the absolute goodness that renders morality meaningful and valid. Combining in himself the "is" and the "ought to be," he is at once the ground and archetype of all true virtue.

One may be inclined to question at this point the consistency of Edwards' thinking. He had previously defined excellence as the consent of being to being. He regarded it, therefore, as having to do with relations. This means that goodness is relative. But if goodness is relative there is obviously no warrant for absolutizing it in God. How is God, the absolute, compatible with excellence, which consists only in relations? Are we not forced here to the disjunction: either God is good, and consequently relative; or he is absolute, and consequently beyond good and evil? Of these alternatives, however, Edwards accepts neither. God, he says, is love, and that in the strictest moral sense. In setting this forth he begins by reaffirming the necessary connection between excellency and relation. "One alone, without any reference to any more, cannot be excellent: for in such case there can be no manner of relation no way, and therefore no such thing as consent."[40] In other words, both existence and morality are fundamentally social. A being that should exist in utter isolation would not be a being at all. He would be simply a mental abstraction. Nor could he be described as moral, since beings, and not abstractions, are the proper and only subjects of morality. An individual, therefore, considered simply as such, is neither real nor virtuous. This is true of finite spirits, but it is equally true of God. He, too, is good only by virtue of his relations; but, unlike those of finite spirits, these relations are not external. God does indeed *exercise* his goodness in relation to his creatures, but it does not consist in this exercise. "He was as excellent before he created the universe as he is now."[41] The relations that determine God's goodness are internal. He is himself a society. " 'Tis peculiar to God, that he has beauty within himself, consisting in Being's consenting with his own Being, or the love of himself, in his Holy Spirit."[42] If God were what the

39. *Ibid.*, III, 103.
40. *Ibid.*, I, 697.
41. *Ibid.*, p. 700.
42. *Ibid.*, p. 701.

Deists suppose he is, a simple being without metaphysical distinctions, then indeed it were folly to speak of him as good. "In a being that is absolutely without any plurality, there cannot be Excellency, for there can be no such thing as consent or agreement."[43] But God is not "without consent of parts."[44] He is at once absolute and social, for he is triune.

Edwards' trinitarian doctrine is a combination of the traditional Christian teaching and the psychological views current in his day. Along with his contemporaries, he had distinguished two faculties in the human mind—understanding and will.[45] Understanding he had defined as that by which the soul "is capable of perception and speculation, or by which it discerns and judges of things"; and will, "that by which the soul is some way inclined with respect to the things it views or considers."[46] Both go to make up what the older psychology had denominated the rational soul, in distinction from the vegetable and sensible. Understanding, moreover, is further analyzable into the four subordinate faculties of sensation, imagination, memory, and judgment.

Sensation, in Edwards' view, provides all the materials with which the mind operates. "All ideas begin from thence; and there never can be any idea, thought, or act of the mind, unless the mind first received some ideas from sensation, or some other way equivalent, wherein the mind is wholly passive in receiving them."[47] In this he was in complete agreement with Locke, who had allowed the conception to control the views he set down in his *Essay*. The two thinkers parted company only when they described the nature of the objects stimulating the sense impressions, Locke describing them as physical and Edwards as ideal. Edwards, however, never abandoned the view that simple ideas are altogether dependent on the senses. It appears again, for example, in his description of the thoughts and attitudes of the saints as being due to a "new sense" imparted by the Holy Spirit.[48]

Imagination and memory Edwards regarded as particular modes of perception. The first he defines as "that power of the mind by which one has an image of the things which are the objects of sense when those things are not actually present to be perceived by the senses"; and the second, or memory, as "the identity, in some degree, of Ideas that we formerly had in our minds, with a consciousness that we formerly had them, and a supposition that their former being in the mind is the cause of their being in us at present."[49] The

43. *Ibid.*, p. 697.
44. *Ibid.*
45. Calvin, Shepard, Hobbes, Malebranche, Cumberland, Watts, Locke, and others had made the same distinction.
46. *Works*, V, 10.
47. *Ibid.*, I, 666.
48. *Ibid.*, V, 155.
49. *Ibid.*, I, 680.

materials of both are provided by sensation, and the mind in both is predominately passive.

Reason or judgment is the *active* principle in the understanding. There is something of the will in it. In judgment the mind not only receives; it reacts. It reflects upon the ideas provided by sensation; it sorts, arranges, classifies, and combines them. It is this faculty of the understanding that distinguishes man from beasts, and constitutes him most like God. "A very great difference between men and beasts is, that Beasts have no voluntary actions about their own thoughts; for it is in this only that reasoning differs from mere perception and memory. It is the act of the Will, in bringing its ideas into contemplation, and ranging and comparing of them in reflection and abstraction. The minds of Beasts, if I may call them minds, are purely passive with respect to all their ideas. The minds of men are not only passive, but abundantly active."[50]

The second faculty of the mind is will. Edwards did not conceive of it as a separate organ in man's soul. He regarded it simply as a mode of the soul's existence, or, in other words, as an affective and therefore energetic attitude of the soul toward the things perceived by the understanding. "It is the faculty by which the soul beholds things—not as an unaffected spectator, but—either as liking or disliking, pleased or displeased, approving or rejecting."[51] It is therefore indissolubly connected with the passions or affections. It is, in fact, identical with these. "The will and the affection of the soul are not two faculties; the affections are not essentially distinct from the will."[52] It is, for example, correct to say that the will is the soul in action, but this is only to observe that the affections are the moving springs in all the affairs of life. "Such is man's nature that he is very inactive any otherwise than he is influenced by either love or hatred, desire, hope, fear, or some other affection. . . . Take away all love and hatred, all hope and fear, all anger, zeal, and affectionate desire, and the world would be in a great measure motionless and dead; there would be no such thing as activity among mankind, or any earnest pursuit whatsoever."[53] The moving, activating, energizing principle in the soul is, therefore, the will, or which is the same thing, the soul's inclination to, or affection for, the thing toward which it moves.

It is with this psychology that Edwards approached the Christian doctrine of the Trinity. His interest in it was more than casual. As he saw in the Nicene Formula more than a curious example of high Greek speculation, so his attachment to it was more than conservative loyalty to Christian tradition.

50. *Ibid.*, p. 682.
51. *Ibid.*, V, 10.
52. *Ibid.*
53. *Ibid.*, p. 14.

He accepted it as a profound truth to which not only as a believer in divine revelation but also as a teacher of morality he was necessarily committed. He is brought to consider it now by the exigencies of his ethical theory.[54]

Edwards had previously defined God as the eternal, all-comprehending mind. This definition serves him now as a point of departure. Being mind, God has both understanding and will. Since he is divine and incorporeal mind, there are, of course, "no such distinctions to be admitted as in ours between Perception or Idea, and Reasoning and Judgment."[55] Yet the manner of the divine understanding, "if it be anything that can be any way signified by that word of ours,"[56] must be by idea. It must be supposed, accordingly, that God "perpetually and eternally has a most perfect idea of himself, as it were an exact Image of and representation of himself ever before him and in actual view."[57] It is in the unvaried presence of this infinitely perfect idea that God's understanding or wisdom consists. He knows all things and has all wisdom, because he has an idea of himself, who is "the all-comprehending being—he that is, and there is none else."[58] But if God beholds himself, he must become his own object. There must be a duality. The idea that God has of himself is a perfect idea, that is, it accords precisely with his being; there is nothing in the thinker that is not found in the idea. Hence God is in a real sense repeated. The case could be illustrated from our own thinking. If we had a perfect idea, for example, of love, that idea would be identical with the thing itself, and if we had a perfect idea of all that went on within us, we would have a double existence. God has such an idea of himself, and the Deity is, accordingly, truly and properly repeated. "Therefore as God with perfect clearness, fulness, and strength, understands himself, views his own essence, . . . that idea which God hath of himself is absolutely himself. This representation of the divine nature and essence is the divine nature and essence again. . . . Hereby there is another person begotten . . . and this person is the second Person in the Trinity, the Only begotten and dearly beloved Son of God."[59]

54. Besides the fugitive and incidental references that are to be found throughout his writings, there are especially three sources for our knowledge of Edwards' trinitarian views. The first is his *Treatise on Grace*, edited by Alexander B. Grosart, and published in 1865, along with other items, in a volume entitled *Selections from the Unpublished Writings of Jonathan Edwards*, and printed privately in Edinburgh. The second is his *Observations Concerning the Scripture Oeconomy of the Trinity and Covenant of Redemption*, published in New York in 1880, with an introduction and appendix by Egbert C. Smyth. The third, and most important, is a publication of George P. Fisher entitled, *An Unpublished Essay of Edwards on the Trinity, with Remarks on Edwards and His Theology*, New York, 1903.

55. Edwards, *An Essay on the Trinity*, in *Representative Selections*, Clarence H. Faust and Thomas H. Johnson, eds., New York, 1935, p. 375.

56. *Ibid.*

57. *Ibid.*

58. *Ibid.*, p. 376.

59. *Ibid.*, pp. 376–377.

The Holy Spirit, or the Divine Love, is generated in a similar fashion. Love in man, Edwards observes, is "scarcely distinguishable from the complacence he has in any idea."[60] That is, love is the highest degree of inclination to or affection for an idea presented to the mind. Love therefore is a movement, act, or energy; it is the highest expression of will. Love and will are in fact indistinguishable in God. "As the sum of God's understanding consists in his having an Idea of himself, so the sum of his Will or Inclination consists in his loving himself."[61] This Will, or Love, is the third person in the Trinity. It is God in act, or God in tension between himself, absolutely considered, and his idea of himself. It is God considered as an affective and energetic attitude toward his own idea. Edwards puts it this way: "The Godhead being thus begotten by God's loving an idea of himself and showing forth in a distinct subsistence or person in that Idea, there proceeds a most pure act, and an infinitely holy and sacred energy arises between the Father and Son in mutually loving and delighting in each other. . . . This is the eternal and most perfect and essential act of the divine nature, wherein the Godhead acts to an infinite degree in the most perfect manner possible. The deity becomes all act, the divine essence itself flows out and is as it were breathed forth in love and joy. So the Godhead therein stands forth in yet another manner of subsistence, and there proceeds the third person in the Trinity, viz., the Deity in act, for there is no other act but the act of the Will."[62]

In the Godhead, therefore, are three persons or subsistences—the Father, or he who loves and acts; the Son, or he who is loved and acted on; and the Holy Spirit, or he who is the Divine Love himself and the Deity in act. All are eternal and necessary, and all are dependent on each of the others. So close is their independence and communion that the Godhead must be said to have only one will and one understanding. Yet each divine subsistence is truly personal; each has both understanding and will; and they form together a most perfect society. "There is such a wonderful union between them that they are, after an ineffable and inconceivable manner, one in another, so that one hath another and they have communion in one another, and are as it were predicable one of another."[63]

Our primary interest in these representations is not their theological accuracy or want of it.[64] Edwards himself was fully aware of their inade-

60. *Ibid.*, p. 376.
61. *Ibid.*, p. 379.
62. *Ibid.*, p. 377.
63. *Ibid.*, p. 380.
64. It was long believed that Edwards' heirs thought the *Essay* heretical and that they had suppressed it in order to safeguard the reputation of its author. His views have been variously called Orthodox, Sabellian, and Tritheistic. For the controversy itself cf. the articles of Edward A. Park in *Bibliotheca Sacra*, Vol. 38, 1881; Smyth's Introduction to the *Observations;* Fisher's

quacy and never supposed that he had given a scientific explanation or a logical demonstration of what must always remain an article of faith. "I am far from pretending to explaining the Trinity so as to render it no longer a mystery. I think it to be the highest and deepest of all divine mysteries still, notwithstanding anything that I have said or conceived about it."[65] The *Essay* must be regarded as nothing more or less than an attempt to enter more deeply into this mystery and so to set forth its meaning for both theology and ethics. Our interest lies in its moral significance.

Edwards' doctrine is ethically significant first because, as already mentioned, God is not a stark one, as the Deists and their Unitarian children supposed, but rather a Trinity of persons constituting in some mysterious and ultimately inexplicable way a oneness of being and a unity of perfection, and thus he can with strict accuracy be regarded as both moral and absolute. Morality is essentially social and as such presupposes relations. Since these relations exist pure and perfect within the very Godhead, apart from all and every relation to any other being or existence, the conditions are fully met which enable one to ascribe supreme excellence to God while maintaining his absolute sovereignty.

A second point of interest is Edwards' emphasis on love as the bond of unity in the Godhead. Love, he says, is so "essential and necessary to the Deity that his nature consists in it."[66] This may strike those as strange who are wont to regard Edwards solely as the grim determinist who preached sulphurous sermons on the wrath of angry and arbitrary Deity. Yet it remains true that there is nothing of Scotus and everything of St. John in Edwards. God, he echoes, is light and God is love, and "whatsoever else can be mentioned in God are nothing but mere modes or relations of Existence."[67] His will, for example, is "not really distinguished from his Love, but is the same only with a different relation."[68] This accords, of course, with his entire psychology. Edwards never conceived of will as some imperious and irresponsible power; it was merely the name he gave to the inclination of the soul which was the soul's movement toward the object of its affection. That inclination depended wholly on the nature of the soul whose inclination it was. What is primary in any being is his quality, not his energy, and this is supremely true of God. Not will, but love, is prior. It is God's character that determines his acts, not his will that defines his character. God

---

Preface to the *Essay;* and Alexander Allen's *Jonathan Edwards*, pp. 341ff. For a masterful analysis and criticism of Edwards' trinitarian views, cf. Jan Ridderbos, *De Theologie van Jonathan Edwards*, Amsterdam, 1907, pp. 258–280.

65. *Essay on the Trinity*, p. 381.
66. *Ibid.*, p. 376.
67. *Ibid.*, p. 379.
68. *Ibid.*

exercises his will, but he is not himself will, any more than he is immutability or omnipresence. On the other hand, he not only has and exercises love; he is himself love. Will is but the instrument of love, or love-in-operation. God is indeed to be obeyed, since his will is inviolable, but obedience is not the highest virtue. Even Satan and the damned shall ultimately obey him. True blessedness consists in the enjoyment of God, and of enjoyment the proper and only object is God's character and perfection.[69] That the sum of this perfection is love, Edwards never tires of reiterating. His elucidation of the trinitarian formula is one deliberate attempt to show that divine love is not a mere sentiment that may at any moment be supplanted by hate, nor merely one attribute among others, nor merely a mode of God's existence, but that it is his existence itself. Love is the very Spirit of God, the third person in the blessed Trinity. It is the mark and sign of the divine society.[70]

A third thing to be noted is that since the Godhead is in very essence a community of persons, it contains in principle all the materials of the social life and thus portrays in broad outline the whole complicated scheme of virtue. Plato had in his *Republic* proposed a consideration of the state in order that by a contemplation of that large society one might see morality writ large and thus the better discern its true nature and scope. Edwards proposed a similar inquiry but appealed beyond the state to the divine community, for what appears in human society in shades and half-tints exists there clearly and perfectly. It is in this kingdom beyond the stars that we first see, for example, what love is. Here love is shown to be spiritual, disinterested, and unifying. In the light of this ideal we can recognize the actual. This, the eternally real, interprets that which on earth is only in the process of becoming. It is the same with happiness. In God it consists "in the infinite love he has to and delight he has in himself."[71] Happiness is seen, therefore, to be inseparable from love, and totally independent of what Aristotle called "the furniture of fortune." Happiness is in no sense a reward of virtue. That would be to conceive of it externally. It *consists* in virtue, since love, the sum of virtue, is itself delight or happiness.

What is especially to be observed, however, is the steadfast hope and unconquerable optimism that Edwards derived from such representations as these. His was an ethics of the infinite. Ideals spoke to him with a compelling objectivity and importunateness. He knew himself under obligation not merely to the dictates of conscience but through these to the inviolable im-

69. Cf. the *Westminster Confession*—"to know and enjoy Him forever."

70. Edwards does frequently speak, of course, of God's hating, being angry, displeased, etc. But he does not regard these as being positive affections in God. God acts from no other principle than love. Love is the sole source of all his affections. Out of love for himself as the sum of all good flows hatred for all that is contrary and opposite. Hatred, like sin, has only a negative existence.

71. *Treatise on Grace*, in A. Grosart, *op. cit.*, p. 48.

peratives of God. This made life serious and morals strenuous, but it gave life its strength and morals its dignity. Behind the human society Edwards discerned the divine. Existing unchangeable in the eternal heavens he saw a goodness of which every earthly good was but the shadow and witness. Behind the society of men stood God, the absolute standard for all relationships between beings. The rules of right, the laws of conduct, and the principles of spiritual intercourse are not, he saw, provincialisms of this planet. They reign beyond the stars. Their seat and and fountain is in God himself. Here lies the root of optimism. Whatever else the Puritan philosophy of life may have been it was neither petty nor pessimistic. The Puritan strode two worlds like a colossus. He lived under the controlling conviction that the moral life had its source and issue in the eternal, and he was unafraid. The good man, in his view, did not stand alone, but had the universe to back him. He was partner in a venture whose success was assured, for God himself was in the enterprise. Hence he never feared the future. He knew that the ideal, though ever recessive here, will not always be in flight. Utopia is no idle dream. It most certainly lies ahead because it certainly lies behind. What ought to be will be, for in God it already is.

Edwards' view of the world consists with his view of God. We have already noticed the distinction he made in finite existences between physical objects and human spirits. He makes a corresponding distinction in God between his natural and moral attributes. What intrigues him in each case is the spiritual and ethical. The fact is significant. He lived in an age when the scientific temper was pressing to the fore. Men were turning with a new and intense interest to the study of the measurable and the ponderable. Astronomic physics had opened up amazing vistas, and in the vastness of the universe it revealed, man seemed puny and insignificant. Nature, accordingly, was taking man's place in the center of things. Men stood enraptured around the impressive Newtonian world-machine, fascinated by its laws and revolutions. With measure and rule and mathematical formulae they set about to see how it worked. They learned in the process to be objective, that is, to suppress the personal element in investigations. Men became spectators and observers, not agents. In short, the physical overshadowed the spiritual, and nature dominated mind.

Edwards' early idealism was a protest against all this. It was, to be sure, not a protest against science as such. Edwards recognized both the legitimacy and usefulness of nature studies. What he could not tolerate was what he regarded as the usurpation by nature of the place that rightfully belonged to man. Many of his contemporaries seemed willing to lay down their title to the central position in creation. Edwards steadfastly refused to abdicate. The physical, he said, exists but on the outskirts of the universe; on the verge, so to speak, of nothingness. Its existence is dependent, and its value instrumental. It exists in the interest of man. Not to matter, but to spirit, belongs the ascendency. The clue to reality, he was convinced, lay in personality. The ultimate forces in the universe are not those of motion and gravity. They are more refined than that, subtler, and more mysterious. Physical categories will never render the universe intelligible because the universe is built on other and vaster lines than physical science supposes. It rests on a spiritual foundation and has a spiritual goal. It exists in the interest of holiness and virtue. It was because the science of the times was obscuring this truth that Edwards protested against it. Men were raising the principles of physics and mathematics to the dignity of principles of life. As a consequence of being mechanically conceived life became fixed, stable, and static. Religion, as an expression of that life, tended to be shorn of its mysteries and to become formal and moralistic. Ethics became prudential, conduct being guided simply by the dictates of a cool and calculating reason. The emotional side of life was ruthlessly suppressed. For the moods of awe and reverence, for worship and soul-stirring affections there was little or no place. It was a spiritually barren age, drab and uninspiring, and Edwards set his face against it.

As he opposed his age on the human front, so he opposed it on the divine. There were few atheists in Edwards' day. The Deists believed in God and had constructed a definite theology. But it bore all the earmarks of contemporary science. It ignored or obscured the personal and moral qualities of God and gave prominence to what Edwards called his "natural attributes"—his wisdom and his power. Deists recognized him as the maker and designer of the world, as the ingenious engineer who had fashioned the complex world machine whose laws it was man's chief business to discover. But they had emptied him of his fulness. God became a formal first cause or prime mover; something distant, awful, and impersonal. Himself absent, he operated in the world only by proxy—through accurate and inviolable mechanical laws. All this amounted, in Edwards' view, to an intolerable depreciation of Divinity. That God was to be honored for his wisdom and power he never thought of contesting. It is what he repeatedly affirms. Nor did he deny that these attributes stood revealed in the processes of nature. Edwards was as sensitive to its grandeurs as any of his contemporaries. What he insisted on was that God is infinitely more than nature is able to mirror. To see him there, or to recognize his power, is but to touch the hem of his garment. It is to see him partially and therefore falsely. God is indeed infinitely wise and infinitely mighty, but this bare admission says nothing really significant about him. He might for all of that be a destructive power and a malignant mind. It is not, therefore, God's natural attributes that make him God. He is God because of his moral qualities. The divinity of Divinity lies in holiness and love. Without these "God himself (if that were possible) would be an infinite evil, we ourselves had better never have been; and there had better have been no being."[72] To truly know God is to know him as a person, as moral, as excellent, and as good. It is to know him concretely and materially, not abstractly and formally. To know him in his fulness is to recognize his wisdom and his power operating in complete subservience to his holiness and love.

That means that all things in which his wisdom and power are revealed exist in the interest of a purpose dictated by holiness and love. That purpose is not far to seek. Both the superiority of men to things, and of God's moral attributes to the natural, combine to indicate it. Both attest the spiritual character of the universe, and the ethico-religious purpose of creation. This thesis, implicit in his view of God and man, Edwards now elaborates in *A Dissertation Concerning the End for Which God Created the World.*[73] His discussion of the subject proceeds on the assumption that God did indeed create the world. The fact was granted by all parties and needed no defense. The question was: Why did God create the world? What end did he seek?

The question is perhaps best understood when formulated hypothetically on the supposition that the world is non-existent. One might then ask: If God were to create a world, what would be his object in so doing? What ultimate end could and would he have in view? To this question, as Edwards saw it, there could be only one answer. God could have only himself in view. He certainly could not act in the interest of his creatures. These are, *ex confesso*, non-existent, and it is absurd to suppose that that which does not exist, not even in idea, is the ground of its own being. But even if we were to suppose the existence of other beings resident somewhere in the primeval void, we would still have to acknowledge God as having respect only to himself in any act of his will. He is the perfect moral agent. As such he has "respect to things according to their nature and proportions."[74] His moral rectitude "consists in his having the highest regard to that which is in itself highest and best."[75] But since he is himself the highest and best, in possession of "all possible existence, perfection, and excellence,"[76] he must himself be the object of all possible regard. He must, if he is to create a world, do it in his own interest. This is what his greatness and holiness demand. If then, as is the case, the world does actually exist, we are bound to recognize it as existing *for* God, as well as *from* him. "As all things are from God . . .; so all

72. *Works,* V, 158.

73. The dissertation was written in the spring and summer of 1755, at which time Edwards also began his *Dissertation Concerning the Nature of True Virtue.* The works were published for the first time in 1788, in one volume.

74. *Works,* III, 14.

75. *Ibid.,* p. 14.

76. *Ibid.,* p. 16.

things tend to him."[77] He is the origin and end of all, the alpha and the omega, the efficient and the final cause. He is the "final term to which all things tend in their ultimate issue."[78] This does not mean that he made his existence the end of creation. That "cannot be supposed without great absurdity. His existence cannot be conceived of but as prior to any of God's designs."[79] Nor did he have an extension or growth of his being in view. That is eternally full, beyond all power to add or detract. What he seeks is his honor or praise. "God's glory is the last end of creation."[80] This is what he regards as being "good, valuable, and excellent in itself."[81] This, therefore, is what he aims at, and this is what all his providential dispensations are designed and calculated to achieve.

From this it is seen that the world has a religious goal. One might say with equal truth, however, that its end is moral. In seeking himself, God seeks his creatures. In aiming at his glory, he aims at their holiness. Distinguishable in thought these aims are identical in fact.[82] "God and the creature, in the emanation of the divine fulness, are not properly set in opposition, or made the opposite parts of a disjunction. Nor ought God's glory and the creature's good, to be viewed as if they were properly and entirely distinct.... God in seeking their glory and happiness seeks himself; and in seeking himself... he seeks their glory and happiness."[83]

There are times when Edwards explains this pantheistically. God, he says, comprehends all entity. "The eternal and infinite Being is, in effect, Being in General."[84] He is identical with universal existence. Love to himself is therefore identical with love to his creatures, and to seek his own welfare and glory is, by that token, to seek the welfare and happiness of men. Yet such explanations are not characteristic. It is not from the existence of God, but from his love or will, that Edwards would have the matter understood.[85]

77. *Ibid.*, p. 26.
78. *Ibid.*, p. 40.
79. *Ibid.*, p. 41.
80. *Ibid.*, p. 50.
81. *Ibid.*, p. 51.
82. Edwards' son and successor regarded this as one of his father's most noteworthy contributions to theological and ethical thought. He says: "For ages it had been disputed whether the end of creation was the happiness of creatures themselves, or the declarative glory of the Creator.... Mr. Edwards was the first who clearly showed that both these were the ultimate end of creation, that they are only one end, and that they are really one and the same thing." Dr. Edwards, Jr., in Dwight, *Life*, I, 613.
83. *Works*, III, 37.
84. *Ibid.*, p. 38.
85. Alexander Allen, *op. cit.*, pp. 331ff., is of the opinion that the *Dissertation* breathes a Gnostic and Neo-Platonic spirit. It is true that Edwards' language frequently lays him open to the charge of Pantheism. He speaks of diffusion, emanation, increase, repetition; and on occasion compares God and the world to the sun and its rays, a fountain and its stream, a tree and its

He speaks repeatedly in this connection of God's fulness, by which he understands "all the good which is in God natural and moral."[86] It is another word for God's love, or the sum of his excellency. This love is mobile, energetic, and communicative. Its very nature is to seek an object on which it can spend its beneficent force.

Edwards describes this tendency of love to impart itself, as a disposition in God "to communicate himself or diffuse his own fulness."[87] Here lies the reason for the world's existence. God, driven by the power of his love, created the world to be the object of his affection and the recipient of that communication of himself, the disposition to which is an "original property of his nature."[88] In God there is an infinite fountain of light. It was his pleasure "that this light should shine forth in beams of communicated knowledge and understanding."[89] God is an infinite fountain of moral excellence and beauty. It was his desire that this virtue "should flow out in communicated holiness."[90] In God is an infinite fulness of joy and happiness. It was his will that these "should have an emanation and become a fountain flowing out in abundant streams, as beams from the sun."[91] To that end he created man, giving him existence in order that he might be the "object of his benevolence."[92]

In all this, of course, God manifested a supreme and ultimate regard to himself. He had regard to himself diffused, or "to his own glory existing in its emanation."[93] Yet, since "himself diffused" is nothing more or less than the communication of his knowledge, holiness, and happiness to the creatures he has made, he must be said to have had an ultimate regard also to them. "Here God acting for himself, or making himself his last end, and his acting for their sake, are not to be set in opposition; they are rather to be considered as coinciding one with the other, and implied one in the other."[94]

---

sap, etc. But these unhappy modes of expression are misleading. The emanation that Edwards repeatedly speaks of is that of God's fulness or love, not of his essence. He emphasizes, moreover, that (1) God's existence is prior to that of the world (*Works*, III, 41); that (2) his creatures can contribute nothing to his fulness (*ibid.*, p. 15); that (3) the world is a product of the will, thus the effect of a choice (*ibid.*, p. 30); and that (4) those views are to be rejected which imply that man in any way shows the divine essence *(ibid.)*.

86. *Works*, I, 20.
87. *Ibid.*
88. *Ibid.*, p. 21.
89. *Ibid.*, p. 20.
90. *Ibid.*
91. *Ibid.*
92. *Ibid.*, p. 38.
93. *Ibid.*, p. 23.
94. *Ibid.*, p. 24. This does not, in Edwards' view, argue God's dependence on the creature. The delight God has in his creatures' happiness cannot properly be said to be what he receives from the creature. "It is only the effect of his own work in and communication to the creature. . . . The sun receives nothing from the jewel that receives its light." *Ibid.*, p. 28.

Edwards never supposed that these goals, once projected, would be automatically achieved through the operation of resident laws, forces, or tendencies. They are moral and religious ends, and thus demand the activity of personal agents. The world is not a machine moving insensibly and relentlessly. It is a sphere in which minds posit ideals and wills undertake to effectuate them. The governing will is God himself. He is actively and immanently directing all things to moral ends. Edwards could never understand the "strange disposition that men have to thrust God out of the world, or to put him as far out of sight as they can."[95] He saw God everywhere—in every natural phenomenon and in every event of life. The universe is his chariot, and in it he "rides and makes progress toward the last end of all things on the wheels of his providence."[96]

It is the strength of this conception that explains the Puritan's attitude toward nature. There is a sense in which he was indifferent to it. He was no physical scientist. The scientist lives in abstractions. He is forced to isolate. At the very beginning of his studies he takes pains to insulate his investigations from all appreciatory attitudes. In so doing he separates man and the world. The latter he regards as a datum. He approaches it as an object existing independently, and as significant in itself, apart from all considerations of value. When he has laid bare the physical causes of a natural phenomenon he has done with it. Description, not interpretation, is his task. Goals and final causes lie quite without his purview. It was different with the Puritan. He approached nature religiously. For him it was not a datum to be investigated, but a voice to be heard. He did not regard it as an independently significant magnitude. It was a finger pointing beyond itself to its creator, whose instrument it was. Study of it was, therefore, not an inherently valuable enterprise. It was valuable only insofar as it enabled one the better to see him who uses it for the moral and religious ends in whose interest the world exists. Nature was not so much a thing to be conquered as a teacher to be heard. So conceived it was of absorbing interest. Every event had its meaning. Let their physical antecedents be what they may, all natural phenomena are events in a vast moral government. All that happens, happens to the end that the society of love, happiness, and holiness may be firmly established on earth.

It is important to observe that these providential dispensations, in Edwards' view, were pedagogical, not judicial in character. He did not look for a balancing of moral accounts in this life. This is the day of grace. The judgment, with its distribution of rewards and punishments, is to come in the future, when all men will be called to give an account of the improvement

95. *Treatise on Grace* in A. Grosart, *op. cit.*, p. 40.

96. *Miscellaneous Observations*, in *Selections from the Unpublished Writings of Jonathan Edwards*, A. Grosart, ed., Edinburgh, 1865, p. 100.

they made of God's dealing with them. Edwards did not distinguish, therefore, between good and bad providences. All God's providential dealings with men are in intention good. Be they pleasant or unpleasant, all are wholesome and gracious in design. Whether they are that in fact and ultimately, depends on man's attitude toward them. If in bright days men grow proud and complacent, and in dark days impatient and rebellious, God's beneficent dispensations turn out to be savors of death unto death. If, on the other hand, men, moved by love to God, are thankful in prosperity, and submissive in adversity, all things work together for their benefit. The good man, therefore, is not to be defined in terms of the particular providences that cross his path, but rather in terms of the attitude he takes toward them. Wealth, success, and ease are no more a mark of virtue than ill-fortune is of vice. These things are in themselves indifferent. They are weighty only as they affect the dispositions of the heart. The Puritan therefore learned to face life bravely and to taste the whole of it. The bitter was as nourishing to him as the sweet. In both he saw the dispensation of a gracious father, who, whether with a smile or with a rod, was disciplining him for membership in the perfect Kingdom. This kept him from courting the sweet as a sign that he stood high in God's favor. He knew that God did not traffic in such signs. Love, either that of man to God or that of God to man, is not deducible from things external. It is altogether a matter of the heart and has its evidence in itself. If it is bound to express itself in action, its validation is outside that action's consequences. "I may pursue knowledge, religion, the glory of God, and the good of mankind with the utmost vigour, but am to leave the honour of it entirely at God's disposal, as a thing with which I have no immediate concern."[97] It might, here and now, be dishonor, defeat, and mortification. Even so it is a means of grace. "Great instances of mortification are deep wounds given to the body of sin; hard blows, which make him stagger and reel. We thereby get strong ground and footing against him and he is the weaker ever after."[98] To the good therefore all things are good, and to the evil all things are evil. As for the saints, "the wheels of the chariot of the universe move for them; and the progress that God makes therein on his throne above the firmament, the pavement of his chariot, is for them; and every event in the universe is in subserviency to their help and benefit."[99]

97. *Works*, I, 86.
98. *Ibid.*, p. 80.
99. *Miscellaneous Observations*, p. 100.

8

Themes in Barth's Ethics

KARL BARTH is an ethicist of the first rank. The ideas he propounds in the field of morals are as important and stimulating as those he develops in dogmatics. For this reason no one who thinks on ethical themes can afford to circumvent him.

Among the Barthian ideas which are engaging the attention of moralists around the world I have selected, more or less at random, six of the most provocative.

1. Barth holds that Christian ethics is not an independent discipline, but part and parcel of dogmatics. He is unwilling to separate a description of man's good life from a description of God's saving acts. He will not sever Christian love from Christian truth. Were ethics to be cut off from dogmatics, the latter would, he thinks, become an intellectual frivolity existing aloof from life. On the other hand, were dogmatics to be cut off from ethics, the latter would have to substitute holy man for holy God, a thing proscribed by Christian principles. In harmony with these ideas almost all that Barth has to say about Christian living is incorporated into his discussions of Christian truth in the *Church Dogmatics*, a procedure which, he recognizes, was followed earlier by John Calvin in his *Institutes*.

2. Barth holds that the divine command roots in the *Divine Election:* "I am the Lord thy God, therefore thou shalt. . . ." The law roots in the gospel, the *Aufgabe* in the *Gabe*. God's claim on man's obedience is founded not in God's mere sovereignty but rather in God's *grace*. God legislates for man not because he is man's maker but because he is man's savior. Ethics is grounded not in an abstract divine "ought" but in an actual divine offer and conferment. The God who establishes ethical authority is precisely the God who is gracious to us in Jesus Christ. The moral imperative rests on nothing else than the evangelical indicative. God claims us, and can claim us, only because he has elected us. Outside of grace there is no obligation.

3. Barth's ethics reflects the same concentration upon Christ as is evident in his *Dogmatics*. In the moral context Christ is the elected and obedient man. Barth knows no man outside of Christ and acknowledges no anthropol-

ogy developed outside the circle of revelation. In the last analysis the man to whom the command comes and in whom the obedient response is made is none other than Christ, the elected one. All other men are embraced in him. Christ is more than man's representative, he is man's self, for in the Christ event is involved the whole essence of man. Christ is the one whose existence necessarily touches that of all human beings. He determines each of them inwardly. He is the only real man and in the incarnation he showed himself to be the very presupposition and condition of man's being. Christ is, moreover, the one in whom God's command is perfectly obeyed and fulfilled because in him God's love is perfectly disclosed and given. In Christ "God has acted rightly *towards* us, and in the same person Man has also acted rightly *for* us." We must say, accordingly, that what men have to do has already been done in Jesus Christ. The *ought* of Christian obligation is embraced in the *reality* of Christ's finished work; the divine claim is both presented and fully paid in him.

4. Also characteristic of Barth is a disinclination to celebrate Christian *sainthood.* So jealous is he of God's grace and freedom, and so afraid is he of spiritual pride, that he refuses to speak, except in the most guarded way, of Christian *virtue.* He lays no emphasis at all on the observable effects of grace in the new life. His recurrent theme is the "hiddenness" of Christian holiness. He does not want to set up alongside Christ a specifically "Christian" righteousness. He says in effect: Expect of me no discussion of the Christian in a partly achieved state of sanctification beyond the act of grace, but only of the existential Christian in the midst of conflict, under judgment, in sin. He puts the accent, accordingly, not on sanctification, but on justification. For him the "Christian" character of man lies not in what he does or does not do, but in what has been done for him in Christ.

5. Although Barth has criticisms to make of Anders Nygren, he shares Nygren's regard for the uniqueness of Christian love, and jealously guards the distinction between eros and agape. Christian or agapic love is quite simply self-giving love. What we have in Christian love is a movement in which a man turns away from himself and toward another. This love does not turn to this other in the interest of the loving subject, but purely for the sake of the beloved object, the other. It loves this not because it is lovable, but simply because it is there as this other, with all its value or lack of value. It loves it freely. In Christian love the lover gives not only what it has or possesses, but also what it is: it gives itself. Barth, accordingly, finds no place in Christian ethics for self-love. "Loving himself," he says, "man no longer loves in the sense of the children of God. Loving himself he no longer loves at all. Love must always have an opposite, an object. What we love—if we love at all—is always something else or someone else." This does not commit Barth to a "curt and dogmatic" rejection of eros, but it does commit him to a

"sober affirmation" of the real distinction between agape and eros, and it does prevent him from trying to fuse the two in order to form a higher synthesis. Christian love for Barth is one thing only: agape. It is never, as such, erotic, hungry, self-assertive, grasping, wanting to possess, to control, and to enjoy. Christian love communicates, surrenders, serves, and creates.

6. In order to throw man back in absolute fashion upon the direction of God, Barth denies that God's command ever comes in the form of a general maxim, or a universal rule, or an abstract law. God's commands, he says, are always concrete, definite, and specific. God does not provide us merely with a rough rule and then depend on us to make an appropriate application of it in varying circumstances. God always speaks directly to our situation. In his command, as in everything else, he confronts us existentially. We cannot in ethics, any more than in dogmatics, have his word beforehand, but only in the moment when it is needed. God's command is not in our possession; it comes to us. His command is not an empty form to which we must give specific content by our action and by the accompanying judgment of our ethical reflection. It is a particular prescription suited precisely to the occasion. God is not only the law-giver, but the applier of the law in every case. Says Barth: "Conscience can only be a reminder and indication that the command is addressed to us in all conceivable definiteness and that we have to render account to it in this its definite form. . . . My decision is whether in my conduct I shall correspond to the command which encounters and confronts me in the most concrete and pointed way." In Barth's view the commands of God are artificially distorted if we try to generalize and transform them into universally valid principles. The command is always specific. There are no commands save those which come to this or that particular man in this or that particular situation. The Ten Commandments, accordingly, since they have the form of General Rules, are not in all strictness to be thought of as commandments. They are delimitations; they mark out the sphere within which we can expect God's command to come to us. They do not themselves declare what must happen within this sphere. What is to happen will take place only in a definite confrontation or conflict with the divine will at a given time and place within the sphere marked out by them.

All of these ideas, which I have merely sketched in broadest outline, are worthy both of further elucidation and of critical evaluation, but it is not my purpose now to undertake the task. The ideas stand there as a kind of introduction to Barth's ethical thought, and as a witness to his genius and originality if not always to his orthodoxy, and they may appropriately be left simply to perform this double function.

Proceeding from this point I wish to indicate that besides being a renowned theoretician, Barth also exercises a profound influence on social and political affairs. He is a thinker whom the academicians cannot ignore, but he is also a force shaping the lives of common people in many lands. In the years 1933–1945 he stood in the very middle of the German conflict; since the war the force of his ideas has effected a significant "breakthrough" in the organizational life of the people in The Netherlands; and he stands currently in the center of an animated discussion concerning the threat of Communism.

I shall in what follows present the briefest possible account of each of these three Barthian "engagements."

Elwyn A. Smith in *The Christian Century* (August 10, 1955) speaks of the Barthian "disdain for activity" and, in reference to the sermons of Barth's disciples, declares, "The listener is expected simply to glory in truth reiterated rather than to shoulder more effectively the responsibilities which his humanity lays on him."[1] Similarly, Reinhold Niebuhr finds the Barthian theology lacking in social dynamic; it is "too eschatological and too transcendent to offer any guidance for the discriminating choices that political responsibility challenges us to." However this may be, it is a fact, as Niebuhr himself acknowledges, that "Barth was the theologian of the anti-Nazi resistance in the whole of Europe."[2] More than any other man Barth rescued the core of the German Church from the flood of Hitlerism which threatened to engulf it. It may be true, as Niebuhr intimates, that his action was dictated "by personal experiences with tyranny and not by the frame of his theology,"[3] but there are those who doubt this. The facts follow.

Hitler came to power in January of 1933. He was supported then and increasingly thereafter by the bulk of the German people, and at a very early date the majority of Church leaders identified themselves with the Nazi cause. But not Barth. Before he or very many others had felt the heavy hand of tyranny he discerned the spirit and ideology of Hitlerism and recognized it not only as anti-Christian but as exercising a religious fascination which, if left unchecked, would pervert the souls of men and destroy the Church. Barth acted in that situation with courage, resolution, and dispatch. What he did in essence was simple, though it was performed at great expense of time and energy. He reminded the Church that it has one Lord, and one Lord only, the Savior Jesus Christ. When Christians in great numbers were about to kneel before the idols of nationalism, race, power, and revenge, he pointed them to the Christ. And as the result of his firm stand a solid segment of the Church spoke to Nazism in the Declaration of Barmen, which in its first Article—framed by Barth—confessed: "Jesus Christ, as he is proclaimed in

1. Elwyn A. Smith, *The Christian Century*, August 10, 1955.

2. Reinhold Niebuhr, "Why is Barth Silent on Hungary?" in *Essays in Applied Christianity*, ed. D. B. Robertson, New York: Meridian Books, 1959, p. 184.

3. *Ibid.*

Holy Writ, is the one Word of God which we are to hear and which in life and death we are to trust and obey. We reject the heresy that, besides this one Word of God as the sole source of her proclamation, the Church may accept any other events, powers, figures, or truths as God's revelation."

Here was Barth in the middle of the arena addressing himself in the context of his theology to a forceful and ruthless social and political movement and arresting it at the borders of the Church. For this he was in 1935 banished from the Reich.

Barth's social and political influence in The Netherlands has been of quite another sort. In this country, where there has been no considerable personal involvement on Barth's part, his theological and ethical ideas have tended to undermine the foundations of Christian Antithetical Organizations. Although the leaders in the *Gereformeerde Kerken* are in general as committed to these organizations now as they were in former days, the effect of Barthian solvents is noticeable in other religious communities and also, it appears, in the younger generation of those who stand in Kuyper's line.

The accent in Barth's ethics is not on the antithesis, but on human solidarity, on the solidarity of men in sin and grace. This alone inclines him to be skeptical about organizations established to articulate the antithesis. The Christian, he says, "is never led astray . . . from the path of fellowship with the enemy. . . . Christians do not need to form a party in the struggle against the wicked."[4] In addition, Barth is jealous of Christ's honor. This causes him to deplore the attachment of Christ's name to human power organizations which, like all historical institutions, exist in sin and lie under judgment.

Moreover, there is prominent in Barthian theology the notion of the apostolate, the idea that one witnesses to the Christ in and with the undivided body of one's fellows, and this element, he thinks, does not receive its due in Christian organizations. No doubt Barth's eschatological orientation also determines his negative stance; in any case he often speaks of a Christianity whose expectation rests on a future life and not on Christian action. We need not, he thinks, be so anxious and intense; "provision is really made that God's opposition to the world's evil will be vindicated."[5]

There are great practical difficulties too, difficulties arising from theological and ethical ambiguities: "How can there be a special Christian party alongside other political parties—a party to which some Christians belong, whilst others do not—a party opposed by other non-Christian parties (which it must nevertheless recognize as legitimately non-Christian)? To

4. Karl Barth, *Church Dogmatics*, Edinburgh: T. & T. Clark, 1957; Naperville, Ill.: Allenson, 1957, Vol. II, Part 2, p. 721.

5. *Ibid.*

institute special Christian parties implies that the Christian community as such has no claim on the support of all its members for its own political line. It implies that it cannot help but allow the non-Christians in the State to consolidate themselves in a non-Christian bloc in order to enforce their own anti-Christian line."[6]

Answers, often telling, are being given to these questions and objections, but a certain breakthrough in The Netherlands has in fact been achieved by Barth, and this testifies, if not to the rightness, then at least to the practical force and influence of his ethical conceptions.

A great many people in Western Europe and America are deeply concerned about the threat of Communism, and some of them are making a great hue and cry about it. Not so Barth. It is not merely that, in marked contrast to his thunderings against Nazism, he speaks here in muffled tones; he is suspected by some of actually sympathizing with the East. What is clear is that he has counselled the Reformed Church in Hungary not to regard the favor or disfavor of the government as particularly relevant to the Church's mission in that land.

In consideration of these facts Reinhold Niebuhr published a highly critical article entitled "Why is Barth Silent on Hungary?"[7] and Emil Brunner published an equally critical *Open Letter to Karl Barth.*[8] Niebuhr thinks Barth's posture in relation to Communism is owing to two defects in his theological framework and approach: "The first is that he is too consistently eschatological for the 'nicely calculated less and more' which must go into political decisions. . . . The second is his extreme pragmatism, which disavows all moral principles."[9] Reference is here to Barth's alleged tendency to judge all historical formations by absolute or final standards, in terms of which all such formations are seen to be "equally" bad; and to his rejection of general rules or abstract laws in favor of concrete divine commands precisely pointed to "the moment of decision" (Barth's "contextualism"). Brunner hazards no guess as to the "theological" reason for Barth's attitude, but accuses him of evading "the problem of totalitarianism" and of refusing to recognize that "the totalitarian state is *eo ipso* an unjust, inhuman, and godless state."[10]

Barth's answer is interesting. To Niebuhr's second charge he replies in words addressed to Brunner: "The Church must . . . concern itself . . . with

6. Karl Barth, *Against the Stream: Shorter Post-War Writings 1946–1952*, New York: The Philosophical Library, 1954, p. 46.

7. Niebuhr, "Why is Barth Silent on Hungary?" p. 186.

8. *Against the Stream*, pp. 106ff.

9. *Ibid.*

10. *Ibid.*

historical realities as seen in the light of the Word of God and of the Faith. Its obligations lie . . . towards its living Lord. Therefore, the Church never thinks, speaks, or acts 'on principle.' Rather it judges spiritually and by individual cases."[11] In these words Barth reaffirms his ethical contextualism and implicitly denies that because he acted in one way toward Nazism he must now act in the same way toward Communism: the Lord's command is not identical in the two cases.

In response to Brunner he indicates why it is not. In the case of Nazism "the central and western European peoples . . . had succumbed to Hitler's spell. He had become a spiritual . . . source of temptation."[12] Therefore he had to be resisted. It is quite different in the case of Communism: "In . . . Western Germany and . . . the non-Russian sector of Berlin . . . I met no man of whom I received the impression (as one did with almost everybody in 1933) that he felt that this 'monster' was a vexation, a temptation, an enticement, or that he was in danger of liking it or of condoning its deeds and of cooperating with it. . . . Anyone who would like from me a political disclaimer of its system and its methods may have it at once. However, what is given cheaply can be had cheaply. Surely it would cost no one anything . . . to add his bundle of faggots to the bonfire? I cannot admit that this is a repetition of the situation and of the tasks during the years 1933–45. For I cannot admit that it is the duty of Christians or of the Church to give theological backing to what every citizen can, with much shaking of his head, read in his daily paper. . . ."[13]

This is Barth's justification of the stance he takes towards Communism.

POSTSCRIPT

Now that Karl Barth has died, I recall with special vividness that time in 1935 when, as a recent seminary graduate, I first dipped into his *Römerbrief* and went on to read the several monographs he published in *Theologische Existenz Heute*. I was studying at the time at a liberal seminary in which the Christian Gospel was presented as little more than a creedless moral posture. I was then not wholly without biblical and dogmatical resources fitted to combat the classical liberalism I faced, but I rejoiced to find in Barth a powerful and contemporary ally in my own little fight in behalf of what I had come to understand as orthodox Christianity. Although I came to read him in the ensuing years with greater critical discrimination, he served in those days

11. *Ibid.*, p. 114.
12. *Ibid.*, pp. 115–16.
13. *Ibid.*

to do nothing but confirm me in my Calvinistic faith. When with his great passion he insisted on God's transcendence, on the necessity of a special divine disclosure, on the centrality of Christ, on the radical indispensability of the Bible, on redemption by grace alone through faith, on the divine judgment resting upon everything that is merely human, and on much of like import besides, he not only led me into a deeper appreciation of my own theological heritage, but he enabled me to understand the very genius of the liberalism which he did more than anyone of his generation to dissipate. For this I shall always be in his debt.

Although Karl Barth's thinking is oriented centrally to the Scriptures and proceeds from the judging and saving activity of God in Christ, it is methodically directed to the life of man in church and world. It is directed to the life of gratitude, which is regulated by the law of God, and which extends beyond pious devotion to man's existence in society and culture. This, however, was not recognized at first. His liberal critics, especially, accused him of being deficient in a moral sense, and of having no room in his system for a meaningful ethic. In this they were of course mistaken. Barth did not complete his *Church Dogmatics*, but the volumes he did write contain so much on the moral life that he may be said to be the most prolific and trenchant writer on Christian Ethics that the twentieth century has produced.

Part IV

PRINCIPLES OF CHRISTIAN ETHICS

9

The Concept of Love: Eros and Agape

THE SUBJECT of this essay is love. By way of preface to a discussion of it, I wish to make two preliminary remarks. The first is linguistic or terminological; the second is heuristic; and each bears on the other.

First, my use of the two Greek words eros and agape to denote the complex thing which in English is called love indicates the linguistic necessity anyone is under who wishes to go beyond the shallow connotations to which the English words "love," "charity," "benevolence," and the like seem, in the public arena, to have been reduced. "Love" as it functions in the vocabulary of many English-speaking people seems to connote little more than sex or sentimentality. The good old English word "charity" is hardly in a better case, since it suggests to contemporary man something like alms-giving. "Benevolence," likewise, has come to carry overtones of patronage. In this situation those of us who speak and write on love have adopted the seemingly pedantic habit of using foreign words like eros and agape, and doing this, it should be observed, not only to transcend the limited meanings of the corresponding English words, but also, by the employment of two words, to acknowledge that love is not a simple, but a complex, and indeed a compound, thing. This, then, by way of terminological justification.

A second preliminary remark is heuristic and pertains to the set of theological categories which determine my outlook on the subject of this essay. What shapes my understanding of love are the concepts of nature, sin, and grace. You will notice that the number of these concepts is three. This is important to observe, not because there can be any real doubt that the biblical drama is structured by these three concepts, or by their cognates—Creation, Fall, and Redemption—but because a study of the history of theology and ethics discloses that these three tend in actual practice to be reduced to two. The shape of classic Roman Catholic theology was largely determined by the two categories of nature and grace, and Reformation theology, in reaction to Thomistic emphases, raised to formative influence the two categories of sin and grace. In this process Romanism tended to minimize the force of sin and depravity, and Protestantism tended to lose sight of nature and reason. The imbalance in each can only be restored, I suggest, by holding nature, sin, and grace in unbreakable relation.

The relevance of these remarks to the subject at hand may perhaps appear if it is recalled that two of the ablest and most influential books to appear on love in the last decades are Paul Tillich's ontological study of *Love, Power, and Justice* and Anders Nygren's massive theological study of *Agape and Eros.*

I find that the distinction which Nygren makes between eros and agape is apt, relevant, and indispensable, and I shall accordingly employ the distinction in my treatment of love. I also endorse Nygren's identification of agape with grace. What in my judgment vitiates his discussion of love, however, is his virtual identification of eros with sin. Eros and agape are the only two types of love that Nygren knows, and, I may add, that I know. But Nygren, illustrating a marked trend in Scandinavian Lutheranism, construes them in terms of sin and grace, paganism and Christianity. He sets them in such stark antithesis to each other that one is obliged to choose between them. It is not a matter here of both-and, but of either-or. What in fact has happened is that in Nygren's vision the dimension of nature has been erased. He seems to know only sinful love and Christian love, and the concept of natural love has virtually vanished from view. Against Nygren I shall contend that though the creation has been shattered by the Fall, and though the natural has been infected by sin, nature, i.e., the creaturely, survives the action not only of sin, but also of grace (sin and grace being only adjectival in their force). I shall contend that, though there is a supernatural love grounded in the grace of God and available only to those who are embraced in Christ (the love called agape), there is also a natural love, innocent in itself and by its nature indefeasible, the name of which is eros. This eros love, because it is creaturely, survives the Fall (sin not being able to destroy, but only to pervert), and this love, because it is creaturely, endures within Redemption (it being the function of grace not to negate but to perfect nature). In short, I shall contend that in thinking of love one must not allow either sin or grace to negate or obscure the natural, the natural being nothing less than the arena in which sin and grace operate.

Paul Tillich is not a Roman Catholic, but he has recognized that Rome has done greater justice to nature than has Wittenberg. Yet, he is not with Thomas; he has moved to the left of him. He has made nature everything. He is indeed not a naturalist in the usual meaning of that term. But neither is he a supernaturalist. He is essentially a monist who thinks himself able to "transcend" the duality of nature and supernature. He moves down to a level in which this duality is presumably overcome; he uncovers an alleged dimension of depth in which all things are basically unified. He accordingly does not recognize two kinds of love, as does Nygren. Love for him is single. It is one. All love is the movement of being toward being. If distinctions are to be made in love, they must be distinctions in quality, not in kind. In this view God's grace in redemption (agape) is essentially the same as man's desire and drive for reunion (eros). Love, for Tillich, is an ontological reality, and what is more, an ontological necessity; it is the "moving power of life" itself. It is the power that "drives everything that *is* towards everything else that *is*." In this monistic, panentheistic vision nature, i.e., being as such, plays the dominant role, and both sin and grace are interpreted in terms of it. Sin here loses its meaning of Fall (it is, in Hegelian fashion, an ascent to maturity), and grace loses its freedom (it is an ontological necessity). Nature occupies the entire field. The only love there is, is eros—agape being, not as Nygren contends, a radically different kind of love than eros, but only a distinguishable mode of it. For Tillich, agape is the depth dimension of eros, a quality of being in general—nothing more than an element in the ontologically determined dynamic drive within all being toward "the reunion of the estranged."

The sum of the matter is that in Nygren nature vanishes under the cloud of sin, and eros becomes unavailable to a Christian. In Tillich, on the other hand, grace (and even sin) is identified with nature, and agape loses its uniquely Christian character as the sovereignly free act of a forgiving God, it being interpreted as nothing more than the ontologically necessary drive of being toward being in quest of wholeness.

I myself would like, in deference to nature and with Tillich, to own and honor the eros which Nygren repudiates, and in deference to grace and with Nygren, to exalt the agape which Tillich denigrates, remembering meanwhile that sin is there to pervert eros and to be overcome by agape.

I shall in what follows be speaking mainly of eros, not because eros is more important than agape in structuring and directing Christian moral existence—the contrary is the case—but because limitations of space force me to give disproportionate attention to only one of two very large magnitudes. This being the case, I shall, for what I hope are sufficient reasons, focus on natural love, or eros, and only through this aperture cast periodic but fleeting glances at agape.

To avoid all semantic confusion I perhaps should explicitly remind the reader that when I employ the word "eros" I use it to name every mode or type of natural love, including the rational-scientific and the mystical-religious love that Plato celebrated, but including a great deal more besides. I assume, in short, that "libido," "storge," and "philia," as well as what Plato called "eros," have the same basic structure, and that on this account they deserve a common name. And the name, sanctioned by current usage, that covers them all is the generic term "eros."

Eros, in all its distinguishable modes, is natural in that it is given in and with creation. This love is grounded in the very character of created being as finite, dynamic, and unequal. The finitude of existence drives towards complementation; the dynamics of life drives towards appropriation; and the inequalities in being drive towards dependence on the one hand and support on the other. Love, i.e., eros, is the name we give to man's innate and indefeasible longing for complementation and support, and to his inexpungable desire to appropriate that which he lacks. Eros, then, is desire, longing, thirst; and in the measure that these are satisfied it is enjoyment. A love like this—desirous and appropriative—can of course become a very vicious thing when qualified by sin, but in and by itself it is innocent and good, being, as I said, an inbuilt feature of our humanity.

It is therefore an age-old and world-wide phenomenon, which made its entrance not with the appearance of Christianity, but at the dawn of history. There has always been, even in areas unsanctified by special grace, the love of young men for fair maidens, the love of friends for one another, the love of the pious for the gods, and the love of all men for themselves. Love of this type is universal; a word for it stands in the vocabulary of all peoples; and there has never been a culture that has not felt its forming power. The Lord has laid it in the heart of all, and he has in his good providence maintained it there in order that by it courtship and family life, friendship and community, may continue to the end of days.

The eros-love of which we are speaking has many modes or dimensions, of which the following are perhaps the most important.

The first sort of eros-love is self-love. One finds in all men a disposition to attend to self. There is probably nothing more natural than this. The egocentric stance and reference of men has therefore been called instinctive. It is in any case indigenous and fundamental. Because one can do nothing at all for either God or neighbor except in so far as one exists, some kind or measure of self-preservation appears prerequisite. A powerful impulse called self-love is accordingly discovered in all men. This induces them to assume a kind of trusteeship over their own being. It drives them not only to maintain themselves against all threats to their existence, but also to develop their resident powers and capacities. By thus actualizing their potentialities they are said to realize themselves. In this self-realization the love of self is perfected. Accompanying this love are various sentiments, among which self-respect is very highly prized by every normal person.

A second type of natural love is sexual or romantic. It is by some called *libido*. Of all other-directed loves none is more natural and thus more universal than this. It is a love that flows between the sexes, and it has a biological foundation. This love is found in all normal persons from the time of adolescence to old age. It is the basis of courtship and marriage, and it underlies the important institution called the family. It draws male and female together in such a bond that under prescribed conditions they become in the end "one flesh," exhibiting in their union something of the oneness that the Church has with its Lord. In this love an ineradicable difference in bodily structure is bridged and made the basis for a human fellowship which when hallowed reaches an unrivalled depth of intimacy and corresponding satisfaction. This love is God-ordained, and it is indispensable to the continuation of the race. It is, moreover, productive of all the beauty and thrilling sentiment that romantic poets justly celebrate.

A third type of love, called mother-love, has also a biological foundation, but it is not sexual in nature. Neither does it exhibit on its face the quality of desire, on which account it bears a kind of analogy to agape. Although this type of love is exemplified most clearly in the love of a mother for her child, it may also be seen operating in a somewhat less impressive form between brothers and sisters, and indeed between all relatives joined by ties of consanguinity. The Greeks, who had a name for almost everything, had a name also for this kind of love. They called it *storge*, which may be translated "natural affection." This love, which is the moral bond of unity between members of one family, is a very precious thing, and it is fortunately in evidence wherever men are found, for it is ingrained in the very being of mankind. If in isolated individuals it is absent, as Paul indicates it may be (Rom. 1:31), the condition is most abnormal and represents the nadir of degradation.

A fourth type of natural love found spread across the world is expressed in friendship. This love reaches out beyond the self and beyond the members of the family and embraces other members of the race. By joining persons not thrust upon each other by ties of blood it establishes a new fellowship which extends the blessings of community. This kind of love was highly celebrated among the ancients, and it is indeed a love which appreciably enriches life, a man without close friends being almost pitiable. An extension of this love in sublimated form is found among acquaintances, among those, that is, who are "thrown together" by circumstance or situation, and who subsequently form the kind of fellowship we discover in neighborhood groups, on college campuses, in veterans organizations, among workers in one factory or patients in one hospital ward, and the like. The "friendships" here formed are normally of a superficial kind, being rooted generally in a temporary circumstance. Yet they are very natural, and while they last (and some of them last through life) they build communities which, although exclusive, are productive of much good. For the special love of friendship the Greeks had a separate word. They called it *philia*. This word was taken up into the vocabulary of the New Testament, where it was used to describe among other things the fellowship of the saints. What we in fact observe in the biblical representation of the Church is a combination of this love with the family-love *(storge)* previously mentioned. The Church in the New Testament is, curiously, a "family of friends," in which Jesus Christ is at once both friend and brother to the faithful (John 15:14,15; Matt. 28:10; Rom. 8:29; etc.).

A fifth type of natural love is spiritual in nature and has on this account been celebrated and developed in most high religions. It expresses itself in moral aspiration and in a dynamic search for other-worldly goods. There is no sex in this, nor any kind of lust. Yet there is soul-passion in it, and something that can be called "desire." Plato, by whom this love was classically elaborated, called it eros. If we would understand what Plato typically meant by eros we shall have to eliminate from the word all elements of physical eroticism. The platonic eros is nothing if not intellectual. It does not hanker after flesh. It does not even seek the temporal and imperfect. It wants nothing but the eternal and unchangeable. It aspires after god, and it thirsts for him as the hart pants after the water brooks. It should here be observed that, whatever may have been the peculiar notes of the Psalmist's love for God (Ps. 42:1–2), this thirst for the supreme excellence is a natural thing discoverable everywhere, also outside the realm of special grace. Of this Plato is a convincing witness. Plato knew and commended a love that drives the lover on to seek a lasting good outside himself and resident even beyond the farthest limits of mankind. Love in his view is a passionate drive toward supersenuous realms. It launches the soul upon a movement toward those celestial and unchangeable entities which he called Ideas, the chief of which are truth, beauty, and goodness. These by their absolute perfection and intrinsic attractiveness lure the soul on, and set up in man that irresistible longing for their possession which has no name but love. This love, or eros, depicts the inner craving that men have for real fulfillment. It represents the tremulous reach of the human spirit for the one unfading object believed able to complete and perfect it.

A sixth type of natural love, and the last to be here presented, is much less dynamic than the one we have just reviewed. This love does not strive; it is quiescent. It is sometimes called the love of complacency, but it has in it all the notes appropriate to esthetic contemplation, and I prefer to call it esthetic love, though the name is of little consequence. Like all the loves thus far considered, it is common to all individuals. It emerges characteristically in the presence of some value—whether of truth, of beauty, of goodness, or of holiness—when this value appears not primarily as an object of desire but as an object of enjoyment. This love wills not so much to acquire and possess its object, as to contemplate and take delight in it. It comes into operation either when the object is already in man's possession and further striving is unnecessary, or when the object is such that nothing but appreciation is appropriate to it. Although this is a universal human love, it is not strange to God, who exercised it when after the six days of creation he surveyed all that he had made and, taking pleasure in it as a master artist, declared it very good. In a similar sense the saints are said to delight in God. They don't pursue him now, and in a real sense they never did, for he was the pursuer, but, being in his presence, they taste of him and find that he is sweet. Or, alternatively, they look on him and their soul expands with joy and they experience peace. As is apparent, this is a mystic love that requires and induces quietude. The hymn of Frederick Faber reflects the mood: "My God, how wonderful Thou art, Thy majesty how bright! Father of Jesus, Love Divine, what rapture will it be, prostrate before Thy throne to lie, and gaze and gaze on thee!"

This then, or something like this, is natural love, or eros. It is the love which sin, with all its negativity, cannot possibly remove; and it is the love which grace, in spite of its radical newness, will, in this life at least, not destroy but rather renew and enhance.

In his endorsement of this love Tillich, in my judgment, is clearly in the right, and Nygren, in his denigration of it, is by that token wrong. Tillich errs, however, in thinking that the Christian Gospel of grace can be construed in terms of eros, i.e., in terms of the value-oriented drive of being itself toward the reunion of the separated. Here Nygren points us in the right direction. Eros, he quite correctly observes, may be fit to shape a pagan culture such as that of ancient Greece, but it is quite unfit to shape the Christian life. The orientation and the natural limitations of eros are such that those who live by it alone remain strangers to the higher life available to and enjoined on those who are in Christ. With this contention I agree. Grace and truth came in Jesus Christ. This means that by his advent, life, death, and resurrection there entered into the world a new kind of love, a gracious, merciful, giving, and forgiving love which infinitely transcends the creational structures in which eros reigns. It is a love which lifts a man up and beyond the narrow confines of creature love, and releases him for self-sacrificial service.

In order to get into focus the wholly new quality of this agapic love, and to apprehend its superiority over eros, we should perhaps retrace our steps and look back, *first*, upon the natural limitations of eros, and *then* upon the structural elements within it which unfit it to be the spearhead of Christian discipleship.

Let it then be observed that, although eros is good in its creaturely existence, its goodness is finite and therefore, even apart from sin, partial and restricted.

1. It is clear that self-love, by which a man is turned inward upon himself, is a very partial love, which by its very nature is only indirectly serviceable to others. Even in its best estate it cannot occupy a central place,

for it affords no gateway to that self-denying service into which Jesus bids us enter.

2. Romantic love is likewise partial. It cannot, for example, be exercised between persons of the same sex, except unnaturally. And it can never serve as a paradigm of Christian love, which in its depths knows neither male or female.

3. Mother-love, though broader than either self-love or romantic love, is nevertheless limited, for it does not extend beyond the family, even though in sublimated form it may embrace the clan and tribe. Like all modes of eros it is discriminatory, which in its farthest reaches agape is not.

4. Friendship, unlike Christian love, is also essentially selective. It is normally exercised only between persons in the same age group, and it crosses the boundaries of sex only at the risk of being compromised by an alien romanticism. Moreover, it is not capable of uniting many, for it reaches perfection in an intimacy that is essentially private—a David is not likely to have two Jonathans. It is, in addition, a grounded love, which agape is not. It does not emerge in the absence of observed and appreciated characteristics in the other; it requires a basis of congeniality. It also needs reciprocation; it dies when unrequited, mutuality being the very mark of friendship. It is here worth remarking, therefore, that one should be careful in drawing theological conclusions from Jesus' statement to his disciples: "You are my friends." It must be remembered that no member of the holy community has become a friend on the basis of congeniality. Into the constitution of the Church some other kind of love has obviously entered. Agape is bigger than even that most salutary thing called *philadelphia*.

5. The platonic eros has really two sides: the rational-scientific side, and the mystical-religious side. The first is abstract, and the second, while not exactly limited, is at best a token of man's creaturely distance from God, and at worst a sign of his lostness.

6. Esthetic love is only a phase of human existence, and in any case, as Kierkegaard has pointed out, it is lacking in moral dynamic and in the outward thrust which agape so characteristically supplies.

So much, then, for the natural limitations of eros.

When now we focus on the structural elements of eros, two of them stand out.

1. *Value*—The first and most distinguishable trait of eros is its orientation to some value. Eros is a love which is exercised only on that which is regarded as in some sense good. Whatever receives this love must be *worthy* of it. It makes no difference how the value of the object is conceived; the important thing is that the object be considered as *deserving* the love it gets. In

the eros-scheme love is always motivated by the beloved; it is kindled from outside the lover; it is evoked by some positive and compelling quality in the object that is loved. Thus, one loves a friend because he is congenial and reciprocates the love; one loves a girl because she is beautiful or virtuous or accomplished; one loves a child because it is an offspring and thus precious; one loves God because he is full of excellence. In short, one loves something because it is in some sense lovable. What is not lovable, one simply does not love.

It would appear from this that, however good eros may be when properly subordinated to agape, it is quite unable of itself to fashion a total perspective acceptable to a Christian. Were natural love, or eros, to be taken as basically determinative, we should have to say that God could not have loved the still valueless non-entities he had in view when he determined to create the world from nothing. By the same token, we should have to deny that he now loves unrighteous sinners. We should also have to reject as absurd the injunction to love our enemies and those who in their person or behavior are unattractive or revolting.

In the persepctive of eros it is only as a carrier or bearer of value that a person becomes a candidate for my love. Love here can never be a genuine concern for others in their actual concreteness. The formula of eros is quite simply this: I love you because you are thus and so. If you were different I should not love you, and when with the passage of time you actually become different, I can and will love you no longer.

But this formula is hardly one by which the Kingdom can be ushered in. It is therefore a very serious thing when it comes to be employed in Christian circles, as it sometimes does, to justify hate for wicked men or to fashion a theology which limits God's love to those who are timelessly embraced in an eternal Christ thought of as the only worthy object of divine affection, and therefore as the only real object of God's concern.

2. *Need*—A second trait of eros relates less to the object loved than to the subject who loves. In erotic love the lover is always one who is in need. He feels, whether because of finitude or because of sin, a want that drives him out to others for fulfillment. Thus, the creature needs God, the boy needs the girl, the mother needs the child, the friend needs the friend. This felt need is not unlike thirst and hunger which craves satisfaction. There is thus in eros a dynamic desire to acquire an object thought able to fill the lover's emptiness, and there is in it too a quiescent delight in the object when possessed.

According to the scheme of eros, what cannot enrich me I cannot want, what cannot enlarge me I cannot desire, what cannot help me I cannot love, for love, by definition, is search for self-fulfillment, or delight in it when achieved. On this basis, of course, no true community can be established, for large numbers of people are in principle excluded from human fellowship. What has no value for a man, what he believes incapable of enriching him or adding to his stature, he simply cannot love.

It is instructive to observe, in this connection, that it was in the name of eros that many Greeks rejected the Christian proclamation of God's love for men, and sinful men at that. The idea that God could love mere men, to say nothing of evil men, was quite unintelligible to them, for is not love *desire*, and does it not presuppose a *vacuum* in the lover? How then could God love? He is the one who is full, who needs and wants nothing, the all-perfect to whom nothing can be added. Indeed, to one who thinks in terms of eros the biblical statement that "God is Love" and that "God loved the world" is utter nonsense. This Paul acknowledged when he said "but we preach Christ crucified . . . unto Gentiles foolishness" (I Cor. 1:23).

Eros is a quite natural kind of love. I therefore do not share the view that it is a sinful thing, although it has, like all created things, fallen under sin's domination. Yet it is redeemable and must, as redeemed, be retained within the Christian life.

But it itself cannot *shape* that life. For that another love is needed, the love revealed by God in Christ, the agape of our gracious Lord and Savior. Agape is not the contradiction of eros, but it differs from it; it is in fact its opposite. It is supernatural love; it is divine. Men would not have known it had it not been revealed, and men can share in it only as they are incorporated into Christ by faith through the operation of the Spirit.

This love does not seek to acquire or possess; it is not appropriative or self-enriching. This love is the very sign and seal that one has already been enriched, fulfilled, and made whole. All, therefore, it can do, and all that in fact it does, is give, impart, create, and redeem. It is not turned in upon the self. It is directed outward, toward the other. It is outgoing and communicative.

Also, this love is not value-oriented, or in any way discriminatory. For it there is no male or female, no black or white, no learned or unlearned, no friend or foe. Not denying the distinctions appropriate to creaturely existence, it is in its own unique operations blind to them. The man who loves with this love treats every man as simply a "neighbor," someone who stands next to him, someone who crosses his path. This love does not ask *who* he is, in order to decide whether or not he should be accepted in love; it only recognizes *that* he is, in order in service to act responsibly toward him.

The conclusion of the matter is that agape and not eros is the love that reigns in the Kingdom of our Lord. But agape redeems eros and makes it serviceable to the ends of that blessed Kingdom.

10

The Concept of Justice*

No ethic, and certainly no Christian ethic, can be elaborated without setting forth the meaning and significance of such important moral categories as love and justice. It is my purpose in this essay to consider the concept of justice, and not to discourse on love, but it is impossible to proceed without inquiring at the very outset whether love and justice are distinct and separate things or simply the same things under different names. Nearly everyone acknowledges that love and justice are related and should, therefore, be associated in the totality of the Christian moral life. But the question is: Is this relation a relation of identity? Is justice but one of the many forms or qualities of love, and should it therefore be defined in terms of love, i.e., in terms of love's most basic meaning; or is justice something quite distinct from love, something which, while it does not contradict love, must, in order to be understood, be given independent status, and contrasted with love?

There are a number of philosophers and theologians who think that justice is at the root nothing other than love. They hold, in consequence, that justice demands love, that persons have a right to and may therefore claim our love. This is, I think, a gross mistake, if by the term "love" is meant agape. It is likewise a mistake, if by the term "love" is meant eros, as this is embraced within the agapically structured Christian scheme. On the other hand, if by the term "love" is meant eros as this is conceived within a monistic ontology of being; if, that is, love is defined as the ontically dynamic drive for the reunion of the separated, then a certain plausibility attaches to the contention that justice requires the actualization of love, for it could then be argued that a being has a right to reunion with that to which it belongs. It could then be plausibly argued that men are only doing justice to themselves when they assert themselves; that they are only doing justice to themselves and others when they effect sexual unions, establish friendships, and form smaller or larger communities; and that they are only doing justice to themselves and God when in rational contemplation or in mystical flight they

*Appeared first in the *Calvin Theological Journal*, Vol. 9, No. 2 (Nov. 1974).

aspire after truth and goodness. It could even be plausibly argued, as Tillich seems in fact to argue, that God is doing only justice when in the atonement he reconciles men to himself, to themselves, and to their neighbors. But, certainly, no Christian is entitled to think of his salvation as only a matter of justice; the justice of God brings death; it is only his agape that saves. By the same token, no Christian is authorized to think even of eros in metaphysically monistic terms and in this way bring it into virtual identity with justice.

In any case, agape is not justice, and justice is not agape. This being so, it is a mistake to hold that a social order, if it is to be considered just, should be beneficent, require mercy, and induce men by legal sanctions to practice charity and be helpful. Of course, persons should love, and social arrangements should embody and reflect that love, and the administration of the law should be tempered and completed by that love, but this is not yet to say that justice is love and that love is only justice. In Christian perspective love (agape) may indeed be thought of as including and going beyond justice, and as in this way comprehending all goodness, but even then it must not be confused with what it embraces and exceeds. But certainly justice is not to be conceived of as the ultimate and comprehensive virtue it was thought to be in ancient paganism. Nor is it to be equated with that comprehensive "righteousness" of which the Scriptures speak. It is not the sum of goodness, but an ingredient in it. It is prior to and subservient to love; the penultimate which supports but does not extend to the ultimate; the basis of, but not the same as love.

It deserves, therefore, not indeed to be set in opposition to love (for the two are compatible) but to be distinguished from and contrasted to love, in order that so it may achieve its own unique identity. It is toward a delineation of this identity that I now proceed.

There is a dispute among students of the subject as to whether justice is best described as being concerned with tribution, attribution, distribution, or retribution, but since most agree that justice is all of these in one aspect or another, we need not here belabor this mooted point. It will suffice, I think, to say that justice is concerned with the distribution of goods and evils to each in accordance with what is *due* to each. Justice has to do with due allocation: goods to whom goods are due; evils to whom evils are due. The formula is: To each what is coming to him. It will appear from this that justice is concerned with moral symmetry, the symbol for it being a balanced scale.

Justice is best defined as "giving every one his due," the term "due" being a wide and neutral term serving to cover all forms of justice. It gives rise, however, to other terms, chief of which perhaps is the term "*right*," which is less neutral and more positive in its meaning. Rights are normally, and usually spontaneously, asserted by those who possess them. They assert their rights by presenting *claims* on what they regard as being due them. The orientation of rights and claims to "goods" rather than to "evils" is reflected in the fact that people do not usually claim the right to be punished or otherwise deprived. In fact, they tend to think that punishments and deprivations are in no way "due" them. It is somewhat misleading, therefore, to define justice as simply "the satisfaction of legitimate claims." What is due a man includes more than he may wish to claim, for the notion of justice includes an element which goes beyond the notion of rights.

This is the notion of *desert*. Desert differs from rights in several ways. "Rights" are usually thought of as somehow inherent in the very constitution of man, as common to the race, and as therefore independent of both individuality and performance. Rights suggest "equality," on which account the call for justice is usually the demand for "equal rights." Desert, however, is individualistic, unequal, and correlated to concrete behavior. On its positive side it has the meaning of *merit*, which suggests the notion of just reward. On its negative side it means *demerit*, which may entail deprivation or just punishment. Justice, it would appear, has as much to do with desert as it has to do with rights; as much to do with inequality as with equality; as much to do with attribution and retribution as with distribution.

A third notion implicit in the concept "due" is "*duty*." Duty is correlated to both rights and desert. When legitimate rights are asserted, when authorized claims are made, duties are thereby imposed upon those who are confronted by these rights and claims. Whoever is presented with a true claim is obliged to respect and satisfy it. The duties of men may therefore be truthfully said to be generated by the rights of other men. This truth is, however, sometimes erected into a general principle which declares that duties are basically and invariably derivative from and subordinate to rights. This principle in its universalized and absolutized form is, however, mistaken. My duty to love, for example, is not generated by the supposed right of another man to be loved. Love is precisely that on which no claims can be made, and yet it is man's highest duty. Duty is indeed always something imposed, and it is sometimes imposed by men through the assertion of their rights; but duty is not always, and it is never basically, imposed by men. It is fundamentally imposed by God. Accordingly, it cannot be simply and unqualifiedly declared that rights precede and establish duties. It is sometimes, and perhaps fundamentally, the other way around: duties establish rights. When God is taken into view, and man's relation to him is considered, a man's duty is seen to be the generator of his rights. I can make claims on men, and assert rights against them, only because I have beforehand been *commanded* by God to live and act in ways which involve casting off man-made restraints, asserting my freedoms, and claiming my rights. My basic right is my right to do my duty. In the final analysis duty appears not as the product of rights but as the creator of them. The notion of desert highlights this side of the rights-duties, duties-rights complex. In questions of State, for example, it would seem that the magistrate's duty to punish criminals precedes and grounds his right to do so.

However this all may be, it is plain that *rights*, *deserts*, and *duties* are involved and deeply intertwined within the over-arching notion of "the due," which is itself at the heart of justice.

Justice says that what is due a man must be granted him. But *what* is due him? What may he rightfully *claim* or justly *endure?* That is the issue which is at the center of the problem of justice. But another question stands close to it, and must also be addressed. That question is: *Where* is it declared what is due a man? What script do we read, or what oracle do we consult, to discover what is due him? And there is still another question of supreme importance—already mentioned in part—and that is this: *How* does what is one's due become one's due? How are (especially) human rights and freedoms *created* and *grounded?* Three questions therefore confront us: (a) the epistemological question concerning the manner in which we get to *know* what is due a man; (b) the foundational question concerning *the reason why* something or anything is due a man; and (c) the material or substantive question concerning *what* is due a man. It is obvious that nothing like justice can be done to these three questions in the space allotted, but perhaps something can be said that will not be entirely vacuous.

A.

I shall begin by considering the first of the three questions, namely: How can we *know*, how can we *discover*, what is due a man?

1. The first answer is: Consult your *conscience*. This answer says, in effect, you don't have to discover what is just; you know it already; you know it innately. You are able by an inner sense to distinguish the just from the unjust, what is fair from what is foul, what you can claim and what you cannot claim. You simply and directly know, for example, that you—and every other person as well—have the right to life (and therefore to food, drink, and medicine), the right to work, the right to personal property, the right to think, speak, and write, the right to privacy, and the like. Now there is truth in these remarks, and I have not the slightest disposition to denigrate the conscience. Conscience, which is given in and with humanness, is a natural and inalienable property of man, and by it he both apprehends moral truth and is laid under obligation to fulfil it. Yet conscience, which is open to divine influences, is open to other influences as well, and this compromises its witness. Its material deliverances being a function of the influences that have played on it, it follows that what it dictates or vetoes is very largely an

echo or reflection of what from the outside has gone into its formation. Conscience, therefore, cannot in and by itself become our guide and teacher in matters of justice and injustice.

2. One can, however, go outside one's self and consult public opinion on the question at issue. There is some advantage in adopting this alternative. Society as a whole is a repository of the moral wisdom of the race, and in public opinion the individual sense of justice is as it were pooled, deepened, and enlarged. Yet it is also pluralized and diversified. One discovers, accordingly, that though public opinion does articulate to some degree the moral awareness which is absent from no community, its witness is often vague, confused, and even self-contradictory.

3. To discover what is due one it is, in any case, more profitable to consult the statute books of States and, subordinately, the statute books of social institutions within such States. The rights of men are catalogued and codified here in what is known as "Positive Law." This law goes far beyond mere public opinion. It is the precipitate of some careful jurisprudential thought and reflection, and it is in process of constant revision by legislators and judges appointed to refine it. To discover what is due to men, to learn what right one has, one could do far worse than resort to the existing and operative legal system. Indeed, it should here be observed that in one sense of justice there is no need, even no warrant, for going beyond the legal system. What is known as "legal justice" or "justice under the law" is fixed and determined by the system. Legal justice is quite simply and exclusively what positive law says it is. Positive law is the very embodiment and standard of this kind of justice. Therefore, when claims are made on the basis of right conferred by statute, and when these claims are honored, justice may be said to have been done, for justice is realized whenever conferred "rights" are satisfied and recognized "claims" are met. Two things, however, are to be observed about positive law and legal justice. First, the rights which are granted by the enactments of legislative bodies are social creations, and their life tenure depends, in democratic societies, upon the public will, and in non-democratic societies, upon the will or whim of some autocratic legislator. The rights can therefore be withdrawn at will, and this being the case, justice can become at last a social variable delivered to radical relativity. Second, legal justice, when considered from a higher point of view, may disclose itself as basically unjust. That is to say, it may, and frequently does, grant a right which is not man's due or withhold a right which is. In considering justice and its scheme of rights and duties, we have therefore to advance beyond the merely legal to some higher law or order.

4. The higher law or order to which men of all ages have resorted to discover what is due a man has come to be known as the "Law of Nature." There are some Christians who do not like to speak of the law of nature, or of

natural rights. These terms seem to them to be overladen with non-theistic meanings, incorporating as they do ideas emanating both from ancient stoicism and modern naturalism. To them it must be conceded that these terms are not the most felicitous and that they readily lend themselves to pantheistic and naturalistic interpretations. Nevertheless, it must be maintained that what these terms refer to—a universally apprehended primal law of justice—does veritably exist. All men have some awareness of it. Even when men cannot say exactly what it is, and what specific rights and duties it establishes, they do appeal to it as a standard, and by reference to it they measure, however imprecisely, the quantity of justice and injustice which is embodied in the institution, practices, and legal structures of society. Moreover, the concept of natural law is not alien to the church. According to the apostle, the reality of this primal law is mirrored in the consciences of man. It is engraved, he says, on their hearts. By this apostolic dictum the existence of this law is certified. But the apostle goes farther and asserts that men everywhere are able to read that law and apprehend something of its content, for they do by nature what the law requires. On the basis of Romans 2, Roman Catholicism went on to construct an unbiblical natural theology and ethics in keeping with an ill-conceived anthropology, but the Reformers, alongside their conscious and forceful rejection of the Roman Catholic constructions, understood, no less certainly than the scholastics, that Paul was here proclaiming the existence of a natural moral law known in varying degrees to all men apart from saving grace. This was especially true of Calvin. "The knowledge of good and evil," he says, "is imprinted by nature on men . . . nor has any amount of barbarism ever so extinguished this light as that no form of law should exist."[1] In another place, speaking specifically of social and political justice, Calvin says: ". . . we perceive in the minds of all men general impressions of civil probity and order. Hence it is that not a person can be found who does not understand that all associations of men ought to be governed by laws, or who does not conceive in his mind the principle of those laws. . . ."[2] This reflects what Augustine once said in commenting on Psalm 58:1. "What man if questioned about justice, when he hath not a cause, would not easily answer what is just? . . . the hand of our Maker in our very hearts hath written this truth, 'That which to thyself thou wouldest not have done, do not thou to another' (Golden Rule). Of this truth, even before the Law (of Moses) was given, no one was suffered to be ignorant." It is therefore the case, as Joseph Sittler says, that "The ideal of Justice—a proper balance of goods, duties, and satisfactions within the human community—it is true that this ideal, and some effort to realize it, is not

1. John Calvin, *Commentary: Harmony of Exodus*, etc., Vol. III, p. 196.
2. John Calvin, *Institutes of the Christian Religion*, II, 2, 13.

foreign to any culture whose story is available to us. . . . Vitalities operative within empirical society have been powerfully generative of the quest for and the creation of various structures of justice."[3]

Yet, the law of nature is not so easily read as some have supposed. At any rate, people who appeal to it for light and guidance concerning what is due to man come away from it with differing opinions about what justice is or entails. Plato and Aristotle, for example, heard the natural law declare that there is no essential equality among men, and that justice requires their being treated unequally—in accordance with the share of reason they possess. The upshot of this was that they accorded slaves no rights at all. More recently the Pope consulted natural law and discovered that it outlaws artificial birth control. Why does this sort of thing happen? There are two reasons, I think. In the first place, natural law lacks the articulateness and the concreteness which characterizes positive law on the one hand and Scriptural law (e.g. the Decalogue) on the other; it is more formal than material; it is more regulative than constitutive of an acceptable order of justice. The Pope has presumably forgotten that, and has drawn out of the law more than it contains. The other reason is that we always bring our own selves to the law and import our schemes into it. All men, including Christians, but especially those men whom the Apostle describes as "natural," accommodate the law, which they cannot avoid apprehending, to their own purposes. In the process they alter and amend the law, often in ways of which they are not aware. Plato and Aristotle illustrate this fact, I think.

5. Where then are we finally to go to discover what is due a man? The Christian replies: To the Bible, which is the source of divine instruction on all moral and spiritual issues, including justice. With this I heartily concur. But where in the Bible do we go? To the Sermon on the Mount, perchance? Or to the pattern of the Israelitish theocracy? Or to the *Haustafeln* in the second half of the New Testament Epistles? Or to the Golden Rule? Or to the Decalogue? Or to the Parables of Jesus? These are not cynical questions. They are serious questions which deserve a carefully considered and responsible answer. But questions of this sort do suggest that persons putting questions to Scripture must be sure that they are appropriate to Scripture, and that the search for an answer is guided by a proper hermeneutic. They may also serve to remind us that the Bible as a whole is less interested in the justice we are investigating than it is in the righteousness of God and the justification of the sinner. At the center of the Bible's concern is the *justitia evangelica*, and not the *justitia civilis*. Unfortunately, I am without space, though not without disposition, to go into these matters, and can only say

3. Joseph Sittler, *Structure of Christian Ethics*, Baton Rouge, La.: Louisiana State University Press, 1958, pp. 78–79.

that all of these Scriptural givens must be taken into consideration and then construed theologically in such a way as both to preserve the natural sense of justice resident in the universal human consciousness, and to deepen and refine that sense through the corrective power of redemptive revelation. I may pause, however, to point out that when theologians in my tradition do appeal to the Bible as a direct and explicit source of information concerning what in justice is due a man, it is to the Decalogue probably more than to anything else that they make their appeal.

Our Lord has taught us that the Decalogue is centrally a statement of what love demands. But since justice is one of the things that love enjoins, it is possible to distill from the Ten Commandments a list, even though it be a partial list, of the rights and liberties men can claim. On the basis of the first four commandments men can claim freedom of religion and worship. On the basis of the fifth commandment parents can claim the right to exercise authority over their children. The sixth commandment can then be taken as establishing the right to life; the seventh as establishing the right of married people to the fidelity of their wedded spouses; the eighth as establishing the right of personal property; the ninth as establishing the right of men to the good name they bear; and the tenth as establishing the right of men to be protected against the threats and aggrandizements of the covetous. This, however, as I have already suggested, is only a partial list of the rights we tend to claim. For instance, there is no indication in the Decalogue of economic freedom: the right to work; or of educational freedom: the right to disciplined growth and development. We might, of course, move on from the Decalogue to other parts of Scripture in an effort to complete the list. We could, for example, go to the Old Testament prophets and learn from, say, Hosea, that the powerless have a right to be protected against the strong. But there is something unsatisfactory about this arithmetical process of numbering and adding up. It seems more fitting to treat the Bible not as a source book of jurisprudence or as a catalogue of discrete human rights and freedoms, but as a disclosure of God's creative and redemptive engagement with man, in which disclosure it is indicated what and who man and God are. It is, I suggest, from a theologically responsible understanding of basic biblical themes such as these that we are to discover what is due a man.

B.

I must turn now to a consideration of the second of our three questions: How does what is one's due become one's due? In what are human rights *rooted and grounded?*

Being here concerned with basic human rights I shall dismiss with nothing more than this slight reference to them the rights and corresponding duties that are grounded in and generated by the (usually temporary) agreements and covenants which are voluntarily entered into by individuals for *ad hoc* purposes (e.g., the agreement to deliver a certain quantity of goods at a certain price). Nor can I consider here the rights and duties that are generated by the much more important covenant called marriage. Alleged covenants of a still more comprehensive scope, such as are contemplated in the social contract theory, I must also pass over with no more than the demurrer that human rights are emphatically not to be regarded as political creations. Also I can do no more than remark that what is due a man cannot be generated or rooted in the impersonal Logos to which the ancients appealed from the time of Heraclitus to the time of the Roman Jurists. All I can do is state and briefly sketch the outlines of the Christian answer to the question we are considering. Two answers are possible, I think, and perhaps both are necessary.

The first answer is: Human rights are rooted in the divine act of *creation.* The Christian says that the basic rights man has are not conferred upon him by impersonal nature, nor by society, but by God. God conferred them not by handing man a certified document detailing them; he conferred them simply by positing man in his creative act. When God made man he made a person, an image bearer of himself. Not only that, when God made man, he made him plural: "Male and female created he them"; and he made him, unlike the angels, racial: "be fruitful and multiply." All of which means that when God made man he made a personal image of himself set in a social context of other such persons. And when God did this he virtually declared to each and every member of mankind: You are a person and you will remain a person, and you are henceforth and forever to be treated by your fellows as a person. This is your inherent, indefeasible right. By this divine declaration every man's very existence takes on the character of a claim. What Tillich somewhere says is therefore true: "In his encounter with the universe man is able to transcend any imaginable limit. But there is a limit for man which is definite—the other man. The 'thou' demands by his very existence to be acknowledged as a 'thou' for an 'ego' and as an 'ego' for himself. This is the claim which is implied in his being. This is his demand for justice."[4] This demand for justice is really twofold. The first is: Since I am a person like every person God has made, I claim the right to be treated like every other person—equally. The second is: Since I am in my own person unique, distinguishable from all others, I claim the right to be treated as myself—unequally. In short, because God created in one complex act both individuals and a race, the human justice he established is equity, the rule of which is:

4. Paul Tillich, *Love, Power, and Justice,* New York: Oxford University Press, 1960, p. 78.

Treat persons both as they are *alike* and as they are *different*. Emil Brunner sees the matter rightly when he declares: "It is only by comprehending the order of creation as the basis of all justice that we can understand why both the humanity shared by all, and the specific nature of the individual, constitute a claim, a right, which must be acknowledged, and in the acknowledgement of which Justice consists."[5]

The second possible Christian answer to the question, How are human rights created and grounded, is this: They are grounded in the divine commandment to love; i.e., they are grounded in the all-comprehensive duty imposed upon us by God.

An individual is a person who, facing God and seeking to respond to his clear commands, brooks no interference from mere man. Becoming a person in God's presence, commissioned by his command to the high office of a servant, he will insist, in the face of every human tyranny and oppression, on his right to serve. He will claim exemption from every temporal restraint which arrests or circumscribes his will to affirm his connection with and obligation to both God and man. He will demand the rights that are rooted in his duties.

C.

To the third and last question I have posed, *What* is due a man, I have space to give only the briefest of answers. It should first be observed that what is due a man is not all that would be good for him; all that would enhance his being and complete him; all that in the cosmic view of things it would be desirable for him to have. For this would be tantamount to saying that what is due him is salvation, redemption, fulfillment, and it is evident that these things are not things to be claimed, but only things to be hoped and prayed for; and when freely and graciously conferred, thankfully received. What is due a man, then, is not what is accorded him by the totality of valid moral principles (of which love is one), but what is accorded him by a particular set of moral principles, i.e., the principles of justice. We are, accordingly, driven to ask what are the principles of justice?

It is commonly agreed that these principles are two: equality and inequality, and in the Christianized Occident it is also generally agreed that of these two the chief is equality. I do not seriously quarrel with this. It must be pointed out, however, that these principles can be accepted and made meaningful only on the basis of a Christian ontology of being such as was hinted at in previous paragraphs. Justice demands equality of treatment indeed, but it

5. Emil Brunner, *Justice and the Social Order*, New York: Harper and Brothers, 1945, p. 50.

cannot, without a proper ontological base, be said that equal treatment is justice. As Prof. Frankena somewhere suggests, a king who boiled all his citizens in oil and then at the last moment jumped into the vat himself would be treating everyone equally, but he would hardly be doing anyone justice.

It should be said, therefore, that not equality and inequality, but personality or personhood is the basic principle of justice. Justice, Christianly understood, demands that every human being be treated according to what he essentially is. And what he essentially is, is first of all a person, i.e., one who bears in his very being the image of God and who in addition has been mandated and commissioned by his Creator to perform an important task in this world. In this respect all men are alike, and on the basis of this increated and indefeasible likeness, and in accordance with this shared high dignity, all men are, in justice, to be treated equally. This means, positively, that in the just treatment of men impartiality should reign. Each should have the same standing before the law. All should have equal access to the opportunities that exist for the assertion of human dignity, freedom, and self-fulfillment. This principle of equality gives the deathblow to the ancient Greek inequalitarian theory that goods and offices are to be distributed in proportion to the amount of reason, intelligence, or wealth different men possess, and also to the modern naturalistic inequalitarian theory that goods and offices are to be distributed in accordance with differences in color, race, sex, or natural origin. The principle of equality says that differences of these sorts are humanly irrelevant, and it dictates that these are not to count in the administration of justice, for they have no root either in the personhood or in the vocation of man.

But man is not only a person, he is also an individual person—each is unique, each differs from every other. This difference is just as deeply rooted in the divine creation and as seriously reckoned with in the divine mandate as is identity. This suggests that the principle of equality must be qualified. If justice is to be done it is not the rule of simple, abstract, arithmetical equality that is to be followed. It is not just to treat all people identically, in exactly the same way. Differences in their situations, needs, and the like must be taken into consideration. This does not mean the abandonment of the principle of equality. It only means that equality does not annul individuality any more than individuality annuls equality. Justice must be equity. Only equity can keep the scales of justice balanced against the weight of absolutistic collectivism on one hand, and relativistic individualism on the other.

A thousand more distinctions and refinements need to be made in considering the matter of justice, but I may conclude by saying that justice is served when each man is given both the freedom and the opportunity to attain to the level of personal achievement of which he is capable.

11

The Dialectic of Love and Justice

In the preceding essays I attempted an analysis of the concept of love and the concept of justice. Now I shall attempt an analysis of neither, but rather an inquiry into how these two virtues comport and interrelate with each other. I hope that on this account the present discussion will be less theoretical and more practical and existential than the previous ones. At issue will be the question: How in the concrete affairs of life can a person or a community be both loving and just at the same time? Or, how in any attitude or action can one combine, or at least keep inviolate and honor, both love and justice?

These questions become acute and critical when we recall that love and justice are in their nature quite diverse. Justice, as we have seen, has an eye for rights and claims, weighs merits and demerits, effects precise distributions, and the like. Love, on the other hand, is a response to neither rights nor claims, and it takes no account of either merit or demerit. Justice is concerned with the delicate balancing of scales. For love, however, scales and balances are an impertinence and an offense. Justice discriminately allocates goods and evils after careful calculation. Love, on the contrary, gives and forgives with uncalculating spontaneity and spends itself prodigally. The genius of love is apparently quite different from that of justice. The laws of operation resident in the one are unlike those in the other. It seems that love and justice by the force of their unique dynamics drive their adherents in opposite directions.

In the light of these facts it is sometimes said that these two virtues can co-exist only if they are isolated from each other and compartmentalized, i.e., if they are assigned to different spheres or at least contemplated as belonging to different spheres. Justice, it is said, reigns in the public arena; love reigns in the private sector. Justice regulates the interactions of impersonal collectivities; love regulates interpersonal relations. Justice is at home in social ethics; love is at home in personal ethics. A variation on this theme declares that justice is what one goes by when operating in the world; love is what one goes by in the church.

There is, I think, an element of truth in these contentions, and I will in what follows pay my meed of respect to them. I believe, however, that the love-justice problem cannot really be solved by instituting divorce proceedings and placing the severed parties in different homes. Love and justice are meant to be and to remain partners in every area of human existence. They are in fact delicately interlocked. There is indeed a tension between them, but the tension should not be broken or disrupted into conflict. Any ethics, therefore, which lays claim to wholeness will be at pains to preserve this polar but undisrupted tension. It is the dialetic of love and justice that such a comprehensive ethic will want to recognize and honor. It is the dialectical unity of love and justice that I now propose to sketch.

I am not entirely sure that I have chosen the best way to go about this business. I considered the possibility of selecting a number of moral issues and then inquiring how variously and yet supportively love and justice stood to these issues. I decided, however, that what was really required was a discussion not of how love and justice bore on some third thing, but quite simply how they stood related to each other. In considering this relation I took, and now take, my position on the side of love. That is, I construe the relation of love and justice from the side of love. I do this because love, in my judgment, is the greater and higher of the two. All that we Christians really want in the last analysis to do is to love in obedience to the command of our Lord. But we are wanting to know how, if we love, are we then to stand to justice. That is the question.

In an attempt to answer this question I have assembled eight different but related things as matter for consideration, and this essay will accordingly touch upon eight successive points. Lest you think that by positing this large number of points I have lapsed into unreformed pluralism, let me quickly add that I have managed to distribute these eight points under three heads and so contrived to salvage my methodological orthodoxy. I shall, accordingly, consider seriatim how love stands to justice (1) in the divine operation of redemption, (2) in human activity within the social arena, and (3) in human interpersonal relations. Under the first of these three heads there is one point only; under the second, five; and under the third, two—for a total of eight. I will at each juncture encase the point to be considered in a relatively short and dogmatically stated proposition or thesis, the better to expose it to your critical scrutiny and appraisal.

It should also be stated that when I use the word "love" I usually and perhaps always mean "agape."

A.

The first thesis, which is concerned with the divine operation of redemption, is this: Divine love does not destroy, but preserves, and operates within, the divinely established cosmic order of justice.

At issue here is a theological question, a question about God. The question is: does God's love, when it is exercised toward and upon sinful man, circumvent or abrogate justice; or does this outreaching love pass through, undergo, endure, and thus sanction and authenticate justice? My thesis is that divine love does the latter; it does not circumvent or abrogate justice; it operates within the order of justice, endures the weight of justice, and thereby ratifies justice. I am by this declaring that the love of God can be exercised on sinners and become available to them only after all the demands of justice have been satisfied. This amounts to saying that, for God, and in relation to a fallen world, the satisfaction of justice is the precondition of love's exercise, the necessary (if not sufficient) ground of active love.

There are theologians who deny this. They assert that God in his infinite free love, in his sovereign and boundless grace, is under no requirement to fulfill the law or to respect the order of justice. Tillich, for example, says: "God's justice is more than proportional justice. God is not bound to the given proportion between merit and tribute. Therefore the divine justice can appear as plain injustice. And he does so in order to fulfill those who, according to proportional justice, would be excluded from fulfillment."[1] My thesis is the opposite of this. It asserts that God cannot, or at any rate does not, love at the expense of justice. God in his love does indeed go beyond justice, but in that love he does no less than justice. The cross of Christ is the sign of this. The cross is at once a cross of judgment and a cross of grace. It reveals the togetherness of God's justice and his love. It is in fact the enactment in a single event of both of these.

The theologian asks, *Cur Deus Homo?* Why did the divine Logos become enfleshed? And why, to save the world, did he have to die? The biblical answer is: in order that justice be fulfilled. In the scriptural representation it is only along the avenue of just punishment that God's love can pass copiously to men. There is no justification of the sinner without the punishment due to sin. God's love is manifested in the fact that he inflicted this punishment not upon the creature who deserved it, but upon himself in the person of his Son. His justice is manifested in the fact that the blow simply had to fall. Someone had to die. This tells us that love can find no passage to a broken world except through a cross. It tells us that grace is not cheap. Before God dispenses pardons, he purchases them, thus preserving the moral order. Without the death of Christ, without his sacrifice, without this obedience to the order of justice, we would still be in our sins, and not even God—or especially not God—could remove or forgive them.

1. Paul Tillich, *Love, Power, and Justice,* New York: Oxford University Press, 1954, p. 66.

B.

I move now to my second point, the first of five points I shall touch upon in the area of social ethics. The thesis is this: Christian neighbor love demands that society do justice to its members. The question here is: If I love my neighbor, what good should I try to secure for him? The answer is: If you love your neighbor, one of the more important goods you should try to secure for him is that which is coming to him, that which is due him. The first, if not the last, thing that love demands for the neighbor is that justice be done to him. When Blacks, Indians, and Mexican-Americans hear Christians talk of love, this, and not alms, is what they expect love to sponsor and confer. And they are right in expecting this. If we Christians would truly love our neighbor, we must see to it that, through the institutions and structures of society, his human rights are met, and that his legitimate claims are satisfied. Love demands that we be at pains to establish, or assist in establishing, a just social order. Love requires that we so structure society that there accrues to our neighbor those goods, service, and freedoms which are his by right.

The possession of a loving disposition toward the neighbor in one-to-one personal relations, and the performance of personal acts of charity, does not absolve the loving man from the task of helping to create impersonal structures of social justice. And the possession of a loving disposition and the performance of loving personal acts never atones for the toleration of social injustices. The very least that love of neighbor means is that freedom and opportunity be given him to be a man.

On another level, it is no doubt loving to tell the neighbor the good news of the Gospel. No doubt it is a case of loving him when we press him to accept the divine acceptance and receive God's forgiveness. But if one stops there, one does not love him enough. One does not love the neighbor enough if one does not also sponsor and defend his earthly right to be treated in the public arena as an image bearer of God with his own vocation.

C.

The third thesis is this: Christian love demands the existence of structures of justice as the precondition for love's own proper exercise. The point may perhaps be expressed more simply by saying: Social justice is a necessary instrument of love.

I am not now repeating what I said in the previous section. There I was saying that to love the neighbor means to be concerned that his humanness is socially recognized and that his rights are legally secured. Here I am saying that I cannot enter into loving interpersonal relations with my neighbor—

e.g., show him kindnesses or have him fully as a friend—unless society is justly ordered. The point here to be observed is that what we ordinarily call loving acts can be properly performed only in the context of certain secured freedoms. Love needs a frame, a defined space in which to operate. Love, in its own interest, therefore demands a structure of freedoms within which it can have a place, and in which it can take place. If I am to love the neighbor, I need room to love him. This is to say that the social institutions and structures in which and through which I meet him must be so ordered that I can meet him. When, as in the old Mississippi ordinance, a white man was by law prevented from drinking a cup of coffee with a black man in a public restaurant, he was prevented by a legal statute from having the opportunity to show love to his black neighbor. That law was not only unjust; it was, because unjust, anti-loving. Love has no free flow or passage where freedoms are limited. Love, it is clear, needs the presence of justice for its operation.

Before moving on to the following thesis, it should be observed that there are several other respects in which Christian love requires structures of justice for its own proper exercise. I shall pause to mention only two of these.

Notice, for example, that I am to love not only my immediate, but also my distant, neighbor—the one who resides in mid-China or on a South Sea island. How am I to love him? I can pray for him, indeed. But how am I to concretely serve him? How am I to reach him? How am I to make him aware of my love, and how am I to make my love actual for him? Obviously, I can meet and serve him only through the medium of impersonal social structures and socially controlled programs, through a comprehensive ecclesiastical mission, a world relief committee, the Red Cross, the Care Program, national diplomacy, and the like. But to be a proper vehicle of my love, to really convey my love, such organizations, policies, and programs must be justly structured and administered. Here again, social justice is a necessary instrument of love.

There is another respect in which this is so. Social justice, more particularly legislative action in the sphere of justice, although it does not and cannot create the attitude and disposition of love, does tend to evoke, encourage, and sustain acts conformable to love. Just legislation and the just administration of the law in the courts, is one of the social methods of reducing not only public discrimination, but also private prejudice. One of the functions of the law is to make us achieve higher levels of morality than we will spontaneously and without such assistance attain to. This is another respect in which social justice is an instrument of love.

D.

The fourth thesis is this: Love, not being the principle of justice, is not the designated instrument for the creation of structures of social justice.

In enunciating this proposition I am impinging on a complicated and controversial issue, one which deserves a lengthier treatment than I can give it now. Nevertheless, I am reluctant to drop the point altogether, for it bears importantly on the relation of love to justice. It centrally concerns the competencies of these two principles or virtues to build ordered societies in a fallen world. The proposition states that love should not by itself undertake the task of political construction, for the reason that, though it may be fitted to create a heavenly city, it is, at least in isolation, unfitted to create an earthly one. Another way of stating the point is this: You cannot live responsibly by a love which is abstracted and divorced from justice, and from the rational and structural elements which constitute justice. Or again: Unless love be so conceived that it also sponsors justice, it cannot be maximally serviceable in this fragmented world, and it can be destructive and even disastrous. The proposition really states that neither love nor justice must be taken in abstraction from the other, but must be held together in the unity of their polar tensions. But the main thrust of the proposition, in my intention, is not against those who want to live by justice alone (I am not too aware of the existence of such people in Christian circles), but against those who want to live by love alone—for example, those Christians who want social morality to be governed by nothing more (or less) than the Sermon on the Mount.

Now, I agree that the Sermon on the Mount is a paradigm of love. I also agree that it is the law of the Kingdom, for in it the nature and structure of the Kingdom is outlined. I am also willing to concede that in the Kingdom love and justice coalesce, as the word "law" in the phrase "law of the Kingdom" suggests, and as the biblical term "righteousness" indicates.

But I should in addition want to contend that, although the Kingdom already is, it also is not yet. The Kingdom was announced and ushered in by Jesus Christ, and it is real; but it is not actual, for we also await its coming. We live in the "between-times." And in this "between-times"—between the emergence of the new aeon and the death of the old—how shall we operate? The thrust of my thesis is that we cannot go strictly by the provisions set down in the Sermon on the Mount. If the love that is enunciated in the Sermon be identical with the highest conceivable justice (the Old Testament "righteousness" and the New Testament *justitia evangelica*), it is still not the civil justice (the *justitia civilis*) by which the affairs of this world are to be regulated. The Sermon depicts a life that can be actualized only in the perfected new aeon, not in this.

Jesus, I think, knew this. He said, My Kingdom is not of this world. And so, when, as is reported in Luke 12, a man wanted him to arbitrate a dispute about an inheritance, he said, in effect, Don't misconceive my mission and make me a judge or divider over you. I have come to proclaim and establish a new Kingdom, which is not of this world. If you are concerned about the just distribution of an inheritance, don't appeal to me; go see the judge. In a similar manner Jesus distinguished, in Matthew 22, between God's realm and Caesar's and bade the Pharisees to respect the tax structure of the Roman Empire and pay the tribute.

Love, it appears, is unfitted by its very nature to supply those fixed structures by which rival claims are adjudicated and balanced.

E.

The fifth thesis is this: Love tempers the administration of public justice. An alternative way of stating the thesis is: Love is required for the proper application of existing law. The key words in these sentences are the words "administration" and "application." They indicate that the focus here is not on the creation of law by the world's legislatures, but rather on the administration of law by the world's courts, and by the judges who preside over them. By the sentences as a whole nothing more (or less) is meant than the sentiment which Shakespeare made Portia express to Shylock: "Earthly power doth then show likest God's when mercy seasons justice." The question here is: Does love have a function in the administration of justice, and, if so, what is that function? What, in particular, is meant by saying that love tempers or seasons justice?

In making reply I wish quickly to acknowledge that if by the word "justice" is meant quite simply justice in all its purity, then to be justice it needs no addendum of love. What is really meant, of course, is legal justice, the law of the land. The thesis is that the administration of that justice, the application of statute law, needs tempering, and that love is required as the tempering agent.

Every law is a rule. Every law, because it comprehends under one rule a multiplicity of cases, is general and abstract. In consequence it ignores the variable situations and circumstances of existential life. Once it has been formulated, i.e., fashioned into an abstract rule, it is closed to imaginative and creative outreaches of compassion. If such outreaches are to be made, and they should be made, for abstract law may not be left to occupy the entire field, then it is not the law, but the administrator of the law, who must make them; the law itself can make no adaptations and adjustments. But for the proper or existential administration or application of the law the judge must have recourse to the sensitivities of love. Love will clarify and heighten the judge's perception of the relevant factors in the concrete situation and impel him so to choose as maximally to validate the substance and intention of the law. Love is able in this way to convert abstract law into civil justice, and civil justice into true equity.

F.

The sixth thesis is this: Love raises positive law to new levels of adequacy. I can afford to be very brief here, since I have already touched upon this point in the section just concluded. The function of love in the present context is to mediate between existence, on one hand, and law, on the other. Law, as we have already noted, is fixed, static, general, and abstract. Existence, on the other hand, is individual, concrete, and changing. "It is the task of love," says Brunner rightly, "to bring these two together in such a way as to prevent the emergence of two evils—the absolutism of abstract legalism on the one hand, and the relativism of unprincipled arbitrariness on the other."[2] Love points existence to law so that existence may be rightly ordered, and love points law to existence so that law may be humane and just. Love in this way provides a standard for all historical schemes of justice, and by its inherent dynamic seeks to raise legal expressions of justice to new heights. As Robert Johann says, "A society can never rest content with the level of justice it has achieved. The sense and order of justice in a particular society . . . maintains what love has achieved. But the love which is at its root is constantly pushing it forward."[3]

I come now to the realm of personal ethics, in the area of which I wish to make two further statements, theses seven and eight.

G.

The seventh thesis is this: In interpersonal relations, love includes justice as part of its content. Or more simply: Love never acts unjustly.

All Christian ethicists recognize that love may be more than just, that love may and does exceed justice, and I shall in fact be declaring this in my eighth and final thesis. But here it is being declared that love is never less than just, that love, though exceeding justice, yet includes it. Conversely, it may be said that justice is the minimal content of love; or, justice cannot be circumvented by active love. To be loving is at least to be just. We have indeed noted this fact when we considered God's redemptive love. It is no less the case in the interpersonal relations of human beings. As Tillich has pointed out: "You can say of a man: 'He is just, but he is not loving or merciful,' but you cannot say of a man: 'He is merciful, but he is not just.'" There is no road of love that bypasses the realm of justice.

2. Emil Brunner, *Justice and the Social Order*, New York: Harper and Brothers, 1945, pp. 96-109.

3. Robert O. Johann, *Meaning of Love*, Paramus, N.J.: Paulist-Newman, 1966, p. 47.

Let us see whether this contention will stand up. Consider the parable of the laborers in the vineyard in Matthew 20. The parable is designed to show what love or grace is. All the workers, those who worked all day and those who worked but an hour, received an identical wage—one denarius. With respect to those who worked only an hour, the householder was surely generous or loving; these workers received more than a just wage. But was the householder unjust to the others? No, he did justice by them; he fulfilled the terms of the contract. The householder would, of course, not have acted justly had he deprived the early workers of their true wages in order to pay the latecomers. Then love would have contradicted justice, and it would not really have been love.

Consider a judge who out of love and pity pardons and acquits a truly guilty man. Is this act of pardon really an act of love? My thesis is that he who pardons a guilty man without due cause is neither just nor loving. What seems like love here is not really that, but something like romantic sentimentality.

The case of Robin Hood is a little vexing. He loved the poor, and to supply their needs he broke a host of English laws, and in so far ranged himself against legal justice. His practice is not to be recommended as a policy, but I am inclined to exempt him from great blame. He was probably trying by love-incited extra-legal and even anti-legal means to balance the scales of justice.

How, though, about one who, in a loving attempt to save a life, steals some medicine or kidnaps a physician to achieve the end of healing? Exceptional cases like this are, of course, the bane of all moralists, but I think the man in question should be dealt with leniently because he acted in an emergency. I believe, however, that his love would be suspect if at the first opportunity he did not make restitution to the druggist from whom he stole the medicine and to the physician whom he kidnapped. If he really loved he would fulfill justice.

It is important, I think, to remember that true love never acts unjustly when we consider our relations to those who are very dear to us—our spouses, the other members of our family, our closest friends, and the like. We love them, we say, and we wish to help and benefit them. But in our efforts to do so we frequently fail to do them justice; we take charge of them; we invade them; we manage them; we reduce their dignity. Helpfulness and service when not tempered by a sense of justice soon becomes aggrandizement. Love, if it is true, is always just.

H.

The eighth and last thesis has already been anticipated. It is, in any case, familiar to all Christians. It is this: In interpersonal relations, love goes beyond, exceeds, justice.

As one who loves I am not free to deny to others their just due, their rights. But I am free to surrender my own. I am free to make no claims. I am free in Christ to be self-sacrificial, and in the extremity to lay down my very life for others. In this way Christian lovers move beyond justice, and a readiness to so move was declared by Christ to be a mark of his disciples.

12

Love and Law: The New and the Old Morality

THERE ARE, broadly speaking, two basic types of ethics: teleological ethics, and deontological ethics. The first sponsors a morality of ends, of aspiration, of the good, and, in Christian contexts, of love. The second sponsors a morality of rules, of obedience, of the right, and, in Christian contexts, of law. Greek ethics is generally of the first sort, and Hebrew ethics of the second. Christian ethics, in my judgment, transcends them both by sponsoring a morality of obedient love. The new morality, however, is in general a return to the first; and the old morality is a return to the second.

A. THE UNITY OF LOVE AND LAW

The new morality is a morality of love. But it does not therefore repudiate law. No ethics does this, or can do this; room must always be provided for a basic imperative. The new morality speaks, accordingly, of a veritable law: the law of love. But this law, in its view, is the only law there is; it is the one and only divine command addressed to men; there are no other "laws." But this means that love *is* law. Love and law here coalesce. Although the new morality does not actually deny law, it really disposes of it by identifying it with love. Love absorbs law and virtually removes it from sight. If beyond the one law of love other laws are recognized, these are held to be nothing but the tracing of love's past course through life, helpful as guides embodying funded experience, but never in the moment of decision-making to be taken as ultimate commands. In sum, love is the only law there is, and this one law relativizes all others—e.g., the "ten words" of Exodus 20. The unity of love and law is here one of simple identity, an identity which in effect denigrates the Decalogue, robs it of its decisive importance, and renders it finally functionless.

The old ethic is an ethic of law. But it does not therefore repudiate love. Love, it acknowledges, is the essence of the law. But precisely at this juncture something happens that brings to mind the new morality. A unity of law and love is effected which is a virtual identification of the two. Law absorbs love and virtually removes it from sight. The new morality play is reenacted here, only in reverse. The new morality takes love for law; the old morality, law for love.

According to the old ethic, if you want to know what to do you have only one place to go—to law. Is there no love then? Of course there is, but it has no longer either content or voice; it has been engulfed by law, and has nothing further to say. Indeed, it never did have anything to say, for love is by nature "empty"; it is constitutionally unable to give guidance. The upshot is that law occupies the entire field. And this law—fixed, constant, and unbending—ignores variable situations and circumstances, stifles every imaginative and creative outreach of compassion, and leaves no room for adaptation and adjustment. Law, in the final analysis, renders love functionless.

But this, surely, is an unwarranted denigration of love. Law, in order rightly to function as a guide, must be informed by the sensitivities of love, just as love, in order to do the same, must be structured by law. Law and love are not to be smelted together beyond recognition, so that one is at liberty to construct, at a whim, either a pure teleology or a pure deontology. What is needed is not simple identity but holy marriage and mutual embracement. What is needed is a loving obedience and an obedient love. Neither the new morality nor the old morality seems to provide this.

B. LOVE

The new moralist could hardly develop a pure teleological ethic of love if he did not first minimize law by reducing it to a set of abstract and unbreakable rules. By the same token the old moralist could hardly develop a pure deontological ethic of law if he did not first minimize love by reducing it, say, to a mere motive. Who could possibly suppose that a man can live responsibly in a complex world by following abstract rules? And who could suppose that moral guidance can be provided by a mere motive; is not the way to hell paved with fine sentiments and good intentions? So, by misapprehending or misrepresenting the nature of law, the new moralist is able to strengthen his case for love. And, conversely, by misapprehending or misrepresenting the nature of love, the old moralist is able to strengthen his case for law.

Now the old morality has developed an ethic of law in which love exercises no guiding function and plays no significant role. We must therefore ask: How is it possible that love—an essential attribute of God, lying at the very heart of the gospel and its claims—can be so completely overshadowed by the necessarily universalized demands of the law? The answer is: It is possible because love is appropriated to the Kantian *Achtung* or reverence, and considered only as a motive without any content of its own. Love is regarded as nothing but an empty formality. It is a mere disposition, either to seek extraneous *ends* (as in the new morality) or to obey extraneous *law* (as in the old morality). It is in and of itself a neutral, unqualified, formless, and unstructured motion toward something extraneous.

But surely love in Christian perspective is more than a motive. It is more than a mere looking out toward something else. It is a settled determination of one's being Godward and manward—toward God in gratitude and toward man in redemptive concern. Like the law, it comes from God; but unlike the law, it resides within from where it structures the whole life of the Christian. It is nothing less than God's grace appropriated and made determinative in and for the new being that the Christian essentially is. It is not only a motion or a mere moving force; it is also, like the law, a pattern and a structure. It is not an erotic emptiness, but an agapic fulness whose lineaments can be described and indeed have been described in classical fashion in the Scriptures, notably by Paul in I Corinthians 13.

Now, because love is the determinate thing it is, it has a power of discernment. It can see or sense or intuit what is to be done in complex situations. It can do this only imperfectly, of course, for the "new being" of which it is the mark and property is still in the stage of becoming; but it can do this nevertheless. Naturally, what it truly discerns is not in conflict with what the law intends, for law and love are married and in essential accord. But the intimations of love are not to be reduced to the letter of the law. If this were possible or permissible, love, or the law within, would be superfluous, which it most certainly is not.

It is because the best and most biblically oriented of the new moralists recognize these things that they must be given a careful hearing. They recognize, as should all Christians, that the new wine of agape sometimes breaks the old skins of a literally construed *nomos*. Love never contradicts law, but it does penetrate beyond the surface words to the inner meaning of the law, and it often allows or dictates what the law *seems* to prohibit. Love is not a mere empty formality. It makes its own contribution to the fulness of the Christian life, and to that life's fund of moral wisdom. It, too, is a guide; one of the two poles by which the Christian must steer his course.

C. LAW

I hope that in my anxiety to preserve a place for love against the encroachments of an all-devouring law I have not been led to read into the law-ethic what is not to be found in it. But I understand it to be saying that the laws of the Decalogue are simple, uncomplicated, unambiguous, wholly transparent, completely understandable rules immediately available for concrete decision-making. "I can know," it says, "what the moral law requires." I shall not challenge this claim to knowledge as such; I make a similar claim for myself, though perhaps at a different level. But I cannot regard the laws of the Decalogue, particularly those of the second table, as simple prescriptions for concrete behavior in particular circumstances. In my judgment the moral laws of the Bible are principles and norms, not rules or practical prescriptions amenable to direct and immediate execution.

The moral life would, of course, be immeasurably simplified if the laws of Moses could be taken as straightforward prescriptions. Then all the commandments, with their implications, would be perfectly intelligible as they stand. Then the sixth commandment, for example, could be taken as declaring, quite simply, that one may never terminate, or be instrumental in terminating, human life. To the law-ethic the commandment, "Thou shalt not kill," is quite plain. It means what it says: Thou shalt not, directly or indirectly, kill a human being—ever, in any circumstance, under any provocation, to whatever end. On this reading of the commandment many puzzling questions which conscientious people are accustomed to ask with great moral seriousness are immediately and permanently solved, or else uncovered as pseudo-problems. On this reading not only war, but self-defense, capital punishment, therapeutic abortion, and similar things, are at once, without hesitation or equivocation, placed in the category of things impermissible. But are things really that simple? What, if this be the case, is the thrust and intent of the many biblical passages which enjoin us to wrestle and agonize in an effort to *discover* God's will. Why pray and search when the whole matter is set down in plain English?

That moral existence is not as uncomplicated as some suggest could be argued in many ways, but it may be sufficient to consider the case of suffering. A Christian rightly regards suffering as an indefeasible part of Christian existence. But it is to be observed that a Christian is alive, and also a neighbor to himself. If he now takes the sixth commandment as unconditionally forbidding behavior likely to issue in the loss of life, how can he will to suffer even to death, as he manifestly ought to will? A man's own life, as well as that of others, is put into his charge. How dare he put it into jeopardy, even in the way of righteousness, in violation of God's plain command—if this be his plain command?

The fact is, of course, that the sixth commandment, and others like it, are not to be taken in strict literalness as concrete and straightforward prescriptions for particular acts of behavior. The moral laws are principles. This does not diminish their authority. On the contrary, it is only as principles that they can be taken as absolute and inviolable. Now the sixth commandment says, Thou shalt always regard it as your duty never to destroy life, but always to preserve and enhance it. But I am a fallen man living among other fallen men in a broken world existing under the power of death. Death stalks me and those for whom I have been appointed guardian. It also stalks those whom the Prince of this broken world has recruited in the cause of death—the murderers who may assault me or my wards. Under these circumstances killing will certainly occur. In the matter of killing, therefore, I am normally not placed before the alternative of preserving or terminating life. Normally I must choose between preserving this life or that, one life or many lives, many lives or more. The concrete moral question, to which the commandment is relevant and for which it is determinative, is therefore this: How shall I, under the conditions of my post-edenic existence and in this particular situation, act Christianly; or, under these circumstances, what shall be the shape of my obedience and the sign of my love?

To answer this question I must have recourse to both law and love. When I face the existential question, Whose life, here and now, shall be preserved or, what is the same thing, Whose life shall be terminated, I must draw upon the two resources available to the Christian—love and law. Killing, in the situation contemplated, will occur; and in that situation I must act. The law will demand that I so act as to make, by my action, the greatest possible contribution to the preservation and enhancement of life. Love will clarify and heighten my perception of the relevant factors in the concrete situation, and impel me so to choose among alternatives as maximally to validate the life-preserving demands of the law. The result of this cooperative effort will be that love, without loss of its existential freedom and sensitiveness, will have been conformed to law; and that law, without loss of its structural integrity, will have been made serviceable to the ends of love.

Meanwhile, of course, I will have killed, for in a world out of joint I cannot avoid killing, directly or indirectly, either myself, or my wards, or my assailant. Have I, then, violated the law? Quite possibly not. It all depends on whether I have succeeded, under the tutelage of love, in preserving the right life, or the greatest amount of life, or the highest degree of life which it is the intent of the law to safeguard.

When the sixth commandment is viewed in this way it is seen to be, not an abstract rule requiring literal and unreflective application, but a living principle existentially related, through the mediation of love, to the concrete and variable needs of men. To meet the needs of men the law does not need to be suspended, but it does need to be opened up by love, and thus made relevant to the situation. In this way both the new morality and the old are superseded.

D. OBEDIENCE AND HUMAN WELFARE

There is an old and very important question in Christian ethics which may be put this way: How can I love both God and neighbor? How can I move at the same time on a vertical and on a horizontal plane? How can I be religious and also moral, pious and compassionate, heavenly minded and socially concerned, obedient and humane?

The question can also be put this way: How does my obedience to law involve me in a loving concern for my neighbor? How does law-observance recruit me for the service of others and impel me to seek their welfare?

I do not wish now to give an answer to those large questions. I wish only to call attention to them, especially to their form. Their form suggests that one can discover viable answers to them only in and through the recognition that an inner and dynamic relation exists between love and law.

The question is this: How does my obedience to law relate to the welfare of the neighbor? It is a question about how, since (according to the ethic of law) I am required (and allowed?) to move in *only one* direction, and to assume *only a single* responsibility, the needs of my neighbor can be met—and by whom.

The ethic of law answers this question not by positing an inner, strictly moral, relation between my obedience and my neighbor's welfare; but by positing an outer, essentially supra-moral, relation between the two. God is introduced. And he is introduced to provide the increment of neighbor-good that my obedience as such neither provides nor is calculated to provide.

In this way, I believe, the two-pronged moral imperative formulated by our Lord is split asunder. That imperative lays a double requirement upon me: to honor God through obedience and to aid my neighbor through an assessment and fulfillment of his needs. But in the ethics of law, as I understand it, I am left with only *one* concern; the other is assigned to God. Reverence for God and obedience to his law are enjoined upon *me;* the welfare of the neighbor is left to the providence of God. The law is *my* responsibility; the neighbor is *God's.*

Proponents of the old morality admit, to be sure, that "what results from keeping the commands of the law . . . is a very large portion of human good." But this, in the context of this ethic, is an *uncalculated* consequence. It is, from the moral point of view, an accident. It is an end which duty does not envision or intend. In view of this ethic the achievement of concrete ends and historical goals is no part of moral existence. It is not we, but God, who establishes a connection between our obedience and our neighbor's welfare. Sometimes, according to this ethic, we can observe no positive connection between the two, and sometimes it may seem that our obedience works evil in our neighbor, but we are not to mind; we are to do our duty and leave the rest to God.

It will have appeared from all that I have said hitherto that this is a view of things that I do not share. I hope that my faith in God and in his providence is as authentic as a Christian's ought to be. I also recognize, with all Christians, that none of men's moral strivings is able to usher in the Kingdom, that our insights into what is best for our neighbor is incomplete and defective, and that all of our acts and intentions stand in need of redemption. But I cannot believe that men are therefore absolved of direct responsibility for their neighbors. We must obey God's law, but always and only in such a way as to make us our brother's keepers. We must seek through the insights and ingenuities of love to effect the good of our neighbors, but never in such a way as to nullify the law. God reigns over all and will, we trust, one day perfect our feeble attempts both to obey and to be compassionate. But today he puts a double burden upon us. He bids us both to remember the commandments and to seek the welfare of the neighbor.

13

The Liberty of Conscience

ANYONE undertaking to write of liberty—whether of man or of conscience—may expect to be received and heard in a different way by at least three different classes of people.

The libertines will applaud the writer's choice of subject and listen carefully in the hope of hearing what will justify their license and abet them in the exercise of a rampant liberty. I hope I shall say nothing in this brief essay to give such people comfort, for I consider their doctrine quite without foundation in the Gospel, which always ties liberty to duty and frees man only in the interest of virtue and selflessness.

The legalists and rigorists, on the other hand, are likely to regret my choice of subject. They will admit that the Scriptures speak of liberty, but since they do not think the accent rests on it, they will not greatly welcome a popular discussion of it. Believing it to be a subordinate and relatively unimportant matter, and somewhat dangerous in addition, they fear its being brought into the open. To them discussing liberty is like playing with fire. They prefer to have a man play safe and let the matter lie. It is too subversive of human authority and conventional morality. I hope I shall not say anything to give such people comfort, for I consider their doctrine of conventionality and safety to be as foreign to the Gospel as is the doctrine of license they justifiably condemn.

The third class of people, the Christians, will, like the libertines, value liberty and welcome a discussion of it, but they will do so for quite a different reason and on the basis of a quite different apprehension of what liberty is. The Christian will value it because he finds it occupying a central place in Scripture, and because he has discerned that without it he cannot rightly serve his Lord. He will, therefore, like to have it talked about. He wants it brought up often because he understands, to use the words of Calvin, that "unless this be understood there can be no right knowledge of Christ, or of evangelical truth, or of internal peace of mind."[1] I hope that in what I shall

1. *Institutes*, III, 19, 1.

say I shall confirm this Christian judgment and thus disclose the mind of Christ.

Before I begin to speak directly about the liberty of conscience, I should like to indicate what I do not embrace under that term, and what I shall therefore not discuss.

I do not embrace under liberty of conscience what is sometimes called freedom of worship or religious liberty. Freedom of worship or religious liberty is a socio-political concept which defines a man's relation to the State. Liberty of conscience, on the other hand, is an ethico-religious concept, and has to do with a man's relationship to God.

This means also that I shall say nothing, or nothing worth mentioning, about the freedom of the will. This is to a considerable extent a psychological problem, and it falls as such outside our present view. It may be observed in passing, however, and only by way of reminder, that Calvinists are not "free-willists." They assert indeed that man is free—that he is a moral agent not caught up in the wheel of things or determined by mere natural antecedents. But they apprehend that this is something else than freedom of the will. Man is free, i.e., he can under ordinary circumstances do what he wills to do. But the will is not free, i.e., there is no extra-volitional vantage point from which the will can determine itself. Man's will responds to his nature, which is what it is by sin or by the sovereign grace of God. All of which leaves responsibility fully grounded, for nothing more is required for holding a man accountable than his acting with the consent of his will, however much this may be determined. But now to the liberty of conscience.

Observe first that the life men live is a life lived in the presence of God. God is everywhere. Whatever else this fact may mean, it means that God is our environment, that he surrounds, encompasses us. It means that every man stands in relation to him, is constantly confronted by him. It means that there is no privacy in the universe. It means that there always is this awe-ful presence, this great unavoidable whom no man can escape meeting and knowing.

And this omnipresent God is Lord. He is our master. He made us, he owns us; he supports us, he commands us. And above him is no one and nothing. He is himself the good who defines the right. He only holds the scales of justice, he alone marks the lines of virtue. It is with this God—this omnipresent Lord—that we have to do in morality, and ultimately only with him, and always necessarily with him. Whatever claims are on us are his claims. Whatever authentic ideals exist for us are ideals he posited. Whatever true goals we may envision are goals he set. Whatever obligations we have are those he laid upon us. His will is our law. He defines us and delineates our perfection. Whatever intimations men may have of right and good, of duty and obligation, are therefore intimations of him.

And whatever sense men may have of wrong, whatever feelings they may have of guilt, are also intimations of him, for since the Fall he is the great and inexorable avenger who greets those who turn from him with a scowl, and fills those who hide from him with anxiety and fear. Men meet him everywhere they turn. They do not leave him by fleeing him; they only go from him pleased to him displeased. Thus God is the measurer of good and right and he is the measurer of guilt and wrong. He is the inescapable Lord of double aspect whom men must meet whether their face be uplifted or averted. It is with this Lord that conscience has to do.

Conscience, which is given in and with humanness, is that native and inalienable property or organ of man by which he apprehends moral truth and is laid under obligation to fulfill it. It is a form of consciousness, and through it every human being apprehends more or less clearly, at least from the time that he becomes conscious of himself, no less than three important moral truths about himself and the world he lives in.

Through it he apprehends, first, that there is a good and a bad, a right and a wrong. He may not know with anything like the required clarity what (materially) is good and what is bad, although some knowledge even of this seems in Scripture (Rom. 2:15) to be ascribed to him, but he certainly does know that some things are right and others wrong. The notions of good and bad are intuitive; their meaning is directly known.

Through conscience a person apprehends, second, that he ought to follow the good and to avoid the bad. This sense of obligation springs directly from that (intuitive) recognition of value just referred to. A person knows that he is obliged to do the right, that something or someone categorically demands this of him, that he is under the constraint of an imperious "ought." He knows he owes something, is in debt to someone who never ceases to address him in the imperative mood.

Through conscience he apprehends, finally, that failure to obey the command renders him guilty, whereas compliance absolves him of blame. There is in him a native sense of guilt and merit, his "conscience bearing witness... and [his] thoughts one with another accusing or else excusing [him]" (Rom. 2:15b).

If it be true that conscience naturally apprehends the distinction between good and bad, is necessarily charged with a sense of obligation, and unavoidably makes judgments of approval and disapproval, it follows that conscience is never essentially and structurally free. It is always and permanently bound.

How could it be otherwise? Is not conscience precisely man's consciousness of being under the governance of some good, some binding good, which, through the conscience, legislates for man? Conscience is nothing if not that through which man becomes aware of obligation. How then should conscience not be under obligation? How could conscience not be bound, seeing it is of its very essence to acknowledge the existence of a claim on itself? What is conscience save a witness to man's being set under the imperious rule of right? Is not its whole being exhausted in proclaiming subjection to apprehended good? The answer to this question is Yes. Conscience is obviously bound.

Conscience, however, does not tell us, or tell us clearly, what the nature of the good is to which it is bound and from which it derives whatever authority it has. It does not, except formally, assess its own authority, or explore its own foundations. Conscience provides no unambiguous answer to the question: What is the Ground and Source of Obligation? Consequently, there are in the field a host of different answers to this question. The utilitarians tell us that the oughts, the dictates, the compulsions of morality are no more than the generalized maxims of social expediency. The hedonists say that they are the precipitate of private selfishness. Plato thinks that all our duties are grounded in and deducible from the nature and structure of man. Kant teaches that the moral imperatives issue from an autonomous practical reason. The Christian, on the other hand, believes on the basis of the Word Revelation that the authentic compulsions of morality are divine commands and, as such, are rooted in the nature and activity of God. This belief cannot be established to the satisfaction of those outside the faith, yet the Christian finds it verified in the whole of his moral experience, and he is compelled to declare that without God our moral intuitions would be unintelligible and morality would be non-existent or else some vain and passing thing.

Conscience, therefore, in the Christian view, is tied to God. This means not only that conscience can perform its function with maximum power only as it remains receptively open to God's ministrations; it means also that conscience is ultimately answerable only to God and can allow itself to be bound by no human authority, however august, that contravenes or goes beyond the authority of God. There is one, and only one, lord of the conscience.

Being bound by God, conscience binds all else. Having been spoken to authoritatively, it itself speaks with authority. When it speaks it speaks in imperatives, communicating in the form of its utterances, though not necessarily in the material content of them, the authority of the divine imperative it was appointed to disclose. When it speaks it always says "Thou shalt" or "Thou shalt not." It communicates its varying content only through this unvarying formula. Is this significant? It is, for in this formula its authority is disclosed, an authority which is quite inviolable. When conscience says

"Thou shalt not" it wants to be obeyed. And its demand is right. It should be obeyed, strictly and unqualifiedly. A man is bound to keep faith with conscience. Not to do so is to surrender one's inner personal integrity, to destroy character, and to subvert all morals. Conscience may never be violated. Its formal authority simply must be acknowledged. This is so not because the conscientious man is always right, but because it is moral suicide to betray oneself and to go counter to one's best insights. And it is sin, being a profanation of the sacred relation the conscience bears to God. No man, having bared his conscience to God, and finding that conscience condemning something, can do that thing without the gravest moral hurt. For witness hear the Apostle, who declares, ". . . he who doubts is condemned if he eat, because it is not of faith. And everything that is not of faith is sin" (Rom. 14:23).

The authority of conscience, which on the formal side is absolute—I mean the authority of its command "Always do your duty"—is on the material side very far from being that. When one wishes to know what one's concrete duties are—to know what is commanded, prohibited, and allowed—the conscience is not the best source of information. There is no doubt that conscience was meant to be the voice of God in man and therefore to speak in all men uniformly. There is also no doubt that "when Gentiles that have not the law do by nature the things of the law, these, not having the law, are a law unto themselves in that they show the work of the law written in their hearts, their conscience bearing witness therewith" (Rom. 2:14,15). Yet there is ample evidence that the conscience, through its deep connection with the fallen heart, and by its direct dependence on an apostate or imperfect will, is radically defective. It does not as a matter of fact echo God's words alone but also those of foreign gods, and so its material deliverances within any individual are ambiguous and within the universal community of men self-contradictory. The reason for this lies not only in the fact that since the Fall the will has paid religious homage to the creature, but also in the fact that conscience in itself is a purely formal faculty. It speaks no words of its own. It speaks only what it hears. Its content comes from outside itself. Many of its more particular maxims are those it has absorbed or adopted from conventional morality. On a deeper level the norms it proclaims are those by which the will is captivated. And since in different men the will is captivated by different things, since, that is, men have different basic loyalties, and since those who have the same loyalties are faithful to them in varying degrees, the concrete dictates of conscience are neither uniform nor authoritative.

One cannot therefore in any uncritical sense let conscience be his guide. Its material imperatives, its dictates concerning what concretely we have to do, are not absolute; they are relative to the influences and pressures that have operated on conscience. It is only the disciplined, the well-formed, the well-educated, the good conscience that we may take as guide, and then only provided we check it constantly and inform it ever anew by the revelation of the good given to us in the inscriptured and incarnate Word of God.

It is the Word of God, specifically the Bible, which is the ultimate guide. It is our rule for conduct as it is for faith, and from its pages we must learn what God's will is for our life. It is to its counsels and imperatives that we must subject ourselves under the direction of the Holy Spirit, who leads the faithful into goodness as well as into truth.

But what, according to the Scripture, does the Lord demand? What must a man do, or leave undone, in order to act in conformity to his will? How must he regulate his life? What obligations rest on the conscience? What does the Bible say? What does it command, prohibit, or allow?

The first thing to be observed is that specific, minutely detailed obligations are seldom laid upon the conscience in the revelation God has given us. If we exscind, as we must, the carefully formulated civil statutes and ceremonial regulations which helped to define the path of duty for the Old Testament saint, there is very little left in the Bible of specific injunction concerning the concrete problems of everyday life. If a man wants to know whether he may attend a modern movie, make use of contraceptives, play cards or dance, swim at the cottage on Sunday afternoons, join the CIO, drink whiskey, follow a career on the stage, or buy stocks on margin, he will look in vain for a ready-made answer in any one of the sixty-six books of the Bible. The Bible is very unlike a law book. For the New Testament believer at any rate it contains no extended list of regulations. It presents no catalogue of rules.

The reasons for this are not hard to discover. There are, I should think, at least three of them.

First, when prophets, evangelists, or apostles speak from the Bible on moral issues, they always do so in the light of two magnitudes—the Gospel on the one hand and the situation on the other. Permanent in this constellation is the Gospel; evanescent is the situation. When, therefore, they make specific moral judgments—as, for example, Paul does about women veiling their faces and keeping their heads covered—it is necessary to disentangle the Gospel principle from the time- and culture-conditioned application of it which he then made under the guidance of the Spirit. The concrete prescription made is binding on no Christian—the change of situation annuls or compromises it. The Gospel principle remains our guide, but, being general, it needs recurrent interpretation and application, for history moves on and situations change. The first reason, therefore, why the Christian cannot live by rule is this: The proper understanding of the Bible precludes it.

Second, no specific rule, embodying a single univocal meaning, could ever be formulated and made to apply in the same way to all people at all times in all places. From the nature of the case a rule is static, fixed, abstract, whereas life, to which the rule is meant to apply, is dynamic, variable, and concrete. No strict correlation can therefore be made between the two. A rule has no capacity, and a man who lives by rules has no opportunity, to estimate and respond to such important moral variables as motive, degree of temptation, age, alternative courses of action, conflict of duties, and the like. A tight prescription can never be saddled upon a vital process. This is why legalists who like to hedge in the principles of morals with ordinances find themselves compelled, in order to keep pace with life's complexities, to heap rule upon rule. They must frame a rule to define a previous rule, a rule for breaking rules, a rule for adjusting conflicting rules, a rule for keeping rules, and so on *ad infinitum*, in a frantic attempt to fix and contain what no mere rule or set of rules can possibly contain. And this is one reason, I presume, why the Scriptures do not press God's claim on us in the form of a multitude of detailed ordinances.

Another reason, I believe, is that living by rules is not calculated to call into play those faculties of will and judgment which it is the purpose of the Lord to develop in us. It is evidently God's will not only that we should do right, but also that we should be right. He is concerned not only that our external deeds, like straight-aimed arrows, should squarely hit the mark, but also that our characters should come out strong and well-rounded. But character, strength of will, keenness of moral perception, and the habit of fervent prayer cannot be formed in one by requiring him to do no more than manipulate a legalistic calculus. Saints are made when men, aided by God's Spirit, guided by the eternal principles of his Word, and stirred by the example of those who have gone before, of whom Christ is chief, are thrown out into the complex world and forced in the exercise of their God-given liberty to discover God's will in study, prayer, and effort, so that at last, after falling often and being forgiven often, they grow into maturity and attain something of the fulness of the stature of Christ.

I asked a little earlier what it was that Scripture enjoined upon the conscience, and I replied by saying that the Scriptures, not being a catalogue of rules or a handbook in casuistry, were apt to disappoint a man who sought in them a ready-made answer to every particular problem that bothered him. This, I thought, needed saying, but it was not a direct answer to the question.

The answer is, of course, familiar to every Christian. What the Scriptures enjoin on the conscience is love—perfect love, Christian love, supernatural love, the love displayed by God in Christ on the tree, the love which only Christ imparts—the love that suffereth long and is kind, that envieth not, that vaunteth not itself and is not puffed up, that doth not behave itself unseemly, that seeketh not its own, is not provoked, taketh not account of evil, that rejoiceth not in unrighteousness but rejoiceth with the truth, the love that beareth all things, believeth all things, hopeth all things, endureth all things. This is enjoined on the conscience. This is God's will for us.

This is not the place to indicate what this concretely means. The very least it means is what is set down in the Ten Commandments, of which it is the distilled essence. This is the place to say, however, that the command to love requires us to leave no area of our life unsurrendered to our Lord, no duty to our fellows unfulfilled. It demands that our righteousness exceed that of the Pharisees, that it soar high above all conventional morality, and that in all things we be perfect.

This is a very great demand. It lays a heavy, indeed a crushing, weight upon the conscience. It binds a man at all four corners; it nails him down at every point. It leaves the conscience with no option save complete surrender. It delineates a single way and bars and barricades all others. By it God lays claim upon our public and our private life, upon our work and upon our play, upon our thoughts as well as upon our words and works. Even our secret thoughts, our hidden sentiments, are judged by it. This demand cannot be contained. It floods the soul and encompasses us completely. By this demand God orders that we be paragons of virtue, that in our person we incarnate the ideal, that we exhibit the very idea of perfect human goodness.

The conscience that truly perceives this is sure to faint. For, perceiving this it perceives at the same time that it is guilty, must remain guilty, and must become more guilty with every passing moment.

In this situation two ways are open to a man. He can ease his conscience temporarily, take the excessive heat off it, by turning his back to God or by interposing between the Lord and his conscience a screen of forgetfulness, a veil of pleasurable indulgences. This will not completely free his conscience from terror and a haunting presence, but it will somewhat assuage the pain and remove the deepest hurt—until the judgment day, when the full weight of the law will fall with a heavy thud on a soul whose conscience will thereafter gnaw at him forever. Or else he can expose himself to the full weight of the law, let the demand for holiness cut right through his soul, fall and lay prostrate under the divine weight of glory, let the conscience be pinned and skewered to the ground, fixed immovably by the weight of an obligation it can never fulfill, and then cry out for mercy. And when that cry is uttered, and before it is fairly voiced, a pair of pierced hands will lift the weight of the law off the almost expiring soul, and the conscience, once pinned and bound, will be set free. This is the first, the basic liberty the Christian conscience enjoys. In this liberty the conscience lies no longer under the law, but under grace. It stands not under the lawgiver but the Savior. It is justified. It is not a conscience that will be justified, but one which is justified—justified in its sin and imperfection, and not only in its present sin, but in its future sins. Tomorrow's sin cannot hurt it. In some deep sense, it cannot sin any more, for no law impinges on it, Christ having interposed himself between the law and conscience.

A man so situated is delivered out of the whole realm of works. His good works do not get him to heaven; his evil works do not drag him down to hell. Grace has supplanted law; faith has supplanted works. The Christian is free, his conscience is not anxious. He can live venturesomely for his King. Must he not love then? Of course he must. The law remains, but it has changed its character. It is now a gracious directive, not an imperious demand. And if it is not kept entirely? Well, there is forgiveness!

Shall we sin boldly then? God forbid! It is the Christian we are talking of. We are talking of a man who is in Christ. How shall he want to sin? He may indeed fall into sin, and he does; but sin, to destroy which Christ died, is his enemy forever.

And yet there is something about the Christian, the man from whom the crushing weight of the law has been lifted, that is wholly unlike the Pharisee. His anxiety is gone; his nervousness is gone. He has equilibrium. He is not asking always whether a course of action is safe. He takes risks, knowing that Satan can no longer ensnare him. Who can separate him from the love of God in Christ? Who can judge him, whom God hath justified? Let no man lay anything to the charge of God's elect. Here is a free man—a free man in grace—who moves with poise and not with a timid and overly scrupulous conscience among men, and pushes on into the world unafraid.

The Christian conscience, while bound, is free in another sense as well. It is free from foreign bondage. It is now in some deep sense its own law, its own master. How could it be otherwise? Christ is his Lord, but he is in Christ, and in so far as he is in the mystic union identified with Christ, in so far he knows no law outside himself. It is only as he is outside of Christ, and in the measure that he is outside of him, that he experiences the everlasting valid law of love as a burden and a hindrance.

Or to put it another way: The law stands there indeed; it is not abolished. But the sinner touched by grace sees it only through the Christ and contemplates it no longer as a command, but as a privilege; not as a demand but as a directive. It is not that it is less valid than before, but it presents itself differently. It is not a tyrant; it is a guide.

In this sense the soul is free. It finds in the law, which in itself is unchanged, that which suits and fits. Just as a fish finds the water no burden, and the train finds the tracks suited to its nature, so the redeemed soul finds the law setting forth and recapitulating what it itself wants and desires. The law, forever valid, stands not outside the Christian's life, but reigns inside it. The autonomy of the law fuses with the autonomy of the soul. The soul is free. It can do what it will because what it wills is the same as what it ought to will.

Finally, the conscience of the man in Christ is free from every human ordinance that is not derived from the Scripture or, which is to say the same thing, that does not articulate the law of love. In the ethical-spiritual realm as in the socio-political realm, the Christian hates all tyranny. He has one Lord and he will not acknowledge another. He will let no man lord it over his conscience. The transactions of conscience are between him and God, and he is determined to keep it that way.

This third type of liberty of conscience usually is discussed in theological and ethical treatises under the head of *adiaphora* or indifferent things. So, for example, we find Calvin saying, "... we are bound by no obligation before God respecting external things, which in themselves are indifferent... we may indifferently sometimes use, and at other times omit them."[2] What does this mean?

It does not mean that there are some things we do which in the doing have an amoral quality. There is no conscious voluntary human behavior that does not possess a moral quality, and everything we do we do in dedication to God, in the way of his service, to his praise and glory, or not. All things are done before the Lord, in his presence, piously or impiously, gratefully or thanklessly.

Granted that whatever I do voluntarily I do responsibly—i.e., morally, either virtuously or viciously—is it a matter of indifference whether at any given moment I do that thing or some other? Am I in the moment of decision ever confronted by two options, the choice of either one of which is a matter of no moral consequence? I think not. I think that at any moment in any concrete situation there is only one right thing to do, one right decision to make.

Granted, then, that whatever I do I must do to God's glory, and granted that at any given moment there is only one right thing to do, what is left of the notion of indifference, the notion of *adiaphora?* What is left, I think, is the notion of a class of things, about which, as a class, I can say two things: There is no commandment, direct or indirect, from the Lord concerning these things, particularly no prohibition; and these things are amenable either to virtuous or to vicious use.

Now, concerning these things no man or group of men (however august) may bind my conscience. Concerning these things I must be free to determine, not what may please me, but what my duty or responsibility is. And if I determine to use or enjoy these things my fellow Christians are bound to respect my liberty.

2. *Institutes*, III, 19, 7.

There is only one limitation on the exercise of this liberty—the law of love. This liberty, like every liberty the Christian cherishes, is not an end in itself. It is a means to virtue. The Christian cherishes it because and in so far as it enables him to perform all the duties of charity and to develop himself to full Christian stature. Now if a weak brother, that is, one who is still immature, is tempted by my example to do something which his conscience condemns, then I am bound to surrender my liberty for his sake, lest he perish for whom Christ died. I may not tempt a man to violate his conscience.

There are no other limitations on the exercise of my liberty in indifferent things. The protests and accusations of the strong, I can ignore. For as Calvin says: "How much attention should be paid to an offence taken by Pharisees, we learn from our Lord's injunction, 'Let them alone; they are blind leaders of the blind.'"

Part V

ETHICS AND SOCIETY

14

The Freedom of Man

EVERYONE wants freedom. Businessmen want economic freedom. Citizens want political freedom. Believers want religious freedom. Teachers want academic freedom and all individuals want personal freedom.

This is understandable. Man has an essential dignity and a native claim to liberty. He was made in God's image. He was not meant to be a slave, and he can never be happy in bonds.

This the Christian knows better than any man and that is why he hates all tyranny. It is the reason for his uncompromising opposition to political dictators, economic collectivisms, and coercive religious establishments. It accounts for his resistance to monopolistic education and programs of thought control. It is the reason why he defends human liberty on all fronts.

In thinking that man should be free from arbitrary restraints in every department of human thought and action the Christian does not differ on the surface from the modern liberal. The liberal, too, loves liberty, and though he is not so sure as formerly just what liberty means and how it can be preserved, he still pursues it with religious, though not with Christian, devotion. It is not surprising, therefore, to find the Christian, in whom the love of freedom is inextinguishable, in at least apparent agreement on many practical issues with the secular liberals of the day. Like the latter he is apt to be an advocate of some form of democracy in government, of free though responsible enterprise in business, of liberty of conscience in religion, of freedom of expression in journalism, of civil liberties for men of every race and color in social policy, and of freedom of thought and inquiry in the schools. He is especially apt to be this if he is a Protestant and aware of the Protestant tradition of liberty, criticism, and non-conformism. The typical Protestant is a doughty champion of human freedoms, and thus in form at least a brother to the modern liberal.

It would be a mistake, however, to suppose that the Christian and the modern liberal are cut from the same cloth. Their agreements are only on the surface. Both want freedom, but their definitions of freedom are radically different, and the difference is bound in the long run to affect policy and practice, and to place them on opposite sides in the battle now being fought to preserve the culture and institutions of Western civilization.

An important feature of that culture is, or has been, the high value placed upon the human personality. Another, though related, feature is the important status accorded to the individual in the social order. A third is the respect entertained for human brotherhood in the social community, and the principles of love and justice which generate and support it. Both Christian and secular interpreters of the contemporary crisis in Western civilization are agreed that these features define as nearly as any the free society which they are seeking to preserve against the threat of Communist collectivism and totalitarianism. They are not agreed, however, on the origin of these features, nor on their abiding ground. The one believes that the dogma of the sacredness of human personality and of individual rights, and the dogma of community, are natural and self-evident truths, requiring no transcendent ground and validation, and being sufficiently guaranteed by a non-religious or secular humanism; the other points to their Christian origin and insists that they can be established only on a theological basis. This difference of opinion is fundamental. The liberal believes that the Christian imperils human freedom by associating it with religious authoritarianism, while the Christian believes that the liberal in rejecting divine sanction for liberty has already lost his grip on it and is enjoying it only by Christian sufferance.

It can be shown, I think, that the freedoms which Western man enjoys are due in largest part to the influence of Christianity. The free society men cherish roots in the religion of Christ. A genetic relationship exists between Christian faith and the best in what has come to be called the democratic way of life. Western civilization has two roots: classical paganism and Christianity, and the first of these—classical paganism—influenced the development of Europe, at least during the first fifteen centuries, only in so far as it was preserved and modified by medieval Christianity. It may be said therefore that the Christian faith is the taproot of our civilization and by that token is the source of what we have come to regard as one of its most hallowed traditions, the tradition of freedom.

It is evident, at any rate, that there is nothing in Greek humanism as such which could account for the development of those liberties which have received acknowledgment in the constitutions and bills of rights of most modern states.

The rationalistic universalism of Greek thought could provide no place for the individual. For Plato particularity was a non-rational moment in an otherwise rational universe. True being was universal being. The individual was not really real and it owed what existence it enjoyed to the negative principle of non-being. Individuality and uniqueness counted for even less in monistic Neo-Platonism where mystic absorption in the all-one, and consequent loss of identity, was presented as the goal of life. In all of Greek thought this inability to establish and validate the individual reveals itself. Even sophism had no true appreciation of the self. It confused individualism with sheer subjectivity and landed in nihilism. Nor did Aristotle, for all his insistence on the empirical and contingent, really get beyond universalism. For him the species and not the individual remained the important reality. In political and social theory this meant the subservience of the individual to the interests of the state in a way not unlike that revealed in contemporary communism.

Of personality, as we of the Western world have come to think of it, the Greeks had no conception. In the thought of the great Greek thinkers being was rational indeed, but it was not spiritual. Ultimate reality was in their view static and impersonal—a form or an idea. It did not create, it did not save, it did not love. By the same token the essence and dignity of man lay not in his capacity to respond to and have fellowship with another summoning him to communion, but only in his capacity intellectually to apprehend and adjust to abstract truth. God in Greek thought had no heart, and by consequence neither did man, for, as Brunner says, "Only the personal God can fundamentally establish truly personal existence."[1]

Where respect for individuality and personality is lacking, there one need not expect to find community. Nor does one find it in classic paganism. Plato, it is true, secured the Greek *politeia* from the threat posed by Sophism, and Aristotle regarded man as a political animal, but neither distinguished as they ought between society and the state and, consequently, neither attached due importance to the one group where love and community has its proper center and point of radiation—the family. More basically still, they had no experience of that love without which true communion is impossible—the divine agape, God's love for sinful and unworthy man. The best they knew was eros, a self-initiated attachment to what was considered good and valuable. But this, from the nature of the case, could not be exercised upon the ignorant, the wicked, and the ugly, and thus large numbers were excluded in principle from human fellowship, and authentic community was never achieved. It is, therefore, not from the Greeks that we derive those features which form the texture of free societies.

With the emergence and growth of Christianity, however, a new set of ideas began to shape the thought and action of the peoples of the West. These ideas were derived from the Scriptures of the Old and New Testaments, and their promulgation and acceptance created a new order in Europe. This order differed in significant respects from the Graeco-Roman order which it dis-

1. Emil Brunner, *Christianity and Civilization*, New York: Scribners, 1948, p. 94.

placed. In particular it created in those whom it formed a truer understanding of individuality, personality, and communion than had previously existed, and thus prepared the way for the recognition and exercise of those liberties which a new and anti-Christian secularism is in our day engaged in undermining.

The absence in medieval society of many democratic freedoms should not mislead us into believing that there is no connection between Christianity and human liberty, or to place undue blame upon the medieval church. It takes time to establish liberty, and it takes time to fashion a civilization. Social organization, laws, and institutions are not formed in a day. If the medieval church did not actually create a polity and culture which we should regard as desirable, it did proclaim truths about God, man, and the world which in due time would move men to organize society in a manner more in keeping with the Christian message and outlook. It placed upon the untutored peoples of northern and western Europe the imprint of the Christian spirit, it formed their conscience, it gave to their lives a Christian framework, it pressed on them the claims of Christian duty, and it aroused in them an aspiration to be free men under God. It told them of their being created by God, of their being formed in his image, of their fall, of the reconciliation effected in Christ, of the hope of immortality, of the obligation to love all men and God above all, and of much else besides—all of it calculated, when properly understood, to make them love freedom and oppose tyranny, even the tyranny of the church itself.

The Church did all this imperfectly, of course. It did it so imperfectly, indeed, that no one instructed in the Scriptures can in good conscience now follow its example. Its greatest fault was that it failed to keep the determinative Christian ideas in strict biblical purity. Instead of developing a truly scriptural anthropology which might have enabled it to fashion even in medieval times a more basically Christian culture, it effected a synthesis with pagan thought and developed a nature-grace schema which obscured and undermined the very fundamentals of the faith. The synthesis, because it was a synthesis of two incompatible religious motifs, could not, from the nature of the case, endure. The pagan and the Christian elements had sooner or later to be disengaged. This disengagement was effected when, at the beginning of the modern period, the Protestant Reformers and the Renaissance humanists broke with the Church, the former seizing the Christian and the latter the Greek components of the medieval synthesis.

It was now that the day of human liberty, long in preparation, finally dawned. The Reformers, particularly Calvin, settled these liberties firmly on their Christian basis. The humanists appropriated and proclaimed them, but they simultaneously lifted them off their foundation and thus, by secularizing them, doomed them to extinction.

It is characteristic of the Reformers that they put human liberty in an ethico-religious context. This is especially true of Calvin. He binds freedom to morals. Freedom for him is a means and not an end. It has only instrumental value. It must serve the purposes of love. This determines its nature, and sets the limits of its exercise. Liberty is granted a man, he says, "in order that he may be the better prepared for all the duties of charity."[2] And again, "Our liberty should be subject to charity."[3] In speaking thus Calvin follows the teaching of the Apostle, who in his letter to the Galatians admonishes, "Brethren, ye have been called unto liberty; only use not liberty for an occasion to the flesh, but by love serve one another" (Gal. 5:13). Liberty, then, is always in order to goodness. It is never merely freedom *from* something; it is always freedom *to* something. It is the freedom to meet one's obligations. It always implies direction, which means commitment to some value or ideal. This means that freedom binds. It presupposes God. Our duties are the generating source and limit of our liberties. But our duties precisely represent God's sovereign claim on us. There can, accordingly, be no liberty that does not take God into account. This is Calvin's conviction and that of every Christian who listens intently to the Word.

It is evident from another point of view as well that for Calvin human liberty is inseparable from God. God is man's creator. It is only in God that man lives and moves and has his being. We are God's subjects. In our subjection to him consists both our humanity and our beatitude. His service is perfect freedom. He it is *cui servire regnare est.* To declare one's independence of him is folly. It is the essence of sin, and the very source of slavery. Augustine had made this very plain long before Calvin. Man, he says, stands under God. Let him seek to escape God's sovereignty and he forthwith comes in bondage to that which has no claim on him. Man will have a master. A God he must and does have. If it is not the true God it will be a spurious one. It is as T.S. Eliot has said: If a man deny Jehovah he must pay his respect to a dictator or to nature or to fate or to some other such thing.

On the other hand, where God is recognized and served, there man's dignity shines forth and his freedom finds increasingly full expression. A man becomes a person only in God's presence. Brunner is in error when he regards the image of God as nothing but a possibility, but he is quite right in declaring: "that which gives man his specific place in the Universe and specific dignity is . . . his relation to the Creator" and "the humane character of man . . . realizes itself only in that answer of man which corresponds to the divine call."[4] This has been shown in history. The Calvinists have been behind no man in acknowledging the absolute rule of God and yet it is from

2. John Calvin, *Institutes,* III, 19, 12.
3. *Ibid.*, III, 19, 13.
4. Brunner, *op. cit.*, pp. 78–79.

among their number that the world's most intrepid fighters for human liberty have been recruited. The Puritans of England are a case in point. Their humility before the Creator gave them poise in the company of men. Their willingness to be slaves of God made them unwilling to be slaves of any creature. Of this fact none is so eloquent a witness as Thomas Babington Macaulay, who in his *Essay on Milton* speaks as follows of the Puritans.

"The Puritans," he says, "were men whose minds had derived a peculiar character from the daily contemplation of superior beings and eternal interests. Not content in acknowledging, in general terms, an overruling providence, they habitually ascribed every event to the will of the Great Being, for whose power nothing was too vast, for whose inspection nothing was too minute. To know Him, to serve Him, to enjoy Him, was with them the great end of existence. . . . Hence originated their contempt for terrestrial distinctions. The difference between the greatest and meanest of mankind seemed to vanish when compared with the boundless interval which separated the whole race from Him on whom their own eyes were constantly fixed. They recognized no title to superiority but his favour; and, confident of that favour, they despised all accomplishments and all the dignities of the world. . . . On the rich and the eloquent, on nobles and priests, they looked down with contempt; for they esteemed themselves rich in a more precious treasure, and eloquent in a more sublime language, nobles by the right of an earlier creation, and priests by the imposition of a mightier hand. . . . The very meanest of them was a being to whose fate a mysterious and terrible importance belonged, on whose slightest action the spirits of light and darkness looked with anxious interest; who had been destined, before heaven and earth were created, to enjoy a felicity which should continue when heaven and earth should have passed away. Events which short-sighted politicians ascribed to earthly causes had been ordained on his account. For his sake empires had risen, and flourished, and decayed. For his sake the Almighty had proclaimed his will by the pen of the Evangelist and the harp of the Prophet. He had been wrested by no common Deliverer from the grasp of no common foe. He had been ransomed by the sweat of no vulgar agony, by the blood of no earthly sacrifice. . . . Thus the Puritan was made up of two different men; the one all self-abasement, penitence, gratitude, passion; the other proud, calm, inflexible, sagacious. He prostrated himself in the dust before his Maker; but he set his foot on the neck of his king."[5]

As the last sentence suggests, the acknowledgment of divine sovereignty enables the Calvinist to put the proper limits upon the prerogatives of the human ruler, and so to guarantee one of the basic elements of true

5. T. B. Macaulay, *Essay on Milton*, M. A. Eaton, ed., Boston: Educational Publishing Company, 1899, pp. 97–98.

democracy—the limitation of power. If God's power is absolute, then that of any human ruler must be relative, and the citizenry has the right and duty to fix the due limits of that power. Calvinists must, therefore, in all consistency oppose absolute monarchy and dictatorship, and, by extension, assert the rights of the citizen over against any possible encroachment of the government. In practice this means that he must seek to have these rights embodied in constitutions or other written guarantees, and that he must advocate the participation of citizens in the formulation and administration of the laws of state. The Calvinist is in principle committed to some form of democracy in government. He is this not only because, as already indicated, he can allow no creature to pre-empt God's sovereignty, but also because he takes seriously man's sinfulness. As Professor Bennett says, "The Christian knows more realistically than the secular humanitarian the degree to which men are tempted by power and so he can warn that in every situation provision must be made for the criticism, the checking, and the displacing of those who exercise power."[6] C. S. Lewis is therefore right when he suggests that the true ground of democracy is "not that all men are so good that they deserve a share in the government of the commonwealth, and so wise that the commonwealth needs their advice, but that fallen man is so wicked that not one of them can be trusted with any irresponsible power over his fellows." Of all this Calvin was very much aware. It is for this reason that he favored some form of representative government. He says quite unmistakably that "aristocracy, or aristocracy tempered by democracy, far excels all other forms" of government and adds: "the vice or inadequacy of men thus renders it safer and more tolerable that many hold the sway, so that they may mutually be helpers to each other, teach and admonish one another, and if one asserts himself unfairly the many may be censors and masters, repressing his wilfulness."[7] There is little doubt that John Knox was reflecting the views of his teacher when he declared: "To bridle the fury and rage of princes in free kingdoms and realms... it pertains to the nobility, sworn and born to be councillors of the same, and also to the barons and people, whose votes and consent are to be required in all great and weighty matters of the commonwealth." Calvin sums it up by saying, "No kind of government is more happy than this, where liberty is regulated with becoming moderation, and properly established on a durable basis."[8]

Closely related to the issue of democracy is the issue of revolution. Calvin's commitment to a democratic form of government does not in and of itself commit him to an endorsement of revolt. One may hold that states should be

6. John C. Bennett, *Christendom,* Spring 1940, p. 171.
7. *Institutes,* IV, 20, 8.
8. *Ibid.*, IV, 20, 8.

so organized as to insure a proper limitation and distribution of power, without holding that an existing government may be overthrown by force—i.e., without holding that revolution may sometimes replace the orderly process of democratic action. It is evident, nevertheless, that Calvinists, when circumstances seemed to require it, have not hesitated to disobey state laws, resist governmental authority, dethrone kings, and banish tyrants. And in so doing they have acted in accordance with rather than against the counsel of Calvin himself.

Calvin was aware, of course, of the apostolic teaching respecting the obedience due to magistrates: "Let every soul be in subjection to the higher powers: for there is no power but of God; and the powers that be are ordained of God. Therefore he that resisteth the power withstandeth the ordinance of God: and they that withstand shall receive to themselves judgment. . . . Wherefore ye must needs be in subjection" (Rom. 13). Calvin was aware of this teaching, but he did not understand it as requiring *absolute* submission, which, from the analogy of Scripture, he knew to be due to God alone. "We must obey our princes who are set over us," he said, "but when they rise against God they must be put down and held of no more account than worn-out shoes. . . . When they seek to tear God from his throne, can they be respected?"[9]

There are passages in the *Institutes* which seem out of accord with this sentiment and which have led some students of Calvin to represent him as condemning revolution. For instance, Calvin says: "Wherefore if we are cruelly vexed by an inhuman prince or robbed and plundered by one avaricious, or left without protection by one negligent, or even if we are inflicted by one sacrilegious and unbelieving, let us first of all remember our offenses against God, which are doubtless chastised by these plagues. Thus humility will curb our impatience. And secondly, let us consider that it is not for us to remedy these evils; for us it remains only to implore the aid of God in whose hands are the hearts of kings and changes of kingdoms."[10]

This passage, it must be acknowledged, encourages a patient and conservative attitude towards unjust politics, but it does not enjoin unqualified acquiescence, and it does not absolutely proscribe revolution. To understand it one must observe that Calvin is speaking in it of private persons. Private persons, he held, may never revolt. They may, in the way of passive resistance, refuse to obey laws that go contrary to God's commands, but they may not, as mere individuals, remove even a tyrannical ruler by force. "The voice of the celestial Judge," he says, "openly condemns the private man who lays violent hands on a tyrant."[11]

9. Calvin, *Sermon* on Daniel 6.
10. *Institutes*, IV, 20, 29.
11. *Ibid.*, III, 10, 6.

Nevertheless, he does regard it as the duty of representative functionaries or subordinate officials to protect the people against the license of kings, and, where necessary, to remove the source of offense. "For," he says, "if there be, in the present day, any magistrates appointed for the protection of the people and the moderation of the power of kings, such as were in ancient time the Ephori . . . among the Lacedaemonians, or the popular tribunes . . . among the Romans, or the Demarchi . . . among the Athenians; or with power such as perhaps is now possessed by the three estates in every kingdom when they are assembled; I am so far from prohibiting them in the discharge of their duty to oppose the violence or cruelty of kings that I affirm that if they connive at kings in their oppression of the people, such forbearance involves the most nefarious perfidy because they fraudulently betray the liberty of the people of which they know that they have been appointed protectors by the ordination of God."[12] In another place he says, "There is no exploit esteemed more honorable, even among philosophers, than to deliver our country from tyranny."[13] Revolution, I suggest, is allowed and commended by Calvin.

Before quitting Calvin one must observe with regret that he did not come to Christian clarity on one of the most important of our liberties—the freedom of worship. The principles he enunciated clearly implied and demanded this freedom, but neither he nor Beza proclaimed it. Abraham Kuyper, in a famous address on "Calvinism, the Original Guarantee of Our Constitutional Freedoms," maintained that the constitutional liberties of The Netherlands had their origin in the Calvinism of the French Huguenots, the English and Scotch Independents, and the American Puritans. His thesis is generally sound and comes well documented. It is demonstrable, for example, that though the constitutions of most free European states were deeply influenced by the French Revolution, yet the Proclamation of Rights issued by the French General Assembly in 1789 owes its ideas and much of its language to the various American constitutions whose religious parentage is beyond question. The enlightenment did not give birth to our liberties; it merely propagated them in secularized form. It is true, nevertheless, as Van Schelven has pointed out in his *Emendations* on Kuyper's Essay (*Uit de Strijd der Geesten*, 1944) that Calvinism has not, in general, stood for either freedom of worship or separation of Church and State. It has come out for tolerance only when it was persecuted or when it underwent a mixing with Anabaptist or humanistic ideas. The Calvinistic Massachusetts Colony in America, for example, afforded no asylum for the dissenting Roger Williams, who was forced to found a settlement of his own in which freedom of conscience and

12. *Ibid.*, IV, 20, 31.
13. *Ibid.*, III, 10, 6.

worship were allowed. It must in all fairness be observed, however, that the Huguenots of the period 1560–80 and the Scotch-Irish Presbyterians in America after 1704 did proclaim religious liberty and in so doing reflected, not indeed the direct counsel of Calvin, but yet the true genius of Calvinism.

The argument for intolerance has, of course, a kind of plausibility. Just as the secularist argues, quite correctly, that the franchise ought not to be granted to the illiterate, the criminal, and the insane, on the ground that a minimum of apprehension of and commitment to shared ideals is requisite for an ordered commonwealth; so the Christian might argue that, since non-Christians live by false principles and values, they are bound to disrupt the true order of things, and ought not to be tolerated. Moreover, he may argue, the honor of God requires that no countenance be given to those who dishonor him. Nathaniel Ward reasoned this way when he wrote, "I dare aver that God doth nowhere in his Word allow Christian states to give Toleration to adversaries of his Truth, if they have power in their hands to suppress them. . . . To tolerate more than indifference is not to deal indifferently with God. He that is willing to tolerate any Religion, or discrepant way of Religion besides his own, unless it be in matters merely indifferent, either doubts of his own, or is not sincere in it."[14]

It seems plain, however, that even apart from the fact that common grace enables unbelievers to make their contribution to a Christian society, both Christian humility and the spiritual nature of God's Kingdom require that tolerance be given to all men in matters of religion. Not being God, no man, not even a Calvinist, may absolutize his own formulation of the truth and penalize dissent by dismissing from the commonwealth those who differ in their views. Moreover, it is by persuasion, and not by force and compulsion, that the Kingdom comes to men, and what protects the church in the last analysis is never the power of the State but only the Holy Spirit as he accompanies the pure preaching of the Word and regenerates the hearts of men. It is as Jonathan Edwards once wrote: "Men's using methods with their neighbors, to oblige them to a conformity to their sentiments or way, is in nothing so unreasonable as in the worship of God; because that is a business in which each person acts for himself, with his Creator and Supreme Judge, as one concerned for his own acceptance with him. . . . And so I suppose that it will be allowed that every man ought to be left to his own conscience, in what he judges will be most acceptable to God, or what he supposes is the will of God."[15] This indeed all Calvinists will allow. It is consonant with their deepest principles.

14. Nathaniel Ward, "The Simple Cobbler of Aggawam," in Perry Miller, *The American Puritans*, Garden City, New York: Doubleday, 1956, p. 100.

15. Jonathan Edwards, *Memoirs*, Sereno E. Dwight, ed., p. cxvii.

Consider now the Renaissance. It came almost simultaneously with the Reformation. This has led Roman Catholic historians to regard both as manifestations of a single spirit. In this they are, of course, mistaken. What is correct is that both Reformation and Renaissance sprang out of the bosom of the Church: the Reformation as an effort to express and give historical continuity to the genuine Christian idea which had never been wholly absent from medieval religion; the Renaissance, in order to articulate the natural paganism that the church had vainly sought to synthesize with the Christian gospel.

The crisis brought on in European civilization by the Renaissance was profound. What happened can be quickly told: The Renaissance man set out to secularize culture, to free it from the influences of religion, to lift it off the foundations of faith. He did this in the name of liberty. Science and philosophy, he believed, must be free and independent. So must art, education, business, politics, and indeed every social activity. They must be neutral, religiously non-partisan, and uncommitted. Religion is good, to be sure, but it is a private affair and should not be allowed to determine thought and govern practice. It cannot constitute the basis or framework of a really free civilization.

When the Renaissance man set out, therefore, to build the modern world, he put Christianity aside as irrelevant, if not as a positive hindrance. But he did not thereby get rid of religion. He merely exchanged one religion for another. For the Christian ideas that had hitherto guided cultural effort he substituted a set of non-Christian ideas. He placed at the foundation of modern culture the religion of autonomous man.

According to this religion there is in every individual a sacred core called personality which is good, infinitely perfectible, and basically inviolable. This basic creed, as interpreted by what may be called orthodox modernity, spelled individualism in very large letters, and the effect of it was to rip the fabric of our culture and to bring about that social disintegration which we are wont to refer to as the crisis of Western civilization.

Think of man as a completely free, autonomous personality and you isolate him and thereby destroy society. God cannot touch him with his grace or revelation, for he is free, and freedom here means precisely inviolability. Tradition can get no hold on him, for should the past enter him it would determine him. There can be for him no sovereign good that engages his will, for he can recognize no law of which he is not the author. He can acknowledge no objective reality which measures and regulates his intelligence. He can only settle down in the solitude of his tiny sacred universe and resist any intervention from the outside.

And so it happens that we have (or did have until the revolt set in) in modern schools autonomous pupils who choose their own subjects of study and pursue them in their own way; in modern families autonomous children who reject the authority of their parents; in modern democracy autonomous voters with no common goal; in modern industry autonomous business that knows no law but the immanent operation of the market; in modern society autonomous man shattered and fragmentized by the force of his own pretensions.

What is destroying him and pulverizing the liberal bourgeois civilization he has constructed is, of course, the lack of true community, and ignorance of what constitutes it. He might have learned from Christianity that individuals can live together in society only if each submits himself to the superintendency of God. But this in his pride he refused to learn and rejected as naive. Had he not done so, he could have saved both his individuality and his community. Now, if outside of Christianity he wishes to preserve his society at all, he can do so only at the price of freedom. He can do so only by abdicating in favor of collective man.

It is the claims of collective man that communism is pressing. Communism is sick of the irresponsible freedoms of the liberal tradition. It detests rugged atomistic individualism. It wants community, solidarity, loyalty, cooperation, cohesion, and it is determined to get it—only it does not propose to get it in the only way it can be gotten. It does not propose to get it in the Christian way—by moving on the vertical plane and attaching every individual to a transcendent object. It proposes to get it by moving on the horizontal plane and uniting individuals by class interests. It proposes to get it, in short, by staying within the Renaissance framework but shifting the accent. Short of returning to Christianity this is all, of course, that modern man can do—shift the accent. But this will not set him free. He is doomed by his secular commitment to perpetual slavery.

There is in the notion of freedom both a negative and a positive element. In current usage the negative element predominates and this negativity is erroneously regarded as exhausting the whole meaning of the term. This is a serious mistake. It remains true, however, that the term freedom does have an inalienable negative aspect. In this aspect freedom means freedom *from*. It means independence. It means immunity or exemption from something. It connotes absence of restraint, bondage, or subjection. It means to be loose from restrictions.

This negativity, far from being a negligible element in freedom, is the very essence of perfect or absolute freedom, such as is enjoyed by God. God is completely free. He is bound by nothing external to himself. He is in bondage to nothing.

Now man is created in the image of God, and because he bears the divine *image* he too has freedom, even freedom in the negative sense of independence. But because he is *created*, his freedom is a creaturely freedom, his independence is a creaturely independence. The adjective "creaturely" is important. It modifies man's freedom. It means that human freedom can never be described simply as exemption from restraint, but only adjectivally as exemption from undue restraint.

This implies, of course, that there are due restraints on him. They are on him precisely because he is a creature and thus subject to God, to God's laws, and to all the ordinances of God. But it also implies that he is entitled to throw off undue restraints. He is entitled to do this precisely because he bears the image of God. Being superior to nature and on a plane with his fellows he may refuse to be victimized by the one or enslaved by the other.

It is this nice balance between liberty and restraint, freedom and subjection, that is the essence of the Christian conception of liberty, and the very basis of genuine democracy.

Because there is a nice and delicate balance here, it has not always been preserved. To many, freedom under law, liberty under restraint, independence within the framework of an ultimate dependence, high dignity while in creaturely subjection, has seemed grossly contradictory and quite intolerable.

The first to think it intolerable was Lucifer, and by putting the thought into operation he became the devil. The next to think so was Adam, and his acting on the principle was his Fall. He wished to be like God. In this context that means he wished to be free, unqualifiedly free, exempt from any and all restrictions except those imposed by his own nature.

To the sinner, fallen in Adam, this desire has ever since seemed somehow right. Freedom, he thinks, is incompatible with commitment. Of course the view cannot be consistently maintained except on the basis of a radical atheism. But very few men have gone so far as to deny that God exists; most men have simply fenced him in. To save his freedom man has restricted God; he has shorn him of his comprehensive and unqualified Lordship. The sinner, untouched by grace, puts God either in an uninfluential and non-determinative spectator role, as in deism; or identifies him with the human spirit itself, as in pantheism; or exempts from his rule and sovereignty some particular part of the human soul, as in rationalism, where the intellect is declared autonomous.

The liberal notion of freedom is negative; it is freedom from. For the Calvinist it is positive; it is freedom for. For the secularist freedom is an end. For the Calvinist it is a means. The Calvinist wants freedom, but he wants it in order to attain a further goal. He wants it in order to attain his true place *under* God who made him and *above* the nature he is called to rule.

It is clear to us Calvinists that we are creatures and therefore not wholly sovereign. We know that we do not and cannot exist in ultimate independence. We know that from the nature of the case we and all men have a master, and that by an inviolable law of our being we all serve one, the true one or a false one. We know, therefore, that the question of freedom is never rightly put until one asks, What Lord do you acknowledge? To what do you tie yourself? To whom or what are you basically and finally committed? And we know that there are only three possibilities here: nature, man, and God.

We Calvinists choose God, or are chosen by him, and we try to live and think by his Word. We bow at this one point and therefore are free at every other—free precisely there and completely there where a human being may and can be free—free of nature and on an equality with men. That is why we are deaf to communism; we have no ear for economic determinism. That is why we resist to the death all tyranny; having given our allegiance to the King of kings we count no man our master—neither the man on horseback, nor the man in purple, nor the man in the mitred cap. We stand in awe neither of the man in the Cadillac nor of the man in overalls. We are not intimidated by academic nonsense, and we do not bow before the sacred cow of science. We are free men. And we are free men because we have our anchor in the bedrock of the universe.

The secularist, on the other hand, who speaks of a human freedom proper only to God, is bound to lose both God and every freedom proper to a creature. On the level of nature he will become the victim of those mechanical monsters—bomb, plane, cannon—that he has the ingenuity to create but not the wit to control. And on the level of society he will fall before a succession of Mussolinis, Hitlers, and Stalins. Having no foot in heaven he has no power to resist the strong men of the earth.

The liberal does not want this slavery, of course, He hates communism, he hates tyranny, and he hates the bondage of machines and gadgets. He hates them almost as much as he hates the sovereign God of Calvinism. He wants to be free of them all. But, of course, he cannot. He has to make a choice of masters.

15

Laws and Lawyers

"LAW" IS an ambiguous term. It has not one meaning, but several. There is not only one kind of law, there are many. From the philosophical point of view, the whole universe is under law, and every concrete thing within it. Indeed, every abstract aspect of the world has its own law. There is, for example, the law of numbers by which two follows on one, and according to which five and five make ten and not nine or eleven. This law must be respected by us in all of our dealings with the cosmos and with one another. Willful violations of it would reduce our scientific calculations to meaninglessness and make our commercial accounts a shambles. There are also the laws of space in accordance with which the science of plane geometry is elaborated and in the name of which we declare that a line has length but no width or depth and that a point has no dimensions at all. The significance of recognizing this law of points will be evident to anyone who remembers the famous paradoxes of Zeno. Zeno maintained, you may recall, that it was inconceivable that a shot arrow should ever reach its target or that a hare should ever overtake a tortoise who had gotten a head start. It is, of course, inconceivable that these things should happen if there are an infinite number of points on even the shortest line (which is true) and if each point takes up some room. But, of course, it is false to say that a point takes up some room; this is to contradict the laws of space; and the consequence of such contradiction is existential nonsense. And so it goes throughout the universe. Law is everywhere, and its violation always creates havoc. There are physical laws of motion, biological laws of growth, psychological laws of sensitivity and response, logical laws of thought, historical laws of development and decline, social laws of courtesy and manners, aesthetic laws of form and beauty, moral laws of goodness and virtue, and juridical laws of justice and right. It is within the structure of these laws that human life is lived, and it is as men recognize and obey these laws that they attain their full stature and give substance and meaning to their existence.

Now, of course, judges and lawyers are directly and professionally concerned with only one of these sets of laws—the juridical. But though it is only one of many sets, it is an important one. It appertains to the society of men as they are organized into a body politic—the State—and it is consequently of immense significance. By it an order of justice is established and fundamental human rights and freedoms are secured. Without it Whirl would be king, and political anarchy and social chaos would ensue. It is to prevent this that lawyers have been set in their office. They are the appointed guardians of the laws, the curators of social justice, the patrons of our freedoms. And if they fail our prospects are bleak and and unpromising indeed.

Now, just what is that law with which they are concerned? What is that juridicial law which they have been appointed to safeguard and articulate, and upon which the socio-political well-being of mankind depends? It is something which has three layers or dimensions, with the first of which they are directly and primarily concerned, but with the others of which they are ineluctably involved. It is *positive law*, *natural law*, and *divine law*.

Positive law is that sum of rules and regulations which society has imposed on itself for the better ordering of its affairs. Sometimes these rules are not written at all, but simply observed over a long period of time by a large proportion of the population and so given status under the name of common law. Sometimes these rules are decreed and enacted by some governing or legislative body and so become authoritative as statute law. And sometimes either one of these, or both together, are so interpreted or combined by the courts as to become virtual law. But all of these together constitute positive law, the distinguishing characteristic of which is that it represents, at least in democratic countries and in free societies, the public will.

Now, it is obvious that this law is established not because people are fond of laws, or courts, or legal sanctions as such, but because they recognize that there is something in the world—in the language of religion called sin—which requires to be socially tempered and controlled so that what is good and right and just may have free course. Positive law represents, therefore, a judgment of society concerning what regulations are calculated to secure the maximum opportunity to do that which is right; and the lawyer and the judge, whose direct and immediate concern is with this law, are called on to implement most scrupulously this social judgment. They are the custodians of the law, and they are in duty bound both to manifest respect for it and to bend every effort to keep it inviolate—not, again, because this law as such is intrinsically inviolate, but because it is set and posited to secure the rights and freedoms of living people. No lawyer, therefore, may—on pain of betraying the people—subvert the law or circumvent it or nullify it by extra-legal means, not even in the interest of securing the supposed good of an individual. For when the law is subverted, the very structure of society is undermined and endangered.

But there is, as everyone knows, another side to this whole question. Society, the people, the public can be mistaken, and indeed frequently is. Therefore, the laws it wants, or the laws it tolerates, may be in fact unjust, and stand in need of amendment or repeal.

It is just at this point that there enters the second dimension of the law—natural law. Underlying positive law, and finding only incomplete and imperfect expression in it is a law laid down in the nature and consciences of men which is both more simple and more basic than positive law. Speaking quite untechnically, but I think truly, this law is composed not so much of rules and regulations, as of principles, principles in accordance with which positive law requires to be formed, and in terms of which it requires to be judged and appraised.

These principles, because they reside in and grow out of the nature of man, are not only more basic but also more universal than the regulations constituting positive law. The latter is quite relative, being variable according to time, place, and circumstances; different societies have significantly different positive laws. But natural law, embodying the universal principles of justice, leaps over natural and ethnic boundaries, and makes a general claim on the hearts and wills of people.

It is to this law that the judges and lawyers in our civilization must especially be true. They may not indeed subvert positive law by an appeal to natural law, but by an appeal to natural law they must—through orderly process—perfect positive law, so that the regulations governing human coexistence in society may reflect not merely what a given people may desire but what they ought to desire—true and unchangeable and inviolate justice.

The Constitution and The Bill of Rights in the United States represent an attempt to articulate these basic principles of law, though even these, from the nature of the case, are only approximations to it. Still, what detailed positive law is intended to secure through appropriate sanctions, are the basic human rights and freedoms that the Constitution and The Bill envisage: The right to speak, to work, to worship, to assemble, and so forth. It is these rights on which the dispossessed minority have an inalienable claim, and which some of our positive statutes prevent them from enjoying. The lawyer and the judge have here a great responsibility: To move and shift the ponderous positive law into ever closer conformity to what is, in the very nature of things, good and right.

But there is beyond the law of nature still another law, not contradictory of the former, but fundamental to it—the law or will of God. There are those, I know, who hesitate at this juncture to speak of God. I do not, and I should like nothing better than to engage in a further discussion of this point, but in the interest of getting on, let us call this law for the moment the *law of the universe*. The suggestion I am here making is that it is not "the will of the people" in positive law that ultimately obliges us, not even "the nature of man" in natural law, but the structure of the universe in divine law.

Here as always the crucial question is a philosophical or theological one. The crucial question is what is the nature of ultimate reality and whither, if anywhere, does it tend. In the last analysis both the laws and the principles of justice must be rooted in the very structure of being. If the structure of being is misconceived, if the nature of ultimate reality is misread, our legal principles and enactments will sooner or later respond to the mistake, and drive both our legal structure and our society into paths of injustice and tyranny, and away from true righteousness and freedom.

The notion of freedom is as old as the human race, and the love of it has animated men in every age of the world's history. But it may fairly be said that nowhere except in Western Europe, and there not until the beginning of the modern age, has a whole society been deliberately structured on the principle of liberty. At the fountainhead of modern thought and practice stand the Renaissance and the Reformation, and from these two sources liberty flowed as a culture-shaping force, the likes of which the world had hardly known before. Both the Renaissance and the Reformation consciously articulated the ideal of freedom, and since the fifteenth and sixteenth centuries these movements have, by their combined force, produced a kind of consensus among Western peoples on the practical issues of liberty.

Freedom is now in crisis around the world. And so, indeed, is law and order. That both should simultaneously be in jeopardy is no accident; law and liberty stand and fall together. And the reason why both are now in jeopardy is plain. The acids of modernity have eaten away the Christian foundations on which they chiefly rested. The freedom under law which is our American heritage has been a freedom under God, wrought out in the crucible of Judaeo-Christian theism. It is only this theism, I suggest, that is capable of preserving it. Liberty and law, freedom and commitment are inseparable, and the commitment which true freedom requires is a commitment in religious faith to the God of Christian revelation.

16

The Ethics of Capitalism

IF BEFORE 1929 there was a widespread conviction that there was something wrong with the capitalistic system, events subsequent to that date established it in ever widening circles. The prolonged depression of the thirties thoroughly discredited the dominant economic order not only in the eyes of chronically disaffected groups but also in the estimation of that large majority of people who are not moved to reflection save by extraordinary catastrophies. Great numbers in the decade before World War II came into conscious opposition to capitalism. Most significant in the revolt was the steady appeal it made to the demands of social ethics. There were those, of course, and they were probably in the majority, who took up the hue and cry for the sake of the loaves, but there were also those who spoke out of an aroused conscience. These urged the adoption of a deeper and broader ethic, an ethic which, embracing economic as well as personal behavior, would move responsible business men away from the depersonalized morality of rugged individualism into an authentic morality of personalized social concern. What they really urged was a return to Reformation and pre-Reformation teaching respecting social behavior and, by that token, a repudiation of seventeenth and eighteenth century naturalism with its intolerance of superimposed ethical restraints.

Much has been said about the connection between capitalism and Protestant ethics. That such a connection exists cannot be doubted. But that a similar connection exists between capitalism and Catholicism is also true, as Sombart amply demonstrates. The emphasis on certain Christian virtues in Reformation times, and an altered stance toward the world, encouraged an already considerable capitalistic enterprise. But the characteristic and not entirely wholesome spirit of modern capitalism was breathed into it, not by the sixteenth century Reformation, but by the Renaissance philosophy which repudiated religious sanctions and declared the natural order to be simply coterminous with the moral order. How the naturalistic outlook, determined by the physical sciences, gave to capitalism its distinctive character and spirit will become clear, I trust, in the course of this essay.

It is common, and usually helpful, to begin a discussion with a definition of the thing to be discussed. In the present instance, however, a definition is almost impossible to provide. Capitalism is so complex, and it has so many ramifications, that analytical description must take the place of definition, and that is, accordingly, what I shall try to provide. I shall consider and appraise capitalism in terms of its alleged moral origins, its elements, its methods, its practices, and its philosophy.

A. ALLEGED MORAL ORIGINS

There is a tendency to regard capitalism as the direct and inevitable outgrowth of the exercise of the so-called middle-class virtues—sobriety, frugality, industry, honesty, docility, and the like. This is obviously an over-simplification. It is true that the industrious and frugal man is apt to be successful in business, but always within limits. These Christian virtues cannot be held responsible for capitalism as we know it, and that for several reasons. First, though really Christian, these virtues are not distinctively so. They form an integral part of Stoic morality, yet their exercise was unattended in ancient times by the industrial fever we have come to associate with capitalism. Moreover, capitalism advanced in direct proportion to the failure of large classes of people to make these moral qualities their own. Take frugality for example. If it were universally practiced there would be no capitalism. As Miss Harkness correctly observes, "had everyone been really frugal economic progress would have been retarded by the diminution of trade due to underconsumption. It was because others were furnishing markets by living in luxury that the Puritans were able to amass wealth."[1] Besides, the advance of capitalism was, as a matter of fact, marked by increasing infidelity to the inner meaning of the virtues to the exercise of which it allegedly owes its existence.

Morality is not a mere aggregate of separate virtues. Only in the context of the whole do single virtues acquire meaning. This was a truth lost to the capitalist temper. It fed on virtues, not on virtue. More than this, it lifted the virtues it acknowledged out of their Christian context, and so perverted them. Christianity had counselled honesty. Business made this prudence. To be successful one had to appear honest. To be regarded honest—that was the important thing. In typical modern business practice whatever artifice and deception one's cunning can devise is admissible if only it is not detected. Because it is likely sooner or later to be detected, honesty is the best policy.

1. Georgia Harkness, *John Calvin: The Man and his Ethics*, New York: Henry Holt and Company, 1931, p. 168.

Christianity had counselled industry. Business made this frenzy and preoccupation. Calvin, though exhorting to industry, had frowned on unceasing engagement with secular tasks. Industry was one of many virtues. Its exercise was accordingly limited by the demands of the others. One was to be diligent in providing oneself and one's family with the means of subsistence and reasonable comfort, but beyond that industry was to be exercised in other ways. Industry was but a means to an end. Business did two things: it made industry an end in itself and gave it a purely industrial signification. To be industrious was to produce. Since one must always be industrious, production must not cease. Thus, by perversion, arose the meaningless habit of producing for production's sake. If it was not for the sake of production it was for the sake of gain, and by the isolation of this one virtue of industry, money-making became the all-absorbing ethical task of the business man. He failed to see that Christian industry had its moral limits.

B. ELEMENTS

Some wish to define capitalism in terms of the elements that constitute it and then to condemn or justify it on the basis of a criticism or validation of these discrete elements. This can hardly be done. In all vital phenomena the whole is greater than the sum of its parts. Capitalism, likewise, is a great deal more than the sum of the economic principles it professes. Indeed, were one disposed to challenge the legitimacy of capitalism one would find little support in Christian ethics for a condemnation of its economic principles as such. Capitalism, for example, believes in capital, and capital is innocuous enough. It is simply that which is saved and set by for future use. Its formation is by "the rate of production exceeding the rate of consumption with consequent accumulation of resources."[2] It becomes economically significant when it is actively employed, when it is made into a fund yielding a return and reproducing itself. Its legitimacy cannot be doubted. No business can be carried on without it, whatever the economic structure may be. The trouble with capitalism has been its intolerance of any social control in the growth and disposition of this capital. It is apparent that money has no inner restraints. Its fecundity is astounding. Capital, like a snowball rolling downhill, grows with each turnover, and unless controlled in the interests of society, develops into the gargantuan monster with which the small man became so tragically familiar in the Depression. The mischief here, as elsewhere, is owing to a lack in capitalism of internal restraint and to a stubborn resistance to outside control. Not capital but its exclusively private regulation must be repudiated.

2. *Encycl. Brit.*, 11th Ed., in loco.

As with capital, so it is with profit and interest. In themselves they are eminently proper. Profit is the offspring of capital. "In all operations of capital there is an element of self-deprival for the present with the risk of ultimate loss of what is one's own."[3] Profit is the reward for the risk. As Calvin says, "Whence do the merchant's profits come, except from his own diligence and industry?"[4] But the significant question is, How great should the profit be? The question engaged the minds of the early ecclesiastics, and they proposed that it be determined by the cost of production. The business man must remember that he is dealing with a brother, and he must not be "a taker of advantages." Business, however, soon forgot these wise counsels. As it grew more complex and depersonalized the market became determinative for price and profit. If one could corner the market, manipulate prices, and make a "haul," that was business. Profit became elastic, stretching between the cost of production and the market. So mysterious was the interplay of blind economic forces, and so delicately poised was the economic structure, that unheard of profits were pocketed with the pious observation that any lesser price would effect the collapse of the market.

The right of private property is another principal element in capitalism. Against it, too, Christian ethics has no objection, though there have been a number of Christian thinkers who have questioned the validity of baronial titles to larger tracts of God's green earth than they could ever work. However that may be, no Christian moralist questions the right of private property in principle. Calvin believed in it firmly. Everybody holds his possessions by a dispensation of God. It is given into his hands as a sacred trust. Had capitalism so regarded property, we should today pick no quarrel with it. But it did not so regard it, and it thereby exposed itself to Christian criticism.

Competition and cooperation are legitimate, and if exercised with due regard for one's neighbor, are a boon to economic felicity. The Christian moralist is, therefore, not committed to a repudiation of these capitalistic principles. It is only when he recalls the mischief done in their name that he hesitates to given his assent. What are trusts and combines if they are not cooperatives? What is a determined policy of underselling by heavily capitalized industries until all competition has vanished, if it is not the exercise of the right to be a competitor? Most of capitalism's bare principles are eminently acceptable. They become vicious because they are not morally conditioned and are without a social reference.

It is the same with the other principles that may be named—individual

3. *Encycl. Brit.*, 11th Ed., in loco.

4. Quoted in R. H. Tawney, *Religion and the Rise of Capitalism*, Magnolia, Maine: Peter Smith, n.d., p. 105.

initiative, freedom of enterprise, freedom of exchange, and freedom of contract. To all cries for their abolishment the Christian moralist is entitled to turn a deaf ear. The Christian holds liberty and individuality dear. He refuses to be caught up in the milieu of the State. But the Christian knows the difference between freedom and license, and he understands too that the individual is an abstraction, unthinkable save in a social context. Because of this he stands opposed to any and all forms of rugged, anti-social individualism.

The fundamental elements in capitalism are acceptable only if they are socially conditioned. In so far as capitalism is opposed to this socialization, capitalism itself must be repudiated. In so far as it is amenable to reconstruction on moral and social lines, it is eminently worthy of salvage.

C. METHODS

Capitalism may also be defined in terms of its methods. It is then looked at under the aspect of its tendency to mechanize and standardize production. Concentration of production, scientific management, and the wage system are from this point of view regarded as essential ingredients in capitalism. They are doubtless justly so regarded. I am not so sure that Christian ethics has much to say here. Technological advance and the resultant mechanization of industry is not an unmixed blessing. It has enriched our lives in its externals. One fears that its influence on the worker has been less salutary. It has definitely depersonalized industry and made machine-tending the bane of the spirit. There is nothing better calculated to shrivel the soul of a man than to have him attach bolt #44 all day long, year after year. When one recalls that thousands earn daily bread in that way, one can hardly repress a desire for the return of the day when every man sat under his own vine and under his own fig tree. To yield, however, would be to indulge an impracticable fancy. Machines are here and would doubtless be here if there had never been such a thing as capitalism. The industrial order that employs them has two obligations to society. It must afford the worker sufficient leisure in which to pursue private projects calculated to counteract the opiate of the machine, and it must make adequate provision for those workers who are supplanted by the machine. Both of these ends will be served by the shorter day and the shorter week. However they are served, the ethical obligation of capitalism is plain.

Considerable criticism, in the name of ethics, has been levelled at the wage system. I cannot compel myself to share the criticism. The wage system has, of course, been in many instances an enslaving institution. Yet it need not necessarily be so, and there is no acceptable substitute, if freedom of contract and freedom of enterprise is to be preserved. The employer is under moral obligation to pay an adequate wage, but he would seem to be under no such obligation to share legitimate profits in cases where the employee did not share the risk. Capitalism would best serve itself and society by admitting the workers to a share in the business, making industry a truly cooperative affair, engaging in planned production, and, by treating the worker as a fellow human being, insuring against the enervating class struggles which have so shamefully blotched our industrial history.

D. PRACTICES AND CHARACTERISTICS

It is always a matter of some delicacy to distinguish between capitalist practices that flow necessarily and inevitably from inherent principles and those which attach themselves from the outside and are not necessary concomitants of capitalistic doctrine. It is obvious, for example, that capitalists have been guilty of profiteering, wild speculation, and maltreatment of labor in respect of wages, working conditions, etc., and that such practices are ethically reprehensible. It is not so obvious that capitalism is necessarily committed to these vices. Those who charge them to capitalism point out, not without persuasiveness, that these practices persistently attend capitalistic endeavor. They do seem to betray a fundamental tendency. Yet that business is being increasingly purged of its more flagrant sins through social legislation argues for a distinction between capitalism and the abuses to which it is liable. It does not conduce to understanding to confound capitalism with capitalists.

There is another set of characteristics which seem to me to be more closely bound up with the essence of capitalism. These are concentration of wealth, periodic crises, and boundlessness. Concentration of wealth cannot but work mischief in society, and successful capitalism cannot avoid it. Money breeds money, and capital adds to capital. This is closely connected with the boundlessness of capitalism. There is a certain fatalism in its movement. A man goes into business not for his health, but for profit. His profits increase his capital. He expands his business and makes more profit. But once having entered on this high road he cannot remain stationary. To stop means to retrogress. There is nothing to do but to push on, continuously expanding. Both Carnegie and Rockefeller confessed to being swept on by this inner necessity. The problem this presents is one that must be solved. It is plain that this concentration of wealth in the hands of a few is dangerous. An economic order that is to win the approval of Christian ethics must effect a more equitable distribution of the world's goods than capitalism has done. There will need to be some control of profit, rigorous anti-trust laws, and restrictions on the amount of capital stock. However the distribution is effected, its moral necessity cannot be doubted.

Chief among the characteristics of capitalism is its reliance on the structure of impersonal relations. In the pre-capitalistic economic order the business man was actuated by the weal and woe of the living, breathing human being. Wealth was not merely for possession; it was for utilization. It was valuable for the creation and preservation of life-values. Intercourse between employer and employee was on the personal plane. The same personal relation obtained between producer and consumer. Production was in order to the demands of the consumer. With capitalism all that changed. The economic order crystalized into a cold and lifeless system. The relation between employer and employee was lifted off the personal plane. In many cases the employer was not an individual at all, but a corporation. The same rigid, impersonal relation obtained between the producer and the consumer. Not the wants of the consumer, not the needs of subsistence, but the exchange value determined the kind and rate of production. That is largely the situation today. It is easy to see what this does for ethics. One is concerned in business not with personal relationships, in which morality finds its true field of exercise, but with markets, prices, stocks, and with labor and consumer as abstract nouns. Because of this impersonality a man will behave in business as he would never think of behaving in private life. He feels that business is business and has a moral code of its own, or none at all. This is the delusion that Christian ethics must dispel. There are encouraging signs of an increasing recognition that there is only one moral code and that it is as applicable to business life as to private life.

E. PHILOSOPHY

Although capitalism has grown by almost imperceptible changes, did not receive economic formulation until Adam Smith, and is amenable to all sorts of modifications, as a large body of legislative restrictions amply testify, yet it is characterized in all times and places by a spirit that is its own. Sombart finds two elements in that spirit: the greed of gold and enterprise. Weber refers its spirit to a deep-seated consciousness of an ethical obligation to labor diligently to make money, and an ascetic self-discipline which drives one to unflagging activity. Sombart lays the emphasis on biological instincts and natural propensities. Weber finds the greatest impulse to capitalism in the ethical teachings of the Reformers, particularly Calvin. Both have doubtless hit on important ingredients in the capitalistic spirit. There are, however, others. The economic theory and business practices of capitalism find their taproots in certain more fundamental ways of thinking. Let us briefly consider them.

Capitalism assumes that the benefit of the individual is the benefit of society. This is radically defective ethical teaching. It accounts for the rugged individualism we have everywhere observed and deplored. The benefit of society will in the long run be the benefit of the individual, but never vice versa. The success and growth of the part does not mean the felicity of the whole. On the contrary the independent development of the part results in a malignant growth on the body politic. It is the fundamentally anti-social teaching of capitalism that must discredit it in the eyes of Christian ethics.

This is closely bound up with another of its fundamental positions. It is that whereby society is regarded as a mechanism adjusting itself through the play of economic motives to the supply of economic needs. Here the materialistic determinism of the then newer physics reveals itself. Society is not construed in personal terms. It is a machine, built on economic—i.e., capitalistic—principles, and operating according to their laws. With such a view there is obviously nothing that will better serve society than a vigorous and whole-hearted devotion to the pursuit of economic gain without any reference beyond. It is this basic assumption that Christian ethics challenges, and it proposes in its stead a personalistic view of society that is to be treated according to ethical not economic standards.

The evolutionistic influence is evident in another basic assumption, that according to which the economic and moral orders are coterminous. Ethics, according to this way of thinking, has no *jenseitig* reference. It is naturalistic. Natural, biological advance is *ipso facto* moral advance. The universe is one, not dualistic. There is thus no contradiction between the economic order and the moral order. The pursuit of gain is identical with the pursuit of virtue. The dynamic which this conviction provided for capitalistic enterprise is incalculable, but its viciousness is plain. It flies in the face of Christian morality.

The basic charge against rugged and individualistic capitalism is its anti-social individualism with its resultant contracted and prudential morality. Capitalism has to learn, as Calvin said, "to regard the transaction not as a private affair, but for the good of the public," and that by direct and conscious contemplation of the public. I incline to think that the contemporary emphasis on the social teachings of Christianity is to be accounted for in no small measure as a reaction to the unethical individualism that has dominated industrial life during the last two centuries. We are learning again that one lives not for oneself. The wants and needs of society must be considered.

Our economic order must reflect that we are our brother's keeper. A social system cannot be built on abstract economic principles. There must be an infusion of conscious morality. As Bucer once said, "Neither the Church of Christ nor a Christian commonwealth ought to tolerate such as prefer private gain to the public weal, or seek it to the hurt of their neighbors."[5]

5. *Ibid.*, p. 142.

17

Nuclear Warfare*

In the area of man's social and political concerns there is hardly a more agonizing question facing the world today than the question of war and peace. Other questions recede into the background when this one is asked because this one affects not merely the quality of our corporate existence on earth, but our existence itself. With the discovery of nuclear energy and the manufacture of the hydrogen bomb there has come into the hands of men a power able to scorch the earth and to destroy or mutilate all life upon it. If states were to resort to war, and in the course of it deploy the thermonuclear power they now possess, they would be able to exterminate each other and in the process involve all or the greater part of mankind in death. This means that when today we seriously put the question of war we place ourselves on the brink of history where yawns the abyss of global chaos. Standing there we are able to hear with new clarity and understanding the words our Lord once spoke to Peter, "All who take the sword will perish by the sword."

Hearing the prophecy, we can hardly fail, of course, to hear the accompanying command, "Put your sword back into its place!" And having heard this we are bound to inquire into its relevance for us. Teetering on the brink of racial suicide we are compelled to ask, If Christ's word about perishing is likely to be realized in our own life and time, must his command to lay up the sword be heeded when we formulate our current plans and policies? Is it possible that history has carried us to the point at which contemporary states are required to appropriate to themselves the imperative once addressed to Peter? Is it possible that in this atomic and space age, with its eschatological nuances and forebodings, Christian states are required to eschew violence just as in the first century, with Gethsemane all about him and Christ's cross looming over him, Peter was required to sheath his sword? Is it perhaps the case that wars are no longer a moral possibility, and that they must be renounced even though without them nothing can be expected but a

*Appeared first in *Christianity Today,* Vol. 7 (1963).

crucifixion? Does the Christian way in this twentieth century lead straight from the abyss, through renunciation, to the cross?

The pacifist has a ready answer to these questions, and his answer may at long last be ripe for adoption, but I myself do not speak out of his tradition. Although I hold that war is never to be glorified and that war always witnesses to man's sin, I acknowledge that man's participation in war can be dictated by a genuinely Christian obedience and concern. I do not concur, therefore, in the pacifist's unqualified condemnation of violent coercion. Historic pacifism fails, I think, to reckon sufficiently with the demonic powers active in historical existence. It also tends to misconstrue the nature and function of the State. And it unwarrantably divorces love from justice, thereby robbing love of its hard core of responsibility. I prefer, therefore, to approach the question of thermonuclear warfare from the side of those who have traditionally held to the legitimacy of war and have elaborated in its support the just war doctrine.

According to this doctrine it is the task of the God-ordained State (Rom. 13:1) to establish and maintain a just political order within which human lives can flourish in accordance with God's creative and redemptive purposes. Since human life can flourish in accordance with these purposes only when men are free to meet their obligations, the State is called upon to recognize and guarantee these necessary freedoms. These freedoms do not have their origin in the State; they flow from mankind's moral task and are rooted in God's command. But the State has been established to secure them, and it is obliged to defend them against perversion and attack.

To this end the State is armed. A sword has been put into its hand by God himself for the maintenance of order and for the punishment of evildoers. The sword is necessary because the world is evil and because lawless forces do in fact jeopardize the freedoms requisite to the full flowering of the moral and religious life. This lawlessness must, in the name of love and justice, be held in check by the coercive power of the State, sometimes by simple police action against criminals operating within the State, and sometimes by military action against foreign nations guilty of international brigandage.

This, in its bare essentials, is the traditional case for the just war, and it is, I judge, in substance sound. Nevertheless, this doctrine does not do what some men think it does. It does not justify every war, nor every kind of war, nor every way of conducting a war approved on independent grounds. Although the doctrine sanctifies war in principle, it does not sanction war in general, and I dare say it does not sanction a general thermonuclear war at all. Indeed, if what the scientists tell us is even approximately correct, it is questionable whether a general thermonuclear war can, in the traditional sense, be called a war at all. It can better be called a meaningless holocaust, which no amount of theological subtlety or ethical ingenuity can justify. If a general thermonuclear war is able to scorch the earth, destroy all or the major part of the technical, cultural, and spiritual treasures of mankind, and annihilate the human race or leave alive only a maimed and wounded fragment of it, as many responsible scientists allege, then a general thermonuclear war is simply impermissible, whatever the provocation. If a Christian must choose between a war like this and slavery or martyrdom, then it is slavery or martyrdom he must choose. No Christian may take part in the mad and wicked act of racial suicide and undertake to put an end to human history.

I understand that there are some Christians who declare that they would rather be dead than red. I am able to put a good construction on their words and in this way to agree with them. But if they mean to say that anything and everything is preferable to existence under communist domination, even the destruction of the planet and the annihilation of its inhabitants, then I quite emphatically disagree with them, and in any case deny their right to act in accordance with their preference. And if they suppose that a total nuclear war can be justified solely as a means of testifying to the worth of transcendental values like freedom, truth, and goodness, regardless of what happens in the realm of historical existence, then I also disagree with them. It is not Christianity, but only romanticism, that could induce a man to fight a war with no historical goal in mind or beguile him into thinking that heaven is served by devastating the earth. A war makes sense when it can be honestly regarded as an effectual political instrument serviceable to meaningful social ends. When it cannot be so regarded, when it does not achieve or envisage a lasting peace settled on the foundation of justice, when it does not intend or effect a righteous and stable political order within which concrete human values are preserved and fostered, and when it destroys the very community in whose interest it was fought, then it makes no sense at all and cannot exact a Christian endorsement.

If it could be demonstrated, as I suppose it cannot, that the war we dread will, if it comes, be of the sort here contemplated, then we all—the traditional proponents of the just-war concept and the pacifists—could make common cause and declare our intention not to fight. We could then urge the government to scrap its nuclear missiles and the whole range of its atomic armament, and agree to deliver ourselves into Russia's or China's hands. I do not now advocate this course of action. One reason is that, not repudiating war in principle, and now knowing that even an atomic blast cannot be contained and localized, I cannot determine *a priori* what premiums—in terms of limited war—I am entitled to pay or to invite others to pay, in order to insure that freedom and self-determination, and the religious and moral values underlying these, shall continue to exist upon the earth. Another reason is that our existing armaments appear to act as effectual deterrents of communist aggression, and as preservers of the peace. Moreover, the United States is the guardian of the freedoms of many smaller nations, and she is the ally of several larger nations with whom her fortunes are intertwined. For her to proceed to unilateral disarmament would be to deliver not only herself but the whole world into the hands of the Soviet Union. This cannot be right.

There is no way out of our terrible impasse but multilateral disarmament. Fortunately, it is becoming increasingly plain, to the Russian people no less than to ourselves, that the world cannot continue to live in the dread shadow of the bomb. Although the possibility of its limited use cannot be apodictically denied, it is very unlikely that, if war breaks out, it will be put under any restraints. But in that case a frightful judgment will fall on the earth and unspeakable devastation will ensue. To prevent this terrible destruction must become and continue to be our first political concern. The best way to prevent it is to secure agreements on a disarmament plan which will give each side a reasonable assurance that faith is being kept. In the effort to secure these agreements our own country, because it is a Christian nation, must take the lead, and all Christians should encourage the government to acquire and manifest understanding of the legitimate aspirations of our opponent, and to exercise such patience in negotiations as may be required to attain the desired end.

What is necessary, too, is that the Christian people of America lend their full support to the United Nations. It is no doubt an imperfect instrument of international peace, but it is the best we have, and it could become much better if all of us gave it our cooperation and support. In our shrunken world the several nations simply must learn to live together. The alternative to this cannot be contemplated with equanimity. Among us all narrowly chauvinistic sentiments should be banished, and the horror manifested in some circles when peaceful coexistence with Russia is mentioned ought to be greatly tempered. To live and work together we need not compromise our convictions or ideals, or surrender our just claims, but we do need to exercise toleration and restraint in peripheral matters and concerns. When this is done, and when we are much in prayer for a world in desperate plight, some easing of the tensions in international relations can be confidently expected.

18

Social Strategy: Christian Power Organizations

MEMBERS OF the Church have recently heard an increased number of voices calling for united Christian political and social action. The call has been not only for the formation of study groups but for the establishment of independent power structures, i.e., for the establishment or strengthening of separate Christian labor unions and political parties. In so far as this call has been evoked by an empirically ascertained state of affairs in neutral unions and parties which is manifestly intolerable to Christians, or in so far as this call has been made in an effort to recruit Christians for engagement in a socio-political stratagem which serves the ends of justice better than the witness of organized or unorganized Christian individuals within neutral unions and parties, the call deserves a careful and sympathetic hearing. It deserves this, for it is quite possible that existing neutral organizations are no longer in fact hospitable to a Christian witness and practice, and it is quite possible that a separate Christian power organization is in fact the best way to press Christ's claims on the world in the social and political arena.

But the contrary is also possible, and the truth of the matter cannot be determined apriorily. Whether or not neutral unions are inhospitable to a Christian witness is a question of fact which cannot be answered by a simple reference to the word "neutral," nor by a simple appeal to theology. Similarly, whether or not separate Christian organizations represent the best strategy in this or any other country is a question of practical wisdom and prudence which cannot be answered in abstraction from actual states of affairs.

Those who call for withdrawal from neutral organizations and for enlistment in Christian organizations do well, therefore, to present both the facts about the behavior of neutral organizations and the prudential considerations that highlight the strategic importance of Christian organizations. It may be confidently predicted that if this is done an alert and interested ear will be attuned to the call.

If, however, the basis of fact and prudence is abandoned, and recourse is had to the principle of antithesis, and if, what is worse, the question at issue is argued in terms of simple fidelity to Christ, the advocates of separate Christian organizations will not get the hearing they would otherwise deserve, and they will, I fear, do injury to their cause.

The first, though perhaps not the most important, matter to be considered is the *nature* of the organizations we are talking about. Our central concern is obviously with the Labor Unions and Political Parties. Now, I have characterized these things as "Power Organizations" or "Power Structures." Some, however, appear not to like this characterization. The word "power," as I use it, seems to have for them a sinister meaning. To call a labor union or a political party a "power organization" is, in their judgment, to give it a bad name; it is to indulge in name-calling. In short, they suspect that when I call a labor union or a political party a "power structure" I am making a charge or registering a complaint against it.

Nothing could be farther from the truth. There is nothing either in my intent or in the term I use that pertains to evaluation, assessment, or appraisal. The term "power structure" is a purely descriptive term, and it is as such that I employ it. I employ it, as it requires to be employed, not to judge but to describe a fact; not to assess but to disclose a state of affairs.

The fact is that labor unions and political parties, whether Christian or not, *are* "power structures." They are this because they have, and of necessity must have, in their possession certain *instruments and techniques of constraint*. Without these instruments and techniques of constraint, without the "force" and "compulsion" that they can bring to bear upon people, they would cease to be what they are.

It should be obvious that without the "strike weapon" a labor union ceases to be a labor union. Without the power to "compel" management to yield to its demands a union is nothing but an educational institute or a propaganda agency; it is not a *union*. A labor union, from its very nature, is unlike a church or a school or a newspaper or a radio station or any other such thing. Churches, schools, and similar organizations teach, proclaim, witness, persuade, convince, and thereby "exert influence," but they do not have the capacity or the right to "constrain," "force," or "compel." This is because they are *not* in their nature "power structures" as labor unions assuredly are.

If labor unions are "power organizations," so are political parties. By the "power" of the ballot political parties seek to reach the point from which they can enact, or help to enact, legislation in support of which the "power of the sword" can be invoked. In the case of successful activity all powers of the State, all the concrete sanctions of the law, all the approved techniques of force—such as fines, imprisonment, and death—can in the end be legitimately appealed to.

Of course, both the "strike weapon" and the "sword of vengeance" must be responsibly used, and a Christian labor union, and a Christian political party entrusted with the reigns of government, will seek to use them responsibly. But neither the one nor the other will want to thrust these "instruments of force" away or hesitate to keep them in reserve. A labor union or a political party that seeks to divorce itself from "force" and the "power of constraint" is one that is engaged in denying its very essence. It is in the nature of these organizations to be "power structures."

I suggest that it can lead only to confusion to argue that the church and the school are likewise "power organizations." One can of course speak of "the power" of the Word, "the power" of the Spirit, "the power" to excommunicate a member, and "the power" to flunk a student out. But there is manifestly a generic difference between these kinds of "power" and the "power of forcible constraint" that a labor union can wield in reference to management, and that a political party can exert through the law of the land and the sanctions of the State.

In summation it may be said, then, that the organizations we are talking about are of a certain kind—the kind called "Power Organizations." There are, of course, other sorts of voluntary organizations, organizations which are *not* power structures. There are, for example, what may be called "Organizations for Contemplation," concerned with study and reflection. There are also what may be called "Propaganda Organizations," which are structured for witness and enlightenment. Included in this group are organizations for the production and distribution of newspapers, magazines, books, and tracts, and organizations for managing such media of communication as radio and television. There are also what may be called "Philanthropic Organizations," such as those that establish and maintain hospitals, distribute goods and monies to the poor, relieve the distressed, and care for the aged. There are, finally, "Educational Organizations," such as schools that train and discipline the young and, on the higher levels, disclose and articulate the basic structures of reality.

About the legitimacy, the need, the appropriateness, and the desirability of Christian organizations of the sorts just enumerated there is, as a matter of fact, no dispute in the Church. No one doubts that separate Christian organizations for contemplation, publication, education, and philanthropy fit nicely into the pattern of Christian living. For whatever reason it is so, the dispute among us concerns organizations of quite another sort. It concerns "power organizations," such as labor unions and political parties.

Having named and described the organizations about which the discussion centers, it remains to consider the spiritual compulsions we are under to establish separate forms of them upon a Christian basis.

The question at issue here is this: What is our Christian duty concerning neutral and Christian labor unions and political parties? Are we inwardly constrained by the Gospel to separate ourselves from non-Christian organizations and to establish or unite with Christian organizations, irrespective of historical conditions and apart from the relativities of time and space? Or are we perhaps obliged by the Gospel to consider the actual and variable states of affairs in the world and to separate ourselves from neutral organizations either not at all or only under certain circumstances; and are we by that token either never to establish separate Christian organizations or to do so only when separation is dictated by considerations of practical wisdom and prudence? Granted that the Christian community is obliged to press the claims of Christ on society and the state, must it therefore be granted that the designated and, in the end, the only acceptable way of doing this is through separate Christian organizations; or must we declare that separate Christian organizations are instruments of Christian strategy that it would sometimes be our privilege and duty to employ and sometimes our privilege and duty to let lie? Granted that the Christian must always live in subjection to his Lord, may he, or perhaps should he, unite with non-Christians toward the attainment of common goals within a single organization established on a neutral basis; or is such cooperation strictly prohibited by Christian principle?

These are the types of questions about which the current discussion centers, and it will be plain to all that a great deal of theology and philosophy, and no small amount of history and experience, go into the answers that are given to them. Yet the answers can, I think, be quite simply classified. There are in theory three possible attitudes one can take toward separate Christian power organizations: one can hold that Christian principle makes these organizations always and everywhere impermissible; or one can hold that Christian principle makes these organizations, if possible at all, always and everywhere mandatory; or one can hold that Christian principle compels one to regard these organizations as strategic instruments that it would be in the interest of Christ's kingdom sometimes to employ and sometimes to let lie. I myself embrace the third position, and in doing so I am compelled to disagree both with the Barthians who generally take the first position, and with certain other persons who seem to me to occupy the second. In what follows I shall briefly characterize the two unacceptable positions, in order the better to highlight the position that I hold.

It is possible to be against separate Christian power organizations on grounds of Christian priniciple. Barth is the living witness of that fact, and so are those of his followers who have initiated and sustained the "break-through" *(Doorbraak)* in The Netherlands. Because of Barth's emphasis on human solidarity in sin and grace he is stoutly opposed to every separation of Christians from their fellow men, save in the Church, the Christian fellowship itself. The Christian, he says, "is never led astray . . . from the path of fellowship with the enemy. . . . Christians do not need to form a party in the struggle against the wicked, but can and must continue undismayed to tread the way of fellowship with the latter."[1] Moreover, because of his avowed jealousy for the honor of Christ's name, Barth wishes to see that name detached from purely human organizations like labor unions and political parties. He asks, "Can there be any other Christian party in the State but the Christian fellowship itself, with its special mission and purpose?... The Church's supreme interest must be... that Christians shall not mass together in a special party, since their task is to defend and proclaim, in decisions based on it, the Christian gospel that concerns all men."[2]

With all of this Emil Brunner is in essential agreement. He, too, is opposed, on the basis of Christian principle, to the formation of separate Christian power structures. Speaking of Christian political parties, he says, "Almost without exception the worst that could befall would be the formation of Christian parties for this would bring in a disastrous confusion between the spheres of Church and State. Christian political parties are in harmony with the style, and legitimate upon the ground of Roman Catholicism; for here the Church as such has a political and economic programme. The Protestant Church as such has no programme; if she were to have one she would already have become Roman at heart. The curse of the betrayal of the Name of Christ broods over the "Christian" social organization.... We cannot take this Name on to any of our little political banners."[3]

When speaking of Christian labor unions, Brunner expresses himself in a similar vein: "... the idea of Christian Trades Unions is and remains a Catholic idea, which is alien to the nature of the Protestant faith, and should remain so. For the object for which the Trades Union is struggling, and for which it should struggle, is indeed something for which a Christian also ought to fight, but it is not on that account by any means a Christian matter."[4] To this he adds, "The name of Christ should only be used where we are certain that opposition to that which we represent is also opposition to the cause of Jesus Christ, that is, never in political groups, or in groups controlled by the principles of political economy."[5]

These quotations may suffice to indicate that continental neo-orthodoxy is opposed to separate Christian organizations not on prudential grounds but on the grounds of faith. Its opposition to these organizations is rooted in principle, and is therefore total and unconditional. It is here affirmed that to build a power structure on a Christian foundation is itself an unchristian act; and it is suggested that no variation in time, place, or circum-

1. Karl Barth, *Church Dogmatics*, II, 2, p. 721.
2. Barth, *Against the Stream*, pp. 45–46.
3. Emil Brunner, *Divine Imperative*, Philadelphia: Westminster, 1947, p. 432.
4. *Ibid.*, p. 673.
5. *Ibid.*

stance is able to render it anything else than impious or mistaken. With the simplicity, rigor, and absoluteness that is characteristic of much principial thinking, no allowance is here made for the possibility that separate Christian organizations may, under certain conditions, effectually implement an authentic Christian vision; nor is the possibility conceived that the forces of evil may so disrupt the solidarity of men as to leave Christians no alternative but to separate from existing organizations and establish their own. As is the case with every absolutistic stance, the Christian is here left with no real options. The whole force of religion and theology, however well or ill conceived, is made to support the dictum: You may never choose to organize separately on a Christian basis.

In spite of my high regard for these eminent theologians, I cannot follow them in this. I find no warrant in the Gospel for so radical a rejection of Christian political and economic groupings.

There are those in the Church, who, though they stand at the opposite pole from Barth and Brunner, share the uncompromising absolutism of these thinkers and declare without reserve that only fixed and eternal principles, and not also the relativities of time and space, may play a role in the determination of these matters.

As in the case of Barth and Brunner, the argument conducted by those who occupy this position is from principle alone. Considerations of time, place, and circumstance are thought to have no bearing on the problem. In this view, the decision to withdraw from a non-Christian organization and to establish or join a Christian organization need not, indeed may not, wait on a careful scrutiny of the facts, a weighing of the variable factors in the situation, and a consideration of the possible effects withdrawal and consolidation may produce. Empirical and pragmatic reflections of this sort are thought to be unworthy of a man of principle and in any case quite unnecessary. What needs to be known in order to make a responsible decision can be known without observation; it can be known from the Scriptures, whose declarations do not require experiential verification and whose truths are independent of changing circumstances. To decide whether or not one may be a member of a neutral union one need not investigate the union in question; one need only ascertain that it is not a Christian union and then recall the biblical teachings about the antithesis, the impossibility of neutrality, and the evil of being unequally yoked together. It is these things that decide the matter, and since these things are constant and invariable, there is no need for empirical research. In this view, accordingly, the necessity of separating from a non-Christian organization and of joining a Christian organization is grounded not in contingent "facts" but in eternal "verities." The necessity is rooted wholly and alone in the fixed nature of man and in the cosmic and stable structure of sin and grace, and not at all in the changing conditions of historical existence.

Needless to say, I find this position quite untenable. It reflects a type a principial thinking which I am bound to regard as simplistic and as a misreading of the Scriptures.

My own position is that separate Christian organizations are neither principially impermissible nor principially mandatory. I hold that separate Christian organizations represent responsible Christian strategy; that they constitute a way or method by which to implement a Christian concern for society and the state; that in some countries and at some times they are the best way to implement this concern, but that in other countries and at other times this may not be the case, the matter depending on the prevailing circumstances. I hold that separate Christian organizations are not themselves a principle nor immediately derivable from a principle, i.e., without the intermediation of important empirical premises. Separate Christian organizations are, I hold, at best a policy, about the wisdom and acceptability of which Christians who serve with fidelity the same Lord may have honest and tolerable differences.

I hold, furthermore, that labor unions and political parties can be neutral. This does not mean that any man can be neutral. Every man is either in Christ or out of him and is, deep down, operating either in the service of the City of God or of the City of the World. But these two sorts of men must cooperate in this world, and I hold that they can do this, and sometimes should do this, in neutral, i.e., non-ideologically structured, organizations established to achieve goals common to Christians and non-Christians.

To get this whole matter into somewhat clearer focus, let us consider at greater length the thesis of those who declare that, wherever possible, Christians must, under the inescapable constraint of Christ, establish Christian organizations in the social and political arena.

It is said by these people that membership by Christians in a non-Christian labor union or political party is principially, i.e., unconditionally and absolutely wrong. Such membership, it is maintained, is always a real, even if sometimes an unintended, rejection of Christ's claim upon the whole of our existence, and it is in essence an enlistment in the cause of those who are in settled opposition to our Lord. It is said that such membership is simply incompatible with a genuine profession of the Christian faith, and that this incompatibility exists regardless of time, place, or circumstance, and regardless of the actual condition of the particular non-Christian power organization being contemplated.

It is important that this thesis be clearly understood. The thesis is not merely that all the non-Christian power organizations that exist in North

America and in Europe are in fact corrupt, in fact inhospitable to a Christian witness, in fact remiss in transmitting a Christian vision to the world, and in fact ineffective in implementing a truly Christian socio-political program, and on that account not a fit home for sensitive Christians concerned to be both loyal to Christ and meaningfully involved in the life of mankind. If this were the thesis, the propounders of it would, I dare say, receive a most sympathetic hearing in the Church and, on the presentation of a due amount of relevant empirical evidence, win many for the cause of separate Christian organization. But this, unfortunately, is not the thesis. Such a thesis is too practical, pragmatic, and non-principial to be enunciated by those whose position we are examining. They are not satisfied to assert, and to demonstrate empirically, that the existing non-Christian labor unions and political parties happen to be materialistic or are contingently and in fact man-centered. They feel they must be more principial than that and assert apriorily—on the ground of faith—that these organizations are essentially and necessarily humanistic, and thus objectionable by their very nature to a Christian.

The premiss from which this startling thesis depends is very simple and very clear. The premiss is this: All non-Christian organizations are anti-Christian. Now, if this premiss were acknowledged to be true by all concerned, then all argument would cease at once, for if anything is beyond dispute it is this: No Christian may be a member of an anti-Christian organization. If all organizations did indeed fall into two classes only, if all organizations were either Christian or anti-Christian, then the Christian course of action would be crystal clear. If the Christian who wanted to be a member of some organization were confronted by the simple either-or here contemplated, he would be without an option; he would be compelled, under the inescapable constraint of Christ, to join the Christian organization and to shun, as the very work of the devil, the anti-Christian organization. Nothing is more obvious than that the Christian may not be against the Christ.

But is it true that a Christian member of an organization must either be a member of a Christian organization or be accounted, if not a veritable enemy of Christ, then nevertheless one who aids and abets Christ's enemies and subverts Christ's cause? Is it true that a Christian who joins a non-Christian union is, at least in his organizational existence, dishonoring Christ's name and repudiating his universal lordship? Is it true that non-Christian organizations are inherently anti-Christian and that a Christian who joins one involves himself in sin through the very act of joining it?

Those whose views we are considering give to these questions an unequivocal affirmative answer, and they give it on the basis of the Bible and theology. Is it not true, they ask, that, unlike Christian organizations, which are for Christ, non-Christian organizations are not for him, and does the

Bible not declare that what is not for Christ is against him? And are we not, they add, all committed to the biblical doctrine of the antithesis, and does the antithesis not divide the world in two and remove all middle ground between Christian and anti-Christian? Do not both Scripture and Reformed theology exclude all indifferentism and all neutrality? Must we not conclude, therefore, that there are no neutral organizations and that those which are generally considered to be such are really disguised enemies of God?

Those who articulate this position recognize that some Christians do distinguish three kinds of organizations: Christian, non-Christian, and anti-Christian. But for this complex set of distinctions they have no sympathy. They cannot but regard the introduction of a middle position between two poles as a fault traceable to the influence of alien modes of thought, and as a palpable lapse into religious neutralism. They are certain that as long as a man thinks biblically and principially he will never come to recognize the existence of a neutral organization that is neither Christian nor anti-Christian but merely non-Christian. In the world as they see it there is room for only two kinds of organizations; a third kind is inconceivable and impossible.

The upshot of this is, of course, that if a Christian who wishes to join an organization does not wish to join a Christian organization, he has only one alternative; he can join an anti-Christian organization and so involve himself in opposition to his Lord. But this is sin, something sedulously to be avoided. If, as a Christian, he is to be in any organization at all, he must be in a Christian organization, and in none other. The only Christian thing to do relative to organizations that are not Christian is not to join them or, alternatively, to withdraw from them in accordance with the admonition of the apostle: "Do not be mismated with unbelievers. For what partnership have righteousness and iniquity? Or what fellowship has light with darkness? What accord has Christ with Belial? Or what has a believer in common with an unbeliever? What agreement has the temple of God with idols? . . . Therefore come out from them, and be separate from them, says the Lord. . . ." (2 Cor. 6:14–17).

For those whose views we are here considering, the general, inherent, and therefore inescapable sin of a non-Christian organization is that, in its constitution, it neither professes Christ as Lord nor proclaims the authority of the inscriptured Word. And its allied sin is that, in accordance with the nature of its constitution, it does not subject its members to specifically Christian norms. As a non-Christian organization it of course does not do this; otherwise it would be Christian. But its not doing this is taken to be proof that it is against the Lord; its not doing this is understood as the No! it speaks to God, as the insult that it hurls at Christ, as the corporate slight of holy things in which it ineluctably involves its members. For those of whom we are speaking the very idea of a non-Christian organization is therefore offensive. They either do not seriously inquire or do not much care whether, in spite of its lack of a Christian profession, the organization pursues goals compatible with Christianity in ways that a Christian can endorse; their eyes are riveted on what they take to be its central negation; they see its lack of a Christian profession as an evil that centrally disqualifies all its good works. They see its lack of a Christian profession as a shameful reproach to Christ, as a positive denigration of the Scriptures, as a sure sign of an arrogant humanism, and as the ultimate guarantee of socio-political futility. They see in its lack of a Christian profession the proof that it is anti-Christian.

It appears that in the last analysis nothing more is needed to condemn the non-Christian organization than the bare fact that it is non-Christian. There is nothing obscure about the reasoning here. Because the non-Christian organization is not for Christ, it is against him; and because it is against him, no Christian can have a part in it. It is as simple as that.

But, of course, this is too simple—even for those who propound the idea. If all non-Christian organizations—all those organizations, that is, which do not profess allegiance to Jesus Christ or take the Christian Scriptures as their guide—are to be regarded as anti-Christian, then a Christian can belong to none of them. This means not merely that he cannot belong to the Republican or Democratic party, or to one of the unions embraced in the CIO-AFL, but that he cannot belong to the Rotary Club, the Lions, the National Association of Manufacturers, the American Medical Association, the American Red Cross, or any other one of the innumerable non-Christian organizations that have been established on this continent.

I know, of course, that this conclusion is unwelcome to those who operate with the alternatives Christian and anti-Christian, and that they sometimes attempt to escape it by distinguishing between "stricter" and "looser" types of organization, but this evasive maneuver will not work. He who appeals to principle must be content to stay with principle. If a non-Christian organization is to be regarded as anti-Christian on the sole ground that it is not Christian, then it follows that any organization that is not Christian is off limits to Christ's followers. And then what is off limits must include so innocent a thing as a secular chess-club—which is manifestly absurd.

If we are to avoid being caught in the foregoing cul de sac we shall have to distinguish between ideologically-structured and non-ideologically-structured organizations. Within the class of ideologically-structured organizations there are two kinds: the Christian and the anti-Christian, and of these the Christian may belong only to the former; he may never join an anti-Christian organization, as, for example, an atheist club. Non-ideologically-structured organizations, on the other hand, are neither Christian nor anti-Christian, but simply non-Christian or neutral. There are many of these in

North America, and indeed all over the world, and all of them are in principle open to the Christian.

Numbered among them are most of the organizations, such as the American Philosophical Association, listed in the previous paragraph. They are invariably communities of interest that profess no religion, commit no one to a specific ultimate allegiance, and admit adherents of various faiths to full participation while in full possession of their faiths. In the past the labor unions and the political parties of America have been just such communities of interest, and in the judgment of many Christian observers they are still that. But whether they are or not is a question of fact, which is to be settled through a process of observation and inquiry and not through simple deduction from some principle like that of the antithesis or merely because these organizations are not specifically and avowedly Christian.

Part VI

THE ETHICS OF SCIENCE AND MEDICINE

19

Christian Ethics and Scientific Control*

When one focuses on science and technology, two features of contemporary existence directly traceable to modern man's scientifico-technical behavior come into view and affright. One is the exploitation and pollution of external nature. The other is the chemical, biological and psychological manipulation of man.

The purpose of this essay is to expose this kind of scientific control to the scrutiny of Christian ethics.

I shall begin by (1) depicting the rise of Western science and technology; attempt next (2) to set forth a Christian understanding of man's relation to nature; and end (3) by commenting on selected features of the current scientific engagement with man.

A. THE SCIENTIFIC ENTERPRISE

Modern natural science has a character of its own, but it is rooted in the past and has a complex lineage. Christian elements are in it and also motifs inherited from the ancient Hebrews. It has connections with the Hellenic nature studies which culminated in Aristotle, and it reflects the Latin sense of order which was transmitted to the Middle Ages by the Roman Stoics. And, of course, it owes much to the philosophical and methodological impulses generated by the late Renaissance, notably by Francis Bacon and René Descartes. In spite of its diverse parentage, however, or perhaps because of it, it has its own unique identity. Its distinctiveness appears when it is compared with the Hebrew, Greek and Christian intellectual traditions.

As the Old Testament amply witnesses, the Hebrew attitude toward nature was not analytical and manipulative, but aesthetic and celebrative. Nature was not primarily a problem or puzzle to be solved nor a set of powers

*Appeared first as "Christian Ethics and Scientific Control," in Charles Hatfield, ed., *The Scientist and Ethical Decision* (Downers Grove: Inter-Varsity Press, 1973).

and processes to be harnessed, but a sign and symbol of the Creator, calculated to inspire praise and, sometimes, fear. Nature to the pious Israelite was Gothic in its structure. It was a finger pointing away from itself toward heaven and God. Most of it witnessed to God's power and goodness, though parts of it—notably the raging seas—disclosed his wrath and the mystery of the divine abyss. In any case, nature was not a thing apart, an object to be held at a distance and investigated or altered. It was God's creation and it was under his providence. Sheep and cattle could be tended, wild and ferocious beasts could be restrained, and the ground could be cultivated—all by the licensing of God—but nature as a whole could only be thankfully and reverently accepted as man's given abode, God's footstool and the arena of his wondrous works. Science, as we have come to know it, could obviously not develop within a world view of this sort, and all men accordingly agree that, though the Hebrews were notable for religion, they produced and could produce no science.

Science, as almost everything else, took its rise, or else came first to self-consciousness, in Greece, It arose, according to Aristotle, out of curiosity. The Greek wanted to *know*, i.e., cognitively to grasp and appropriate the structure, the anatomy, the essence of things. The desire to know these essences might direct a platonizing mind to the contemplation of the pure celestial exemplars of them or direct an Aristotle to a scrutiny of their embodiment in corporeal existents, but, in either case, the interest was in essences, and the satisfaction of the interest was in understanding. There was no end beyond this. Knowledge was not for power or for any other sort of utility. Knowledge was only to satisfy curiosity; knowledge was for the sake of knowledge.

Technology, accordingly, did not develop in Greece. Nature was there to be read and understood, not to be manipulated. More than that, nature—in the sense of mutable phenomena in process—was less the proper object of knowledge than the medium in and through which the proper object of knowledge, the eternal, immutable essences or forms, could be apprehended. Knowledge in Greek thought, whether Platonic or Aristotelian, meant "union with the unchangeable," with the "really real." For this reason, science, as we have come to know it, did not flourish in Greece, even though under Aristotelian auspices the Hellenistic world produced a Ptolemy, Galen, Euclid and Archimedes. There were other reasons, including a disdain of "hands," why Greece did not produce science, but an account of these must wait until we consider the Christian attitude to nature.

Christianity, which is centrally oriented to Jesus Christ, did not, in spite of Marcion, disdain the Old Testament or the Hebrew mind. Nor did it, in spite of Tatian and Tertullian, disdain the Greeks. Christianity is the result of God's gracious act in Jesus Christ and not the natural product of Israel and

Hellas. Yet Justin Martyr and Clement of Alexandria were not wholly wrong: Christianity has made these two streams its tributaries. This has several implications which are not presently germane. What is of interest now is that in its distinctive view of nature and science Christianity included elements from both traditions.

By combining the Old Testament concept of *creation* and the Johannine-Greek idea of the *logos*, Christian thinkers came to recognize and assert that nature is shot through with rationality and that because of its intelligibility it not only can but should be "known." Lacking a radical doctrine of creation, the Greeks never attained this insight. Besides the immanent Logos there existed for them an independent and essentially intractable "matter" which could not be completely "formed" or rationalized. A corporeal thing or natural process could, therefore, never be rightly "known"—not even by the gods; irrationality and unintelligibility are natural and therefore inexpungable components of all phenomena. This is another reason why a natural science, as distinct from a philosophy of essences, was never developed among the Greeks, but could, and did, flourish on Christian soil.

The biblical doctrine of creation served also to drive out of nature the ancient sky, mountain and fertility gods which, in the heathen view, constituted or inhabited it. It rendered nature secular and thus made it available for inquiry. Because of the absence of the creation doctrine among the Greeks, science could even there not really get off the ground. In the Greek view, nature was not something that had been made *ex nihilo*. It was an eternal, self-generating organism involved in ceaseless circular growth. It was the living, throbbing, but impersonal reproductive matrix from which all things—even the gods—arose and into which they were periodically resolved. The Bible, on the contrary, de-divinizes and de-sacralizes nature. This does not mean that it deprives nature of its life cycles, its vital processes and its web of dynamic relationships with all God's creatures, including man. The Bible does not reduce nature to a machine. But it does declare that nature is creaturely and nondivine, and it thereby licenses science.

From the Bible, too, came the insight that nature is the ward of man. This is not a Greek idea. For the Greek, man was a part of nature, wholly caught up in it and obliged to conform to it; he was to live according to nature. In Christian thought, however, man is conceived as in some sense transcending nature and as obliged to care for it. The notion of transcendence involves "dominion" and the notion of care involves "control." As everyone knows, these concepts lend themselves quite easily to perversion. They can be made to authorize a despotic and exploitive rape of nature. In classical Christian thought, however, "dominion" was hedged about with moral restraints and regulated by religious "praise" (Ps. 8:9). It was recognized that man was put in charge of nature, not as an ultimate master but as a God-appointed servant, steward and husbandman, charged with a development and healing ministry. Consequently the "control" which is allowed and even enjoined must be exercised by man in godly fear, and, in strict obedience to the law of love, man must direct his dominion toward the true well-being of all God's creatures.

Hebrew, Greek and Christian impulses did not of themselves suffice to produce the science and technology that emerged in the seventeenth century and came in the following centuries to dominate Western culture. Needed was an additional impulse. As it turned out, this impulse was provided by philosophy, more particularly by the philosophy of Descartes.

Descartes professed Christianity and remained until his death a member of the Roman Catholic church. But his philosophical conceptions, which gave expression to the anthropocentric humanism of the Renaissance, not only moved science away from the Hebrew "celebrative" and the Greek "contemplative" stances, it also moved it away from the Christian stance of an "understanding, preserving, developing and healing ministry" performed in obedience to God and in accordance with his law of love.

What happened was this: Descartes posited two substances, the *res cogitans* and the *res extensa*, the thinking man and the space-time world outside of him. He not only distinguished these two things, he separated them; and, what is more, he placed them over against each other, meanwhile according to man not merely an ascendancy over nature but a power of determination over it. To justify and accelerate man's ascendancy he diminished nature by regarding all of its components, including living things, as automata—mere "things" as manipulable as stones. To implement man's ascendancy he devised a new logic which divorced subjective reason from transcendental and transcendent attachments (cf. Plato and Augustine), and brought into being a means-end calculus which, concentrating on means, either forgot about ends or adopted them from sub- or extra-rational sources, like, for example, the "desires" of a comfort-loving public.

In this way technical reason came to replace ontological reason, and men came to be locked in the means-end structure of phenomenological reality, without transcendence, and thus without extra-phenomenological canons of value. By the same token the Creator God, in relation to whom the created universe has its unity and wholeness, was replaced by the thinking man who unified the world by subjecting it to a logical calculus employed to make nature serve exclusively human ends, where human meant "divorced from both God and nature." Lost in all this was man's own immanence in nature and his mediatorship functions within it. Nature, having been reduced to a mere object, an abstract cognitive *Gegenstand*, a mere pole in the logical subject-object nexus, could be manipulated at will.

This view of things did not of itself produce technology, but it provided a philosophical justification for its unlimited use when and if it should come. Technology came when increased population, growing urbanization and expanding economic wants drove men to tap what seemed to them to be the limitless resources of nature. Descartes' view of nature and knowledge was itself an impetus to produce tools for "control," and the inclination to do so was abetted by Francis Bacon's contention that "knowledge is for power." But deep down it was the human desire first for the satisfaction of basic needs and then for creature comforts that triggered the technological explosion. In response to growing popular demands, partly spontaneous and partly induced by announced possibilities and tempting promises, engineers and other artisans brought nature into the service of man and began to supply the mechanical conveniences with which our present world is filled. So began the industrial revolution.

Based on a Cartesian view of nature and supported by a utopian idea of progress, technology went from strength to strength, creating new wants in the very process of satisfying old ones. Meanwhile most men were unmindful of the fact that nature's resources are finite and fast dwindling, and that industrial wastes were polluting the very air, water and land on which human existence depends. But now we have come to realize that we are in an ecological crisis, and we are puzzled to know how the doom that threatens us can be averted.

It will be my concern in the next section to consider the theologico-ethical understandings which might provide us with a perspective on the observed developments and with standards for evaluating them. I proceed, then, to consider the man-nature relation: the ecological problem.

B. THE MAN-NATURE COMPLEX: ECOLOGICAL PROBLEM

There are many ways of organizing Christian truth, but the organization adopted in any instance must be focused on the issue at hand. I am not sure that my organization is maximally adapted to set forth the man-nature problem, but I have, for good or ill, undertaken to arrange the discussion under the heads of Creation, Fall, Redemption.

(1) *Creation*

The aspect of the problem that is suggested by the concept of creation is the cosmological one of status and position. The question here is: Is man immersed in nature, or does he stand outside it? The question is very old, but it is being asked with new urgency today. In ecological discussions it is dividing men into "inclusivist" and "exclusivist" camps. In a book entitled

Crisis in Eden (Nashville: Abingdon, 1970), Frederick Elder (a self-styled inclusivist) classified Herbert Richardson and Harvey Cox as exclusivists. They are represented as advocating the divorce of man from nature and as favoring the creation of an artificial in place of the natural environment (city vs. wilderness). Elder represents himself and his associates (notably Loren Eiseley) as wanting to think of man as "an inextricable part of nature" and as called to be in harmony with it, rather than to exercise dominion over it. Seen in historical perspective the issue here is one that has always figured in the monist-dualist quarrel.

In the context of the present discussion, a dualist is one who lifts man above and beyond the matrix of nature and thus authorizes him either to flee from it into ideal realms or else to turn upon and assault it. We have already met such a dualist in Descartes. In this particular he betrays a certain kinship with the ancient gnostic and docetic sects which, unlike Descartes, disqualified nature (the corporeal universe) as in some sense evil. Some members of these sects avenged themselves on nature by abusing the body and fouling the fields, thus anticipating the twentieth century. Others, by mystic contemplations and ascetic practices, elevated themselves above the gross reality of nature. If these latter could not be charged with doing positive injury to nature, they could nevertheless be charged with indifference and neglect.

The present growing resentment against a dualistic understanding of the man-nature complex can, therefore, be appreciated. The demand now is for monism. Demanded is that man and nature be brought back together and contemplated as interdependent and complementary parts of one all-embracing whole. The call is for oneness, harmony, unity and equality. If the call for holism debases man, disclaims his assumed centrality and shatters his pretensions, this, we are assured, is unavoidable and salutary. The present crisis requires that man's kinship with all creatures, and his inclusion in a comprehensive ecological system, be emphatically affirmed.

The monism that underlies these representations calls attention to a truth that no one may ignore, but the monism itself is no more acceptable than the dualism it wishes to replace. Monism always comes at the price of reductionism. Some inclusivists, accordingly, reduce man to the status of nature's lowest common denominator, thus substituting a materialistic or dynamic naturalism for the humanistic idealism they have rejected. Others hominize the whole of nature and thus resuscitate the hylozoism and animism of the primitives, or they develop a pantheistic romanticism marked, among other things, by a pious devotion to daffodils and water fowl.

Christianity knows nothing of a dualism, unless the ontological gap which separates the Creator from the creature be so called. Nor does it recognize a monism, unless it be the unity of all things in the Creator and Redeemer. In any case, it has broken with all intra-cosmic dualisms and monisms. Within the cosmos it recognizes individuality and diversity on the one hand, and interrelatedness and interdependence on the other, but neither separation nor identity anywhere. This applies with special force to man, who is unique in God's creation.

On the one hand, man is dust and thus bound in with nature and with all that nature does and contains. From this point of view all of God's space-time creatures are his kin, he and they are embraced inextricably in a common whole, and with them his fortunes are wrapped up. On the other hand, man is a person who by God's special endowment is able (and enjoined) to relate not only to all creatures horizontally but also to God vertically, and so become the mediator between the two. Herein he resembles the Savior Jesus Christ, in whose image he was made. It follows, I think, that if some formula is required to express man's relation to nature it must be framed in analogy to that of Chalcedon: child of nature and child of God. Here immanence is attended by vicegerency. Here that is given which while not disrupting the ecological nexus, maintains the priority and the unique responsibility of man.

(2) *Fall*

The question has more than once been raised about whether through the Fall of man the structures of the cosmos were bent or broken, whether its processes were slowed down or increased, or whether other basic changes took place in nature. I dare go no farther here than to express the opinion that the cosmical structures and processes have throughout time remained essentially the same. It seems clear, however, that nature is caught up in disruptions and that man and nature are involved in conflicts which go beyond the polarities and tensions indigenous to the created world and which, therefore, testify to the presence of sin.

Fortunately, not *all* is conflict; there is unity and coherence, too. What actually appears is *ambiguity*. This ambiguity arises because, though sin is in its very nature alienating and disruptive, it can operate only within and through the stable structures of creation. Evil requires the good in order to be at all, and conflict requires order. This order is maintained by Providence, not indeed apart from Christ in whom the continued existence of the world has its ground and warrant, yet prior to the ultimate redemption of the whole creation. It is on account of Providence that, in the realm of what Bonhoeffer calls the "penultimate," even those who are not (or not yet) in Christ and are not impelled by Christian motives and purposes are yet (by the common grace of restraint and enlightenment) so under God's direction that hostilities are tempered, and that some degree of order and cooperation is maintained throughout the whole of nature.

If, accordingly, one asks whether nature is malignant or benign, the answer must be that it is both. Its benignity relative to itself and towards mankind is disclosed in its capacity for, and nizus towards, self-renewal and self-replenishment. This feature of nature provides ground for hope and optimism in the present environmental crisis. We can know that, if we stop our aggrandizements, nature will largely of itself regain the health which we have destroyed or undermined. But nature is also "malignant" in that, when untended by a superior intelligence and will, it can and does create the deserts, jungles and various noxious things which threaten or discomfit men, that is, those creatures who, being of a higher order than the surrounding nature, are required to build cultures and civilizations.

That man in the state of sin has assaulted, plundered and polluted nature is plain for all to see. But there has, in the past and present, been reverence for it too. And now, whether out of respect for nature's own individuality and identity or out of concern for their own survival, men are disposed to end the war and heal the wounds of nature. Thus good and bad are—also in the human stance, and even apart from saving grace—commingled. These ambiguities and ambivalences have caused some men to take up a position in the middle distance. They have proposed that we declare a truce with nature and strike a balance between the rival claims of nature and human culture. They have proposed that we establish a garden-village between the city and the wilderness, and thus let man and nature live in peace and in territorial integrity. On the level of the penultimate there is doubtless merit in this proposal, but it falls far short of the redemptive plan and purpose that was proclaimed and initiated by Jesus Christ.

(3) *Redemption*

The Christian's relation to nature is, on the creational level, the same as that of any man: He is nature's child, and he is its finite lord. On the level of the Fall (which preserves the creational level) the Christian, like every man, is caught up in the ambiguities of existence and must make prudential decisions in the light of the situation and with regard to the available options. But to be a Christian means not only to be a man and involved in sin; it means to be *in Christ* and to be a willing and active participant in his ongoing work of cosmic redemption. This means that the Christian in his relations with nature is controlled by a purpose which in principle lifts him above the levels of tactics and *ad hoc* decisions and puts him in possession of an all-encompassing strategy: the Christian strategy of involvement, judgment and renewal. These elements in the strategy do, of course, but recapitulate the redemptive events enacted in the world by God in Christ: the incarnation, crucifixion, and resurrection. The Christian is called to repeat in his own life and person these acts of God.

In the incarnation God entered into created reality and, without losing his identity as God, became in a mysterious way at one with it. The Christian must do the same with respect to nature. He must veritably and passionately "identify" with it, recognize it as his own flesh, accept it in all of its disruptions and perversions and make no attempt either to escape or nullify it. However, he must not, in his involvement and commitment, forget that in his being he is a product not of nature but of God, that he participates in the *logos,* and that a redemptive role has been assigned to him that, of all God's creatures, only he can play. One thing, and that the most germane, must still be added. Since, in respect to his being, the Christian is incarnate by nature and not by love and choice (as is the Lord), he must now, in still stricter imitation of Christ, become redemptively incarnate. He must, as Christian, deliberatively renounce his technological power and glory and self-sacrificially espouse the cause of nature, not in order to give nature an unwarranted ascendancy but to prepare both it and the race of men for the coming of the Kingdom.

In the crucifixion of Christ God both passed a judgment on the world and opened up a channel for his grace. The judgment that he passed was primarily on the force of sin and death which had invaded his domain, and it was secondarily on the whole structure of reality which these forces had perverted and despoiled. In the judgment laid upon sin, the divine No! assured sin's final banishment. In the judgment on man and his environment there was a promise that a new creation would replace the old. The Christian must do the same with respect to nature. No invader bent on destruction and perversion should be tolerated; every excessive depletion and every pollution should be avenged. But nature itself must be laid under judgment, not for annihilation but for redemption. Redemption here entails the restructuring and redirection of nature in order that it may be made fit for the effective proclamation of the gospel to all who inhabit it and in order that, under Christ's direction, it may be prepared for the final consummation.

In the resurrection of Christ the future of the world is guaranteed. The resurrection assures us that, no matter what nature does and no matter what men do, God's good purposes will prevail. This truth should, of course, tempt no Christian into complacency, but only enlist him for cooperation in the realization of a goal that, by the determination of God, will certainly be reached. Nothing can compel and nothing can hinder God's grace; his good purposes will prevail. But Christians may know that their engagement with nature and the ecological problem are taken by Christ himself as faith in him and his purposes, and as contributing to the realization of the new paradise he has projected.

It should also be observed that, if we are in Christ, we are constituted, as he is, priests, prophets and kings. It has always been the function of a priest to conserve the things that God has given, and we may thus conclude that, in respect to nature, we have been charged with a custodial responsibility. Because conservation can atrophy into conservatism, Christ has also made us prophets who criticize the status quo and urge men on to better things. And because what God has given and allowed us to develop must be put into the service of the Kingdom, he has appointed us kings or administrators who, in their ministrations, are concerned for nothing so much as the moral and spiritual development of man, the whole man in his ecological context.

Here it should be observed that it is not nature as such, or in isolation, that God is concerned to preserve or develop. What he intended when he created the world, what he purposed when in his Son he died for it, and what in Christ's resurrection is guaranteed, is a community, a fellowship of persons, a kingdom or city set down in a redeemed and renewed environment, a new heaven and a new earth. None of us, nor all of us together, can bring that city and its pacific and indispensable environment into being. Only God in Christ can do that. But we are enjoined to work, both upon men and nature, with the Kingdom in view, that so we may "prepare the way of the Lord."

C. THE MAN-MAN COMPLEX: THE BIO-MEDICAL PROBLEM

Arising out of science and technology is another matter that is bothering sensitive Christians. It concerns man's scientific relation to and control or manipulation of man, and it yields what has become known as the bio-medical problem. Science, armed with technical reason and accustomed to treat a cognitive *Gegenstand* as a mere object, has asked the how question as this relates to human processes such as cerebration, reproduction and social response, and has not only employed manipulative techniques upon man but is making him the object of scientific experimentation.

What I have to say about this lacks the thoroughness and precision that the subject deserves, but perhaps enough will be said to bring the matter into the open.

Because man is a social being with intelligence and will, he not only *is* related to other men, he *has related* himself to them in various ways, out of various motives and to various ends. His having done so is a token of and a witness to his humanity, address and addressability being integral features of humanness.

What concerns us at present, however, is that specific type of relating which is known as scientific and which takes the form of control. Whether this type of relating is really an address in the best and deepest sense of that term is a question we shall have to bear in mind. At this juncture I shall let it lie and do no more than remark that it is very old. Besides the unstructured and spontaneous person-to-person encounters of human beings and besides the social encounters mediated through groups and institutions, there have always been "control-encounters" as well, and these have from earliest times been regulated and directed by sciences developed for the purpose of such control. So, for the control of groups, jurisprudence and military science were developed. On the side of mind, the sciences of philosophy, ethics, rhetoric, aesthetics and the like were developed to shape and direct the three faculties of the soul—intellect, will and emotion. And, of course, on the side of body there developed the sciences of pharmacology, physiology and anatomy, from which flowed the art of medicine. In the construction of these sciences and in the perfecting of control techniques, moral issues sometimes surfaced, as, for example, when inoculation was proposed or when cadavers were utilized for anatomical studies. But, on the whole, scientific control on the one hand and ethics on the other have quite peacefully co-existed.

With the rapid increase of bio-medical knowledge in the last decades, however, and with the amazing refinement of tools and techniques of physical and psychological control, the ethical issue is again rising to the surface—so markedly, indeed, that physicians who stand midway between the theoretical scientist and the lay populace, and who must perform at that level, are asking anxiously for moral guidance.

What, then, are the specific questions being asked? What are the problems which need solving? What are the practices, actual or proposed, which require Christian analysis and assessment? At a Colloquium on Ethical Dilemmas from Medical Advances held under the auspices of the American College of Physicians at San Francisco in 1967, the members of the Colloquium considered the moral issues that arise in the following areas:

1. scientific experimentation on human subjects;
2. the choice of who is to live and who is not to live (contraception, abortion, and infanticide of monsters);
3. the artificial prolongation of life (by such means as dialysis and transplantation of organs);
4. the patient's right to die with dignity (prolonged resuscitation, euthanasia);
5. the psychochemical manipulation of human intelligence;
6. the genetic effect of medical advances and possible planned manipulation of the genetic basis of the human race; and
7. the effects on human beings of overpopulation, environmental pollution and testing of nuclear weapons.

This is a very formidable list of issues (even if it does not include *in vitro* conception, androids and other things), and I must here declare, even though it is presumptuous and indelicate to do so, that I shall, as much for want of competence as for want of space, address myself neither to all of them nor to any of them. What I do propose to do is to comment on what I think are some typical features of the current scientific engagement with man. My remarks on these features will, at the same time, disclose what I think must be respected and/or kept inviolate in man's nature and being by any science wishing to exercise control over it.

1. One feature of science, and not merely the science of man, is its apparent inability to arrest its own momentum and to stop short of putting into practice the knowledge and skills it has acquired. This is another way of saying, I suppose, that knowledge, for most members of the scientific community, is never merely for contemplation but also always for utility. This *does* make *prima facie* sense, but it also raises a moral problem. Is it true, as Karl Rahner has said, that "there is really nothing possible for man that he ought not to do"? I suggest that it is not true. "Can" does not imply "may." Between the ability to do something and the moral permission to do it lies a whole area of ethical reflection, an area which science too often overleaps, or over which it is insensitively carried by its own momentum. Unfortunately, this attitude is generally carried over into the larger community. A woman is told, "Abortions can be safely done." She replies, "I very much would like it done." In many instances it then gets done; the moral issue is screened out.

2. In the sciences engaged with man, man is, when made an experimental subject, sometimes animalized; and this means, once more, that the religious and moral dimensions of his being are ignored and also that he is unclothed. A case in point is provided by the studies in the physiology and psychology of sexual intercourse undertaken by Drs. Masters and Johnson. Their subjects were sometimes unmarried and, in at least one instance, total strangers to each other. But since this was a scientific experiment, this circumstance was considered either irrelevant or calculated to enlarge the scope of the investigation and increase the value of the findings. What offends in all this is that the inquiry was made on the assumption that there is no moral law of chastity and that there is no privacy. But, of course, the assumption cannot be granted. God does forbid fornication and adultery. And he also wishes to reserve a place for privacy. And the preeminent place he has reserved for it is in sexual union. In this sacramental union of love and commitment, which symbolizes Christ's oneness with his Church, no witnesses may intrude. In the experiments of the doctors the canons of morality and the canons of reserve were violated, and in the process man was brutalized.

3. In the sciences engaged with man, man is sometimes *robotized.* In Anthony Burgess' novel, *A Clockwork Orange*, this is dramatically portrayed. In the story the antisocial behavior of Alex is removed by conditioning procedures administered by the State. We are dealing here, it is true, with a

story only, but the story was written to alert the public to the fact that science does now have the resources to by-pass the will and reduce a man to something like a puppet. That this sort of manipulation is within the power of science does not justify the employment of such power or demonstrate that man is actually something other than a responsible person with free will. If it demonstrates anything, it demonstrates that demonic forces are still loose in the world and can bring man into temporary captivity. Science, however, should not ally itself with the demons.

4. A reigning idea in the sciences engaged with man is that of *psychosomatic unity*. One need not immediately quarrel with that idea. It goes back at least as far as Aristotle and was transmitted to the modern world by Thomas Aquinas. One is entitled to prefer it to what is called the "ghost in the machine" theory of Plato. Yet Christians who embrace the psychosomatic theory should realize that they can do so only if they find a ground for *psyche* and a ground for *soma* above these two, in God. Otherwise, one is bound to fall either into idealism or into materialism. With Plato and Kant currently in disrepute, I suspect that most non-Christian scientists fall into materialism and locate the foundations of life, intelligence and spiritual aspiration in matter. This misleads many scientists into thinking that man can be structured, renewed and advanced by biochemical means. This is as mistaken as the idealist thesis that matter is mere appearance and that the body is a function of the soul. Actually mind and body are equally real and legitimate aspects of the cosmos. They are related to each other in various ways, but the relation that holds between them is not one of unilateral domination but one of mutual dependence. Both are created and neither is absolute. Each is correlative to the other. It is only by recognizing this and not by exalting one at the expense of the other that the true unity of the cosmos, and of man, is seen. That unity lies not in the lordship of one cosmic aspect over another, but in the Lordship of God over all and in that divinely ordained structure in which each finds its peculiar place and function.

5. A conviction governing a great deal of the scientific concern with man is that man is not a finished product of creation but is an unfinished, malleable and open-ended something, which, having been produced by mother nature, is being moved by evolutionary forces into a promising future. It is this conviction which justifies for many scientists the various forms of genetic engineering. Bio-medical science, in this context, is not concerned, as it was in the past, simply to support or heal; it is concerned to program and direct, and in this way to be as creative as nature itself. A Christian should, I think, not ignore the dynamic aspects of human existence, but neither should he lose sight of the static structures which set limits to man's nature and within which the elements of potentiality are confined. Because man is divinely

structured I find it hazardous, if not impious, to tamper with the genetic core. To tamper with the genes seems to me to outrun God into an unknown future and to exercise an elective discrimination mere men do not possess.

6. Even though bio-medical science is still captive to the spirit of specialization and is still attached to the abstract method which tends to ignore the religious and moral dimensions of man, there seems nevertheless to be a growing awareness in parts of the scientific community of the need for interdisciplinary studies. Insofar as this awareness exists it may represent a breakthrough in the consciousness of investigators that man is indeed a whole, that he runs the gamut of the created universe, that he is a microcosm, and that by the nonsynthetic, noncomprehensive procedures of classical natural science he can be neither understood nor preserved as human.

20

Toward a Human Medicine

I AM NOT a physician and am therefore disqualified from speaking in any professional way about the technical, diagnostic, and healing procedures of medical practice. When, as a layman, I nevertheless make an address to the subject of this essay, I do so in the expectation that the reader will place the emphasis, not on the word "medicine," but on the word "human." I shall centrally be asking, "What is man?" That is, what is man that the medical fraternity should "be mindful of him"?

The Judaeo-Christian conception of man is that of a personal being who is first of all an individual. Now an individual, if human, is not a mere atom of existence; he stands within a complex network of relations. But he also stands apart; he is singular. Each man, every man, is distinct, unique. As such he forms an impenetrable boundary to all other existences. Being "separate," he has his own private identity, an identity that may not be ignored, compromised, or invaded, but only respected. Because every man has his individuality, no normal man craves long-run anonymity. To exist means to stand out, and if a man exists he wants to stand out, even when he is not outstanding. He does not want to be lost in the crowd, be absorbed in the mass, or be reduced to a number. He wants to be identified, named, singled out. When in our treatment of someone we fail in any measure to fulfill this need, we to that extent diminish and dehumanize him. This sometimes happens within the medical community.

As an individual, moreover, man is never a mere thing, an object. He is a subject, an active, dynamic center of will and power. He is a focus of energy. The human individual is alive, propulsive, and creative. He is marked not so much by passivity as by activity. He is not so much a patient as an agent. In an engagement with a thing, an object, there is no need to elicit the thing's consent. The thing can be manipulated at will, for it itself has no will, no freedom, no creativity. It is otherwise with man. There is no way, except in extreme emergencies or when a man is in an unconscious state, that one can legitimately bypass his inherent agency and spontaneity. Doctors know this, of course. They know that for healing, not operation, but co-operation is needed, but this is sometimes forgotten, and when it is the medicine is less than human.

Moreover, the human individual is rational. He possesses, is an active embodiment of, reason. Now, to possess reason is to be able to think, and human beings, as we all know, are able to do this. But reason is not exhausted in thinking. Thinking merely as such, is a kind of technical competence. It is not to be despised; it is in fact indispensable to the conduct of human affairs. But it is not uniquely human; the higher animals seem capable of manipulating a simple means-ends calculus. But they are not on that account rational in the true and human sense of the word. Reason, as this is embodied in human beings, extends not only to the cognitive, but also to the affective and evaluational dimensions of existence. Reason in man is not only technical; it is this, but more; it is ontological. Reason in man is an ability to grasp the shape and structure of the universe, and to put himself in touch with that overarching order under which he resides. It is by reason that man is able, not merely to move in prescribed ways from premises to conclusions, but to discern, and if not to discern then to posit, a universal law, and the ends of human striving appropriate thereto. To be rational is not only to know how, but to know what, and to know why. To be humanly rational is, in short, to be constituted not merely narrowly scientific, but metaphysical and moral.

These remarks on rationality are meant in part to remind the physician that the sick man under his care has the gift of intelligence (however great or small) and that account must be taken of this. The so-called patient must be addressed as a hearer and giver of reasons. Proposed procedures, and their actual or possible consequences, should be discussed with him, not simply imposed. And every effort should be made to assure that the consent elicited from him is an *informed* consent. But these remarks bear even more directly on the physician's own grasp of rationality. He is a scientist, and as a scientist he is by training and practice tempted more than most individuals to equate know-how with knowledge and technical mastery with wisdom. Under these circumstances he does well to remind himself that reason or rationality is a much broader and deeper thing than the technological competence that modern philosophy and science has made it out to be.

I have thus far considered man as an individual, in abstraction from the relations he sustains. There is therefore more to be said about him. But I shall pause here to sum up what has been said. I have ventured to declare that in the Judaeo-Christian view man is an individual and as such unique, dynamic, and rational; that he is an individual and as such distinct, creative, and transcendental; that he is an individual and as such inviolable, agential, and valuational; that he is, in short, a centered-self, or person. If this account of man be correct, and I think it is, it sets certain norms for practice, also for medical practice. It means that man is never to be so approached, confronted, or handled as to ignore or violate his unique self-identity, his true agency, and his attachment to and engagement with transcendental norms of being and acting. He is to be treated always and only as a person—never as an anonymous entity, never as a mere patient or object, never as a shallow existent without those dimensions of depth and height by which he sets himself upon ends and is constituted religious and moral.

Man, I suggested, is an individual. But individuality is not atomistic particularity. One *is* an individual, one *becomes* an individual, with all the notes of individuality I have already recorded (identity, agency, and rationality) only in relation. In the Judaeo-Christian view there are three relationships within which the human individual is ineluctably caught up.

The first of these relationships is that between himself and God. The Judaeo-Christian man understands himself to be in an unbreakable ontic (even though a disturbed moral) relation to a transcendent self, who because he is a self cannot be invaded, and who because he is transcendent cannot be comprehended, but who because he is God is an unavoidable presence in man's consciousness. Man, in this view, though estranged from God, is not a stranger to God; and God, though offended by man, is not careless of man. God, in this view, is self-existent, and does not *become* God in and with his relationship to man. Man, on the other hand, is man only as he is related to God. It is because of God's creational activity and his providential ordering that man exists and endures, and that he is *what* he is. Human self-hood is accordingly centrally constituted and perpetually guaranteed by the God-man relation. Man is and becomes a person *coram deo.* It is before the face of God that man attains to self-identity, agency, and rationality—the essential ingredients of responsibility. It is possible, of course, to deny that God exists, and consequently to deny that humanness is basically constituted by an ontic relation to the transcendent, but for theists this does not alter the fact; it only obscures for the denier the depth dimension in every man, and thereby diminishes his dignity. In the Judaeo-Christian view man has dignity, for in his very being he is attached to God, and in his constitution he resembles God. He is *imago dei*— on which account there is a kind of sacredness about him which in each one's dealing with him must be kept inviolate. All this amounts to saying that man is a symbol and mirror of that which transcends the relativities of time and space. On this account we owe each man respect. It means, furthermore, that man's being (and that includes his body) is neither at his own disposal, simply as such, nor at the disposal of a physician or surgeon. We have indeed been made stewards of ourselves, but we are obliged to be responsive and responsible stewards, for we are not our own, but God's, and we are answerable to him for what he has given us in pawn.

What does this entail for the practice of medicine? I hazard the generalization that no procedures should be adopted which tend to horizontalize and secularize, and so de-humanize, the patient. I further opine that the art of the physician is likely to be most effectual when it is exercised in concert with the chaplain, the curator of souls. More importantly, it is to be observed that man being what he is—a being in touch with God—is never to be treated as a means, not even as a means toward increased "scientific" knowledge, but only as an end. The experiments conducted on the cure for syphilis in which a control group of syphilitic patients went untreated for scientific purposes, goes counter to every moral value, and offends humanity. It reduces man to a means, and thus dehumanizes him. As for the matter of dignity, the medical instructor who entered the hospital room trailed by a bevy of interns, and unceremoniously uncovered a sheeted woman and began pointing, was apparently unconscious that it was a person—and not a thing—he was pointing at. The story is that the woman—in defense of her dignity—gathered the sheet about her, and obstructed observation. I must acknowledge that I admire her for that, for she recognized that one may not be undressed before being addressed.

There is a second relation that must now be considered, and it bears with maximum directness on the work of the physician. Man is related not only to God, but also to nature—to the inorganic and organic world about him. Man is, in fact, rooted in this world. It is not only about him; it is in him. Man is physical. Man's kinship with nature in his body is a state of affairs that no amount of idealism or asceticism can manage to obscure, and authentic theism has never wished to deny it. Man in the Judaeo-Christian view is an embodied soul or an ensouled body, a psycho-somatic unity, with the closest of ties to nature. This is why so much can be done for him by natural science and by the arts and techniques of medicine and surgery. But in this view man is not a mere *product* of nature; he is more than a congeries of molecules. Implanted in nature, he yet rises above it. Participating in the vitalities of *bios*, he participates also in the realm of mind, and mind is not matter, not even the most complicated matter. Of course, neither is matter mind. A proper view of man is provided neither by idealism nor by materialism. Man is neither mere *psyche* nor mere *soma*, but the two indefeasibly combined in a psycho-somatic unity. Not in the same way as God, but in analogy to him, man is both immanent in nature and transcendent to it. This is why he can both fall victim to the determinations and ravages of nature, and in freedom rise to superiority and victory over it. In fact, this is why science, and in particular medical science, is possible at all. Were man simply immersed in nature, no rational control of nature would be possible, for nothing rises above its source—and man's source is God.

This state of affairs involves, I judge, entailments for the practice of medicine. Because man is neither (merely) a physical and chemical congeries of atoms, nor a living vegetable, nor a sentient animal, but something which, while akin to these things, supersedes them, the approach to and the treatment of even man's body cannot be simply that which is appropriate to inanimate things, or even to animate things—like animals—which in the hierarchy of beings lie below him. Man, even when contemplated as an organism, must be contemplated as an organism-plus. The *bios* of man's life is not that of even the highest animal. It is attended by psychic, social, and religious relations and dimensions that are transcendent to nature. Man is quantified, chemicalized, physicalized, and vitalized, but he is also spiritualized, and this affects and qualifies all the processes that take place within him. Even the physiology of an animal is different from that of a human, for human physiology is caught up in a matrix foreign to, because transcendent to, that of the animal. It would seem to follow that when a physician treats the body of a man, he does not really treat the body of the man unless he attends to more than the body. The body of a man is palpably not a mere body, but something which has super-bodily dimensions. To treat man only as a body is to treat him abstractly. And this dehumanizes him.

The third relation in which man stands is social. The individual, while being a centered-self, distinct from all others, with his own identity, is nevertheless racial. He is set in the context of other persons, all of whom belong to him, and all of whom in some sense constitute him. A self, if human, is not a self except in the company of what is not *his* self, but that of another. The ego demands the other ego for its very existence. The life of a man is inextricably intertwined with that of other men. No man—not even the most forsaken—is an island; he is part of the main. A man comes into the world through parents—ideally through the loving conjunction of an enduringly wedded man and woman intending a family, but in any case (at least until now) through the conjunction of man and woman. Every man, therefore, has kin, and in the treatment of him this may not be ignored. As an individual a man needs and deserves to be treated as separate and unique, not en masse. As a social creature, however, he needs and deserves to experience belongingness, acceptance, and embracement by his family, the physician, the hospital staff, and everyone else. To the extent such embracement is absent, the man is humanly impoverished.

I fear that with the trend toward scientific-medical specialization, and with the demise of the family doctor, the social side of the healing art has not come into its own. It is good, therefore, to hear that some medical schools have lately introduced special programs to train general practitioners who will make house calls and become once more a friend to the family.

21

Abortion*

THE FOLLOWING discussion of abortion is conducted by way of the question and answer method. It originated in response to a written questionnaire, and I have not thought it desirable to change the format in this republication. I hope the shape of the discussion will not appear to the reader as artificial or pedantic.

What is abortion?

Abortion, as it enters into current discussion, is to be distinguished from "miscarriage," which is the accidental and usually unwilled loss of the embryo or fetus. "Abortion" proper is the act by which the fruit of the womb is voluntarily and artificially removed at a time when such fruit is not independently viable. It is the deliberate, provoked expulsion from the womb of the mother of a living embryo or fetus which cannot survive without it. Abortion may be effected either through drugs (pharmaceutically) or through instruments (surgically).

What is an embryo or fetus?

The term "fetus" refers in general to the young of an animal or the offspring of a human being, before birth, that is, in the womb. In the first three months of its existence the fetus is usually called an embryo; thereafter, a fetus.

How does the sixth commandment apply to the abortion question?

In the broadest and most general terms, when we speak of abortion we are speaking of *terminating the existence of something*. This puts it immediately in the context of the sixth commandment: "Thou shalt not kill," that is, "Thou shalt not terminate the existence of something."

When we turn to the sixth commandment, however, we discover that in it bare literalness it is incomplete. It needs a twofold supplementation for proper understanding.

First, an object must be supplied, i.e., the "something" must be

*Parts of this contribution appeared in *The Banner* (June 4, 1971) and in *The Reformed Journal* (March, 1976).

specified. It seems plain that the commandment does not mean to say that we may not kill "anything." It is evident that we may (and should) terminate the existence of evil; we should kill cruelty, injustice, pride, and so on; we should mortify "the flesh." We may also kill weeds (use herbicides), and insects (use insecticides), and animals (resort to hunting or butchering). It appears that the object we must supply is humans, making the commandment read: "Thou shalt not kill humans."

Second, a condition must be supplied, i.e., the situation must be specified. In a sense, the commandment must be relativized, making it read: "Thou shalt not kill humans . . . *unless*, or *except*, or *without due cause.*"

Most of us believe that the State is authorized, under certain circumstances, to kill a criminal (in police or juridical action), or to kill an enemy soldier (in military action). Most of us believe that any of us is authorized to kill another when this other, without warrant or authority, radically threatens the life of the wards we are committed to protect. Most of us believe that at least in one situation a fetus may be killed, namely, to save the life of the mother when without intermediation the life of both mother and child will be lost.

It appears that the moral issue in abortion is whether the sixth commandment and other teachings of Scripture allow the expulsion of the fetus under other conditions and in other circumstances as well.

What are the basic issues in the abortion debate?

Apart from the medical or operational issue, there are, I think, three questions that are central in the debate:

1. Is the "something" we are talking about (the embryo or fetus) a human being, or something else?

2. If the fetus is a human being, is it, under the conditions of our existence, ever permissible or desirable to terminate its existence?

3. What role should society or statute law play in the regulation of abortion practices and procedures?

What is the answer to the first of these three questions?

That is a large question, and we shall have to pursue it for a while. The first thing to be observed is that the fetus is an in-between entity. It is obviously not a simple ununited spermatozoon, nor a simple unfertilized ovum. It is also not a postpartum baby or infant. It exists somewhere between these things. That is why people have disputed about its exact nature or status, and about whether it can be destroyed without moral fault.

What about the destruction of spermatozoa and ova?

That question pertains not to abortion but to birth control. It relates not to foeticide (the killing of the fetus) but to *germicide* (the killing of the sperm or ovum, particularly the former). Roman Catholic moralists have usually condemned germicide, the wasting or spoliation of the spermatozoa.

For this reason, among others, they have opposed the use of contraceptives and have regarded onanism (coitus interruptus) as a sin. Protestant moralists, however, have tended to recognize that since the sperm on the one hand, and the ovum on the other hand, carries only half of the genetic structure needed to produce a child, the destruction of either through contraceptive devices (or through onanism) is morally justifiable.

What about the destruction of the infant?

There has never been any doubt in Christian circles that this is a sin to be shunned with horror. From the beginning all Christians have condemned infanticide as practiced, for example, by the ancient Greeks and Romans.

If infanticide is wrong, and if germicide is right, what of foeticide, the destruction of the fetus?

In the history of ethics and of law, judgment here has depended on whether one assimilated the fetus either to the infant (the postpartum baby—the actually human) or to the sperm and ovum (the potentially human). Of course, the fetus is neither an infant, nor a sperm, nor an ovum, but the last two together—a fertilized ovum. It is neither an actual human being, nor the mere bare potentiality of humanness (as are the sperm and ovum), but something in the process of becoming human.

It is this in-between status of the fetus—this "becomingness" residing somewhere between being and non-being—that makes it hard to judge whether or not we are here dealing with an object that the sixth commandment has in view. Science, philosophy, theology, and law have had their say.

What does science say?

I am neither a scientist nor a physician, and I must speak here with reservations and extreme tentativeness.

Science, it seems, has determined that from the very moment of conception the fetal tissue constitutes a complete genetic package, and that nothing more is needed for its humanness than time and nourishment. If this be so, it tells significantly against regarding the embryo as being at any stage a mere blob of protoplasm.

There are complications, however. There is, for example, the puzzling bio-chemical problem in the case of identical twins. Involved here is a *single* fertilized ovum which splits as late as five days after conception, to form eventually two separate fetuses. There is, in addition, another problem. It has been established that a fertilized egg will never become an embryo or fetus unless it becomes attached to the uterine wall. This may take up to eight days, and very often it does not happen at all; many fertilized eggs are simply washed away in the menstrual stream.

This problem about uterine attachment bears on the use, in contraceptive contexts, of the "loop" (intra-uterine device). Some Christians condemn its use on the ground that it does not prevent fertilization of the egg, but does prevent an already fertilized egg from attaching itself to the uterine wall, and thus destroys it. This, they believe, is a plain case of abortion. I cannot condemn the use of the "loop." I am thereby saying, I suppose, that I do not regard the fertilized ovum as something in process of becoming human until it is implanted in the uterus.

What does philosophy say?

The Stoics tended to think that a child *in utero* had no separate existence. The fetus was not *homo*, nor *infans*, but merely *spes animantes.* It was regarded as merely a part of the mother, as the fruit is part of the tree until it falls.

More interesting, and more influential, is Aristotle. Aristotle distinguished three souls, or animating principles: the vegetative, the sensitive, and the rational. The vegetative soul made plants to live, the sensitive soul made animals to live, and the rational soul made humans to live. Or better, plants have a vegetative soul; animals have a vegetative *and* sensitive soul; and humans have a vegetative *and* sensitive *and* rational soul. But one lives before one is sensitive, and one is sensitive before one is rational. This leads to the notion of an evolutionary process, with three distinguishable stages: plant, animal, man. Applied to our subject, this philosophy poses the question: Does the fetus go through these three stages? Is it first a vegetable, then an animal, and only later a human?

What does theology say?

Christian theologians tended, like Aristotle, to make distinctions between periods of gestation (though some theologians and councils did not) and to speculate on when the embryo becomes animate, i.e., when the soul enters the organism.

In the seventeenth century some theologians held that a separate life comes into existence only at quickening, i.e., only when the mother first feels movement. Much earlier, and more moderate, Augustine believed that the body is created before the soul (cf. Genesis), and he distinguished between the *embryo informatus* (before endowed with a soul) and the *embryo formatus* (after so endowed), although he did not indicate the time at which the change or transition occurred. These are his words: "The body is created before the soul. The embryo before it is endowed with a soul is *informatus,* and its destruction by human agency is to be punished with a fine. The embryo *formatus* is endowed with a soul; it is an animate being; its destruction is murder and is to be punished with death."

Thomas Aquinas held a similar position. He taught that an embryo in its early stages was not a human being. It must during a period of time (forty days in the case of a male and eighty days in the case of a female) attain a certain degree of organization before it can become the seat of a rational principle. A contemporary Roman Catholic thinker, Joseph Donceel, declares: "With St. Thomas I teach that at the moment of conception there originates a vegetative organism that will slowly evolve into a sentient organism to become, at a moment I cannot determine, a rational organism, a real human being."

What does traditional law say?

In England after the fifteenth century common law declared that human life began at the moment of quickening. Abortion was therefore a criminal offense only after the fetus was quick.

Does the Bible say anything concerning the nature and status of the fetus?

Hardly anything. Texts are sometimes cited to prove that the Bible regards the embryo as human from the moment of conception, and that it therefore considers the destruction of the fertilized egg as the destruction of human life itself. Cited are texts like Genesis 25:22, where Esau and Jacob are said to have struggled together in the womb of their mother; or Jeremiah 1:5, where the Lord declares "before you were born I consecrated you"; or Luke 1:41, where John the Baptist is reported to have leaped in the womb of his mother Elizabeth. But these texts, couched in the religious language of faith, do not, in my judgment, speak with any directness to the question at issue.

The only text that does bear on the problem is Exodus 21:22–25, where the law provides a remedy when two men are fighting and a pregnant woman is injured so that she has a miscarriage. The law provides that "if no harm follows," then the man who hurt her is to be *fined* as her husband and the judges decide. The case contemplated here is not wholly germane to our question, for we have to do here with accidental miscarriage and not with deliberate abortion. But the clause "if no harm follows" is not without interest; it does seem at least to discount miscarriage as "harm."

How would you sum up the discussion we have been having on the first of the three basic issues in the abortion debate: Is the embryo or fetus a human being or not?

Because of what I have called the in-between status of the fetus I do not regard its destruction as tantamount to infanticide. What is destroyed in abortion is not a human being; at most it is something in process of becoming human. This, of course, is a great deal; and the fetus therefore deserves everyone's respect and protection. But one is not entitled to speak too quickly and too loudly of murder when the question of abortion is raised, particularly when it concerns the embryo in the very earliest stages of its existence.

Let's go on, now, to the second of the basic issues we have discriminated: Is it—under the conditions of our existence—ever permissible or desirable to terminate the existence of a fetus or embryo, even if there were no doubt concerning its status as a human being, that is, even if it were certain that the fetus or embryo is a veritable human being at every moment of its existence?

My answer to this question is: Yes, under carefully stipulated conditions. This amounts to saying that, in my judgment, no unbreakable rule may be laid down prohibiting all forced abortions. It is to say that the law of the Ten Commandments is to be brought into vital connection with the human situation and with the demands and insights of love, and that only subsequently can a truly moral decision and judgment be made. Because one must distinguish circumstances and situations one must also distinguish various kinds or types of abortion.

What types of abortion do you distinguish, and what is your judgment about each of them?

Let me tell you first about the kinds of abortion that I condemn.

I am radically opposed to what I call "arbitrary abortion"—i.e., abortion performed on women who request abortive procedures simply because they find it inconvenient or otherwise undesirable to have a child.

I am also opposed to what I call "demographic abortion"—i.e., abortion used simply as a means to restrict the size of the family, as a means of birth control, as a substitute for (or as a supplement to) the pill or contraceptive devices.

I am equally opposed to what I call "personal abortion"—i.e., abortions calculated to forestall nothing but personal embarrassment or social discredit, the pregnancy being due to socially and biblically proscribed immoralities such as fornication and adultery.

In all these cases, and perhaps in others, there is nothing to justify the taking of so sacred a thing as a life in process of becoming human.

What types of abortion do you justify?

Well, obviously, I justify what is known as "critical abortion"—i.e., abortion calculated to preserve the life of the mother when continued pregnancy radically threatens her life, and of course that of the fetus too. This sort of abortion is approved by all Protestant moralists, and is also sanctioned by the laws of every state in the union.

Are there any other types of abortion that you justify?

Yes, there are. Not every Christian will endorse my judgment, and among these dissenters are people whose friendship I cherish and whose Christian sensitivity and integrity I deeply respect.

Although I am not as certain about any of these as I am about critical abortion, I am disposed—on the ground that the value of unborn life must be weighed against the value of the life of the already born, and on the ground that we are not called on to increase by our generative activities the increment of evil already in the world—to classify as allowable abortions of the following additional types:

"Forecastive abortion"—i.e., abortion calculated to prevent the birth of a child who, because of the occurrence of German measles or because of the use of Thalidomide, and so forth, is likely to be horribly deformed or deranged.

"Social abortion"—i.e., abortion calculated to forestall dire personal and social consequences, the pregnancy being due to criminal behavior on the part of the father—rape or incest.

"Therapeutic abortion"—i.e., abortion calculated to preserve the physical and mental health of the mother when continued pregnancy will significantly and continuously undermine these.

I have named these three types in the order of their moral priority. I am more certain of the legitimacy of the first and second than I am of the third, but when all the conditions here recorded are maximally and assuredly present, I believe that these kinds of abortion are to be Christianly permitted.

We come, now, to the third of the three issues we discriminated: What is the role of society and statute law in all this?

I believe that the State—and strictly speaking only the State—has by God been given jurisdiction over life and death. Matters of this sort cannot be left to the desire or will of individuals, but must be regulated and controlled by duly enacted laws. Society, through the State, must function as the guardian and protector of fetuses as well as of the already born. The State must protect the potential as well as the actual members of society from arbitrary manipulation, and it must do so by clearly indicating by which duly authorized persons and under what conditions such manipulation may take place.

What do you think of the most recent Supreme Court ruling on abortion?

In 1973 the Supreme Court of the United States made a far-reaching decision on abortion. It declared, among other things, that in the first three months of pregnancy a woman may legally seek, and a physician may legally perform, an abortion on no other ground than that it is desired. This decision was applauded by many—not least by the radical wing of the women's liberation movement—but it startled and aggrieved many others, especially those whose consciences had been formed under the influence of the Gospel.

What offended the latter—and what offends me—is that the decision fails to pay sufficient respect to the emerging human life which is present in the womb. Such life is precious and should not be terminated without due cause. The simple desire of the prospective mother (and father) to be rid of the fetus is not a sufficient reason to effect its destruction. Abortion "on demand" suffers from arbitrariness and is on this account morally unacceptable. There must be grounds for the demand before abortion can be ethically justified. The fetus, not being the property of the mother, but a relatively independent being in the process of becoming human, may not be disposed of at will.

Therefore, soon after the Court's decision, concerned citizens understandably marshalled their forces in behalf of the fetus and set up Right to Life movements across the country. The movement has done much good. By way of education it has called attention to the sacredness of human life and to the legitimate claims on protection that accrues to the innocent and defenseless. More than that, it has supplemented education with political action. It is currently sponsoring a right-to-life amendment to the Constitution.

The amendment provides for a definition and extension of the word "person" as this appears in the fifth and fourteenth amendments of the Constitution. The proposal is that the word "person" shall henceforth be understood to denominate not only the postpartum individuals which the Supreme Court adjudged to be in the purview of the Constitution, but also all unborn embryos and fetuses "at every stage of their biological development"—presumably even at the point of conception.

What is your attitude toward the proposed amendment?

I have observed that many fellow-Christians with whom I sit around the communion table, some colleagues, and a significant number of the seminary students with whom I am still associated, are ardent supporters of this proposal. I regret that on this issue I find it hard to join their company.

My first difficulty concerns the language that my friends are using. There is an established vocabulary in the area of genetics and obstetrics, but a revisionist tendency is undermining the linguistic establishment. In recent years the descriptive word "abortion" has too often and too quickly been taken as a synonym of the valuative word "murder." It is now proposed that the biological words "blastocyst," "embryo," and "fetus" be equated with the philosophical and theological word "person." I find this language shift too facile, and not a little confusing. Analysis is impeded, and issues are obscured, when verbal conventions are unnecessarily violated. It is odd to say that squirrels bury oaks when it is acorns that they store. I think it similarly odd to call a fertilized ovum, simply as such, a veritable though microscopic person.

Conceivably, even probably, at least some supporters of the proposed constitutional amendment are not wanting by the use of the word "person" to make an ontological or theological judgment about the status of an embryo in the hierarchy of being, but only pragmatically attaching themselves to the existing language of the Constitution in order to secure for the embryo the legal status and protection accorded by our fundamental law to all individuals born of human parents. If this be the case, the move is not in itself an improper political maneuver, but it has a number of questionable entailments.

As already indicated, the proposed amendment would legally oblige us to adopt the term "unborn person" to name a fertilized ovum even before implantation, i.e., before it meets one of the necessary (indispensable) conditions for ever becoming a baby or even an embryo. This I consider to be inadmissible.

In addition, the amendment provides that "no unborn person shall be deprived of life by any person . . . except to prevent the death of the mother." This provision should by itself give pause to the Protestant and Roman Catholic sponsors of the amendment. Will Catholics now, in contravention of their ethical tradition, allow the fetus to die in order to save the life of the mother? And why should Protestants, in accordance with their ethical tradition, prefer to save the mother rather than the fetus? Must not the tradition at least be rethought, inasmuch as now the issue of death is between two persons, and one of them is innocent besides?

But there is more. If a fertilized ovum is a person, and always to be so regarded, then a DNC performed by a physician on a woman after criminal rape may itself be adjudged a criminal act, it being, or possibly being, the deliberate killing of an innocent person. It would appear, in addition, that backed by the amended Constitution states would be legally able to proscribe the use of intra-uterine devices to prevent pregnancy, or punish a woman for taking a morning-after pill. This is hardly the sort of legislation which is to be recommended or authorized.

Part VII

JUDGMENT AND PARDON

22

Judgment: Divine and Human*

THE ENGLISH words "judging" and "judgment" have a variety of meanings. In logic "to judge" is no more than to establish a mental relation between two or more terms, and a "judgment" is simply a proposition which affirms or denies a connection between concepts. In psychology "judgment" is only another name for perspicacity or sagacity, a quality which is ascribed to one who has the gift of discernment and a capacity for sound appraisal. In the Old Testament the word "judgment," generally in the plural, is sometimes used to designate the Torah, i.e., the sum of God's testimonies and ordinances. But the central context of the term is in jurisprudence, where "to judge" means "to test or try," and where a "judgment" is a "judicial decision." This is the context—the context of justice—in which the words are chiefly employed in the Bible.

Back of this, however, and providing the ultimate context of the words, is, on the one hand, the righteousness of God (a blend of justice and love), and, on the other, the moral and spiritual posture and behavior of men and societies residing in a fallen world. In this ethico-judicial context the framework of judging and judgment is the divinely established moral order; the central concepts are those of good and evil, right and wrong; and the operative principle is that what a man sows that he shall also reap. The standard of judgment, however, is not the bare law, but the law and the Gospel. What ultimately decides a man's eternal destiny is his attitude to the Savior Jesus Christ. By faith in him a man is justified and acquitted (Rom. 3:24–26); by disbelief in or rejection of him a man remains under law and is by that law found guilty and condemned (Gal. 2:16).

In the Scriptures God and Christ are presented as judges who, in terms of Gospel and law, pass a verdict on men, their sentiments, and their actions, and who in history and at the end of it either vindicate or condemn them.

According to the Scriptures God is the judge of all the earth. He is the

*Appeared first in *The Zondervan Pictorial Encyclopedia of the Bible,* Merrill C. Tenney, ed., Grand Rapids: The Zondervan Corporation, 1975.

judge, and fitted to be this, because with him is ultimate authority, unlimited knowledge, supreme righteousness, ineffable love, and unrestricted power.

God, as the Scriptures witness, is the creator of heaven and earth. He is thus Lord of the universe. His jurisdiction knows no bounds, and his authority is absolute. Because he is God he is the very standard of justice and equity, to his judgments all men are obliged to conform, and from his decisions there is no appeal.

God is the great discerner. Being the ultimate determiner of good and evil, he perceives with unerring accuracy the distinctions between these. He is also the great discriminator. With absolute nicety he sifts the elements in men's behavior, and like an expert winnower, separates and weighs the good and evil ingredients in the human moral complex. And he is omniscient. Nothing is hid from his sight. Piercing beyond the superficial and external, he sees into the depths and perceives the intents and purposes of the heart.

God is always found on the side of the good. To evil he addresses no word but No!, and to every good his word is Yes! Indeed, it may be said that his affirmations and negations are what constitute good and evil, for he is the final determiner. In any case all his judgments are just and righteous. Because he judges rightly, the oppressed and aggrieved find in him their advocate and support. In this sense his judgments are often saving, and are as such a token of his love (Dt. 32:36; Ps. 10:18; 2 Thess. 1:5,6).

God's justice most clearly coalesces with his love in the act by which he delivered his only Son into condemnation and death in order that through his sacrifice and merits men may have pardon and life (Rom. 8:32; Gal. 1:4). The Old Testament saint knew that God saved by his righteousness (Ps. 31:1), but in Christ it is made unmistakably clear that mercy and forgiveness flow to men through the judicial sentence passed by God on the Son of his love (Jn. 11:51,52).

The power of God to execute the sentences he imposes and to protect those whom he vindicates is limitless. Those whom he judges are veritably judged, being gripped or upborne by his omnipotence. No one is strong enough to snatch the lambs from his bosom or to withstand the vigor of his wrath and the force of his sentence (Ps. 54:1; Rev. 18:8).

Christ came into the flesh to inaugurate and establish the Kingdom of God which had been promised beforehand and which is to be consummated at the end of the age. He came, therefore, not in judgment, but in grace (Jn. 3:17). Yet, since in his person, message, and deeds he is the touchstone of destiny for all, his very presence in the world was a judgment. By his redeeming presence the world was judged (Jn. 9:39), and its prince (Jn. 16:11), and all who disbelieved (Jn. 3:18). Moreover, although he refused during his earthly ministry to be a judge in mundane matters (Lk. 12:14), he will reappear in glory at the last day to preside at the great and final assize in which all will appear before his judgment seat to receive from him the divine and irrevocable verdict upon their lives (Jn. 5:22–30; Acts 10:42; Rom. 2:16).

Although the men of Nineveh will arise at the judgment and condemn the evil generation which sought a sign from Jesus (Mt. 12:41), and although Christ gives his Church the keys of the Kingdom (Mt. 16:19) and declares that his enthroned disciples will judge the twelve tribes of Israel (Mt. 19:26), and although Paul says that the saints will judge the world and angels (1 Cor. 6:2,3), God in Christ will not therefore vacate the judgment seat. Repentant gentiles will no doubt shame the unbelieving Jews on the day of the Lord, and the lives and testimonies of the redeemed will be to those who are not in Christ like the accusations of their conscience, but, with the saints concurring in his verdicts, Christ alone will be the Judge.

Although the great day of judgment is still in the offing, divine judgments have long been on the earth, and judgment is daily being passed.

In the past it was by the judgment of God that the antediluvian civilization was washed away by the flood (Gen. 6:5–7), that Israel was sent into exile (Jer. 20:4), and that the several nations in the prophecies of Amos were scourged or destroyed. Chief and most fateful of all such judgments was, of course, that which brought condemnation and death to all mankind on account of Adam's trespass (Gal. 5:15,16).

In the present, because God maintains the moral order, his judgments still fall on men and nations. More importantly, just as during his life on earth, so yet today Christ is set for the rise and fall of men, and the judgment that is implicit in his person is even now separating men into two camps. It is by virtue of this fact that believers can in the present, before the final judgment, know and rejoice that for them there is and will be no condemnation (Rom. 8:1,38).

But a day is coming, which no man knows (Mt. 24:36), when the Lord will come in majesty, put an end to history, gather before him all those who ever lived, and seal their destiny with a decisive and unalterable verdict (Mt. 12:36; Jn. 12:48; Acts 17:31; Rom. 14:10; 2 Cor. 5:10).

Not only are judges in human courts of law authorized to make judgments in civil and criminal cases, but all men everywhere are permitted and even obliged to assess human claims upon truth, beauty, or goodness, and to appraise the character, conduct, and teaching both of themselves and of their fellows.

But judgment that is uninformed, impulsive, superficial, premature, or biased is strictly forbidden in the Bible. Bigotry and censoriousness is emphatically denounced. Christians are urged, when they judge, to do it in a constructive spirit and in accordance with authentic norms. All other judging is contraband, particularly the sort that preempts Christ's prerogative to determine a man's eternal destiny.

23

The Nature of Forgiving Biblically Described*

A. FORGIVENESS: GOD

THE BIBLE is a book about God, and when it speaks about anything—also about forgiveness—it speaks about it in the context of God, and not primarily of man. Three things may here be observed:

1. Forgiveness is a divine prerogative; only God can finally forgive. Forgiveness is a work of God alone. It is deep-down a supernatural act. It comes from heaven.

   a. This is illustrated in two events in Jesus' life.
      (1) Matthew 9:2–6 (Mk. 2:5–10; Lk. 5:20)—"Jesus said to the paralytic... 'Your sins are forgiven....' The Scribes said... 'This man is blaspheming....'" Jesus responded, "'But that you may know that the Son of Man has authority on earth to forgive sins....'"
      (2) Luke 7:49—In the house of Simon, Jesus said to a woman of the city who was a sinner, "Your sins are forgiven." Whereupon those who sat with him at table asked, "Who is this, who even forgives sins?"

   b. This means that no person can remit another's sins. We can remove the obstacle to our own fellowship with him; we can be reconciled to him. We cannot reconcile him to God, i.e., really "save" him, really put him in accord once more with the universe. The saying in John 20:23—"If you forgive the sins of any, they are forgiven; if you retain the sins of any they are retained"—is therefore not to be interpreted in the Roman Catholic sense. The words doubtless mean that "as they are inspired by the Holy Spirit (vs. 22) the followers of Jesus, established in the Church, will be able to judge (or are authorized to

*This contribution was constructed as an outline to guide discussion at a conference.

judge) which categories of men have sins forgiven, and which not" (R. R. Morris).

2. Forgiveness is not something that is logically implied in the concept "God." It is not a necessity of the divine being. Divine forgiveness is simply free grace, to be regarded with awe and wonder. "Forgiveness is not deduced from an idea of God, but is disclosed as his act in the event of salvation" (Bultmann). "We can know nothing of forgiveness unless it is explicitly revealed to us. It is as an unimaginable revelation, as a gift which could never be taken for granted, as a free, gracious gift, that forgiveness is proclaimed in the Bible" (Brunner). "In him we have redemption through his blood, the forgiveness of our trespasses, according to the riches of his grace, which he lavished upon us" (Eph. 1:7).

3. Forgiveness is the concentrated essence of God's action in behalf of man; it is the sum of God's gracious activity usward. A study of the Scriptures discloses that "forgiveness of sins" is identical with "justification," "redemption," and "salvation."

   a. The word "forgiveness," favored by Luke and used widely in the Synoptics and in Acts, is used only sparingly by Paul, who prefers "justification" and "reconciliation." But whether the term "justification" is used, or "forgiveness," the reference is to the same powerful, supernatural, and all-inclusive event which may be called "salvation."

   b. "Forgiveness of sins" is the total conferment of God on men, including the cancelling not only of past sins, but also of those of the present and future; and not only the cancelling of sins, but also renewal of life, the creation of a completely new situation, and a restoration to a living fellowship with God.

   c. Luther accordingly said of the words of the Apostles' Creed "I believe in the forgiveness of sins" that "all the other articles lead up to the single article on forgiveness of sins, and come together in this article, as it were in a circle" (in a sermon on Peter's Denial).

B. FORGIVENESS: LAW

The second dimension in which forgiveness finds its meaning is *Law*—and the related concept of *Justice*.

1. The term "Law" is simply a word to describe God's Holy Will to establish a Kingdom of Love, and represents his determination not to be thwarted in his sovereign purposes.

2. All men reside under this Law and are judged by it. In terms of it they are righteous or unrighteous, vicious or virtuous, guilty or innocent. Since the Fall, outside of grace, all men are, of course, unrighteous, guilty; they are in opposition to God's purposes and under condemnation; they are under the sentence of death.

3. Forgiveness, as the Scriptures reveal it, is to be understood in this setting.

   a. God, who forgives, is and always remains a *Judge*.

   b. And what God the Judge does when he forgives is what is done in court; he pardons a criminal, releases a prisoner, remits a penalty, absolves the guilty, acquits the sentenced one.

4. The "legal" or "juridical" sense of the words "to forgive" and "forgiveness" is common to both Old and New Testaments.

   a. The three Hebrew words for "forgiveness"—*Kaphar*, "to cover"; *Nasa*, "to lift up or away"; and *Salach*, "to send away"—do indeed invite a *sacrificial* interpretation and conjure up an image of an altar in the temple, but it may not be forgotten that "the Old Testament cultus, especially the sacrifice, was a legal action instituted to restore and to proclaim the right covenant relation between God and man" (Markus Barth).

   b. The three (or four) Greek words for "forgiveness"—*Apoluo*, "to loose"; *Charizomai*, "to be gracious to"; *Aphiemi*, "to let off"; and *Paresis*, "a passing by"—do have a predominantly *juridical* sense and evoke images of courts, legal processes, judges, and the like. This does not mean that the sacrificial meaning is absent here, but the accent is on the juridical. The most typical New Testament words for forgiveness—*Aphesis* and *Aphienai*—are concepts taken from the realm of law, and they suggest acquittal, a notion which brings "forgiveness" into the closest possible connection with "justification." It may be remarked in passing that those who were responsible for Jesus' death are regarded as murderers rather than as priests. It was Christ himself who was the Priest and the Lamb.

5. The upshot of this brief discussion of law and the juridical is that "forgiveness" is unthinkable without "judgment."

a. He who forgives says "You are guilty," "You are wrong." He who forgives never ceases to be a judge. It is not the innocent whom one forgives; nor the whole whom Jesus saves. God "justifies the wicked," he saves *sinners*. By the same token when we forgive our neighbor we appraise him as guilty. "The willingness to forgive does not involve treating the original offense and the resulting injury as though they never happened or were unimportant. Forgiveness is sternly realistic. When every allowance has been made, when every legitimate excuse has been accepted, the verdict still must be—'This was wrong.' Otherwise there would be no call for forgiveness" (Anon.).

b. By the same token, to receive or to accept forgiveness is to *recognize* oneself as in the wrong, to *confess* one's guilt. It is a logical impossibility to be forgiven without such a confession. He who forgives and he who receives forgiveness must concur at least in this: there is guilt and it lies precisely here.

c. So significant is this fact that it sometimes appears that the mere confession of guilt is able to wipe it out. This is not really so, of course, but experience seems to teach that in courts of law when the evidence runs strong against a defendant a plea of "guilty" will excite the judge to leniency, and one recalls that "John the Baptist told the people (Mk. 1:4,5) to confess publicly their sins, lest the fire-bringing judge destroy them by his imminent appearance" (Markus Barth). It seems, too, that in our relations with our fellows nothing is so calculated to trigger a forgiving spirit in us as an admission of guilt by the offending person.

d. But confession alone will not justify forgiveness or remove guilt. For that something else is required. In the Biblical representation what is required—or at any rate what is supplied—is a death and a resurrection, a cross and an empty tomb.

C. FORGIVENESS: ATONEMENT

Forgiveness in the Bible is nonexistent without Christ. Christ means more than one is able to say, but he does mean that forgiveness, i.e., exemption from the effects of wrongdoing, cannot be had for nothing. There is no cheap grace. It is impossible simply to forgive—just like that. Someone must pay, or else the moral world-order would be overthrown.

1. Christian theology has therefore always looked to the cross as the ground of forgiveness—both of God's forgiveness of us, and of our forgiveness of our fellows. It is not my intention to elaborate here a theology of the cross; and there are no doubt many ways of conceiving of the happening on Golgotha. But one way of thinking of it—amply set forth in Scripture—is to think of Christ as bearing the sentence of death for us. His was a substitutionary atonement. He was the Lamb of God who, bearing the sins of mankind, took away the sins of the world and made forgiveness possible. Without this death, this sacrifice, we would still be in our sins—and not even God, or especially not God, could remove or forgive them. What happened, of course, is that God punished himself, absorbed our guilt, and so blotted out our transgressions.

   The cross of Christ is the ground, the legitimizing foundation for our forgiving our fellow men. We may, and must, forgive for Christ's sake—there is no other justification for our forgiving action. But I suspect that, like God in Christ, we, too, cannot really forgive anyone unless we take a "cross" upon us. We cannot obviously "atone" for the sins and hurts committed against us, but we must—if we are truly to forgive—be able to bear the shock of them and in some real sense absorb them. Some suffering, some humiliation we must undergo, i.e., some refusal to hold the offender to account, some refusal to assert ourselves, some willingness to pay out of our own account the debt remaining. In doing this we shall, of course, not really be hurting—we will be entering into that new life of which Christ's resurrection is the ground and guarantee.

2. It must be noted, in the second place, that it is not only the cross which is the ground of forgiveness; so is the resurrection. There is a very important word of Paul which says: "If Christ has not been raised, your faith is futile and you are still in your sins" (1 Cor. 15:17).

   a. This expression can be easily explained in terms of the cross, i.e., it can be explained as meaning that the resurrection simply completes the cross and vindicates its efficacy. It does do this, no doubt, but it probably also does more. The resurrection is, as it were, an additional or independent ground for the possibility and reality of forgiveness. (I owe this insight to Markus Barth.)

   b. The apostles in Acts accuse the slayers of Jesus of murder and in the same breath preach to them the forgiveness of sins. Why? Because the *corpus delicti* no more exists! Jesus is alive! The murderers are acquitted. They are free! There is no charge against them, for Christ lives!

3. All this means that since Christ's death and resurrection, acquittal, pardon, exemption, forgiveness, release exists, is there, is real. Men have only to believe this, grasp it, enter into it, appropriate it. This activity is called in the Scriptures *Repentance* or, alternatively, *Faith*, which we must next consider.

D. FORGIVENESS: REPENTANCE

1. Justification is through faith; forgiveness of sins is through repentance. Faith and repentance are not grounds of justification and forgiveness; they are appropriations of these things. Without them the circle is not closed. That is why for full and complete forgiveness there must be this movement into it. There must be seizure; there must be repentance.

2. Repentance is insisted on again and again when the Scriptures speak of forgiveness. For example, Mark 1:4—"John the baptizer appeared in the wilderness, preaching a baptism of repentance for the forgiveness of sins." Luke 24:47—Then Christ said to them: "Thus it is written, that the Christ should suffer and on the third day rise from the dead, and that repentance and forgiveness of sins should be preached in his name to all nations." Acts 2:38—"And Peter said to them, 'Repent and be baptized every one of you in the name of Jesus Christ for the forgiveness of your sins.'"

3. Repentance has to do then with the reception of forgiveness.

   a. Repentance is not the doing of penance, but it is a resolute turning away from the bondage of sin, it is accepting release from captivity, it is putting aside evil habits, renouncing erstwhile wrongs, and it is entering into freedom, into newness of life, and into *communion*.

   b. This communion of man with God, and of man with man, is what forgiveness is about. It involves, as repentance, both mortification and vivification; a dying unto sin and a living unto Christ. It involves recapitulating the death and resurrection of our Lord.

   c. From this point of view repentance *is* forgiveness, it is salvation, it is peace, fellowship, and communion. And on the human level—

between man and man—it is reconciliation, the absence of resentment, forgetfulness.

d. Repentance and forgiveness means that hurts are forgotten, remembered no more. The fact can still be recalled, but the fact has in forgiveness lost all power to hurt; its capacity to separate and estrange is gone.

4. There are passages in the book of Hebrews (6:1–8; 10:26–31; 12:15–17) which declare that "it is impossible to restore again to repentance those who have once been enlightened," and there is a word of Jesus which declares that "every sin and blasphemy will be forgiven men, but the blasphemy against the Spirit will not be forgiven" (Mt. 12:31,32; Mk. 2:28,29; Lk. 12:10).

   a. The texts in Hebrews describe men who represent the nadir of folly, who in the presence of pardon and open doors choose to remain captive, and so be without hope. These texts declare "that, outside the freedom and holiness given through Jesus Christ, there is absolutely no other chance to repent, to be forgiven and to be liberated for a free man's life in the community. The sin committed "voluntarily" after the hearing of the good news is described as a new crucifixion and public mockery of Christ that will inherit nothing but condemnation and fire" (Markus Barth, *Acquittal*, p. 80).

   b. And as for the sin against the Holy Spirit, this unforgivable sin is not any specific act of sin; it is the continuing blasphemy against the Spirit of God, the act of one who consistently rejects God's gracious call. There is a parallel to this in interpersonal relations, where the offending party resolutely refuses to accept forgiveness, and communion becomes impossible.

E. FORGIVENESS: RESPONSIBILITY

1. When God forgives a man, he lays a burden on him. God's mercies are yokes—light indeed, but yokes nevertheless. His *Gabe* is for those who take it always an *Aufgabe*. It is not a gift first, and then a command. It is both at once. For he who accepts forgiveness accepts responsibility in the same act. To be forgiven is to be forgiving. To be forgiven, to enter into forgiveness, is to be humble, self-effacing, without resentment, no longer judgmental, understanding, helpful.

   Moreover, to be forgiven is to be in the fellowship of God, indeed to be in Christ, i.e., to have his mind and spirit. Hence it is to be, like Christ, forgiving. This is why forgiving our debtors and being forgiven our debts are always joined together in the Scripture. Our forgiving our debtors is not, in the Lord's Prayer, a ground for God's forgiving us. It is simply that these two involve each other. Christ's remission of our sins is the reason we forgive, but our forgiving is the sign and witness of our having been forgiven. In the absence of a forgiving spirit we forfeit every claim to having been forgiven.

2. The number of times we are to forgive the one who sins against us is infinite—seven times seventy—the number of completion. This is to say that our readiness and disposition to forgive must be constant and uninterrupted. From our side the channels of communication must always be kept clear. This means that our patience should not wear out, nor our concern harden and atrophy.

3. Of course, this forgiveness or readiness to forgive must never degenerate into *condonation*, into acquiescence in wrong-doing. The forgiving spirit, and the offer of forgiveness, is compatible with censure, if not with censoriousness. It is also consonant with a call for repentance and amendment, and in some cases—as with a son or daughter—with chastisement and discipline.

4. But when all is said and done, it remains true that having been made free through forgiveness, we are to seek to make others free in the same way. We are, as Luther says, to be little "Christs" to our fellow men, granting them amnesty and annulment and enticing them to enter into communion, leaving behind them their anxieties and guilts.

5. It should be observed that just as it is only Christ who can release us from our ultimate load of guilt—the sin we have committed against God—so in human affairs it is only we, and not other persons, who can forgive those who have sinned against us. In this sense we are indispensable, or nearly so; we are the particular answer to his special need. We must therefore always be available to him, more concerned about his welfare than our own, active in creating a new situation in which he may find new resources and prospects.

24

Does God Hate Some Men?

THERE ARE those, it appears, who argue against the universal love of God on the ground that God hates some men. The argument goes this way: "God hates some men, *therefore* he does not love all men." My concern in this essay is primarily with the *material* premise of this argument; I wish centrally to inquire whether we are biblically justified in saying that God hates some men. But I wish also to consider in passing whether we are *logically* justified in connecting this assertion with one about God's love.

Beginning with the latter point, which need not detain us long, let me say at once that I have no quarrel with the *logic* of the argument. I agree that in its true and pregnant meaning hate is the antithesis of love. Hate and love are contradictories; they exclude each other, when considered in relation to the same object. It is logically sound, therefore, to declare that if God hates some person, he does not love him; and if God loves some person, he does not hate him. If it can be established that God hates *some* men, it will have to be conceded that he does not love *all* men. Conversely, if it can be established that God loves all men, we are thereby prevented from saying in a truly meaningful way that he hates some of them.

This is not to say that love and hate cannot co-exist in God; it is only to say that both attitudes or dispositions cannot be taken up toward one and the same object. God can love one thing and hate another, but he cannot love a thing and hate it too. Those who object to the assertion that God loves all men agapically on the ground that God hates some men are therefore blameless on the score of logic. They correctly apprehend the contradictory nature of love and hate, and they rightly discern the incompatibility of these in reference to a single object.

But are they right on the question of fact? Is the material premise of their argument sound? Is it true that God hates some men? This is a substantive question and not a matter of mere logic.

Yet the material or substantive question is a question that cannot be answered without considering the logico-linguistic question of meaning. Words are one thing; meanings are another.

If we could go by the form of words alone the issue under consideration could be quickly settled; there could not possibly be a quarrel as to whether God hates some men. Does not the Bible clearly say in Malachi 1:3 and in Romans 9:13 that God hated Esau? And does it not say in Psalm 5:5 and in Psalm 11:5 that God hates evildoers and those that love violence? And are we not plainly told in Proverbs 6:10 that God hates a false witness and a man who sows discord? What more could a reasonable man possibly wish in order to be convinced that God does truly hate some men? How is it even remotely possible in the face of this clear evidence to entertain so much as the tiniest doubt about God's hating persons?

In answer to these questions it must be said once more: words are one thing; meanings are another. Are we, for example, really to hate our father and mother and wife and children? Of course not! Even apart from natural affection, our Lord's command to love our neighbor takes care of that. Yet did not our Savior say that unless we do hate these people we cannot be his disciples? We are driven, therefore, to inquire what in Luke 14:26 the word "hate" really *means*. That it does not, and that it can not, mean what we ordinarily mean by hate is plain. No Christian would dare venture out into the world and declare to the public, without elaborate explanations, that, whereas most men have affection for their mothers, Christians have none for theirs and in fact hate them in obedience to their Lord. Similarly, it is not evident from the mere appearance of the word "hate" in the Psalms and in the book of Malachi and in Paul's letter to the Romans that what is actually meant is hate in its spirituo-moral meaning.

We are obviously not contradicting the meaning of Luke 14:26 when we declare that one may not hate his wife and children. By the same token we are not contradicting the meaning of Romans 9:13 and similar passages when we declare that God hates no man. In order to understand these texts we must get beyond their words to their real meaning. As everyone knows, when our Lord said that in comparision with him our relatives should be hated, he meant to say that they should not be preferred to him, that they should not be allowed to usurp that central place in the Christian life which is reserved for Christ alone. It should be equally plain that the meaning of "not preferred" or, more concretely, "not elected"—which has nothing at all to do with hate in its moral and spiritual sense—is to be discovered in the word "hate" when predicated of God with reference to Esau. And as to evildoers, the divine "hate" that is said to go out to them represents no more (and no less) than the fact that God places them under judgment.

I regard Satan as a case apart, and I am not in this essay considering God's attitude toward him. But concerning men I feel bound as a Christian to declare that God hates no man.

Of course, by the word "hate" I do not refer to such things as wrath and judgment. These things the Scriptures veritably predicate of God as he encounters sinful and recalcitrant men; and it would not only be a misrepresentation of God's self-revelation, it would involve a significant impoverishment of theology to ignore his indignations and his punishments, or in any way to minimize them. Wrath is, moreover, basically compatible with love, as we directly know from our dealings with our children, with whom we can be indignant while cherishing them. The same is true of judgment. Judgment, even final judgment, provided respect is had to the reality of freedom, is quite compatible with love, as every earthly judge can testify. In any case, that the God of love is angry with the sinner, and that he visits on some of them the just rewards of their freely committed sin and resolute impenitence, is abundantly plain from Scripture and must be declared in any complete theology.

Let it be said, in addition to this, that when I deny that God hates any man, I do not wish to be understood as denying that God hates. I am not among those, if those there be, who regard hate as being something which cannot coexist with love. Precisely because God is Love, he hates all that which is not conducive to the realization of his loving purposes with men. He hates all evil, and every evil thing. There is in him a mighty and resounding No! which always since the Fall accompanies his Yes! His negations are, of course, reactive, as his affirmations are not; they are responses to what he does not centrally intend. But they are, relative to a sinful world in revolt against him, as real as his affirmations. There is hate in God as well as love.

What then is hate? This is the point at which a *definition* is needed. It could be said, indeed, that the whole issue before us is one of definition. If someone does not share my understanding of what hate is, then it is possible, even likely, that, whatever be the form of our words and assertions, we have no genuine quarrel. There are those who appear to equate hate with wrath, disapproval, judgment, and the like. I do not. I believe, on the testimony of Scripture, that God is indignant towards transgressors, that he does not approve of them in their concrete evilness, that he brings men under judgment, and that in his mysterious sovereignty he justifies and reclaims some men while others continue, without divine pardon and renewal, in their sin and awful estrangement. All this I believe, but I do not believe that God hates some men. Why not? Because of the very nature of hate. What, then, do I understand hate to be, that with the apostle John I should regard it as an unallowable attitude of persons toward persons?

Like Christian love, hate is more than a mere feeling; it is a settled disposition rooted in the center of one's being. It is the fixed, passionate, and gleeful determination to negate, to extirpate, to destroy. Its symbol is the No! Hate is "murderous." Its nature is to kill. The one who hates not only happens to kill; he avidly seeks to kill; and he delights in killing. He kills not reluctantly, but gladly. Hate wants ardently that its object be removed. It craves that its object be reduced from being to non-being, and be forever gone or rendered totally ineffectual.

If its object be not some thing, some power, some sentiment, or some opinion, but a personal being; and if the death or annihilation of this being is beyond its power to achieve; then what hate envisages is the pain, suffering, and deep unhappiness of its object. Hate is concerned to visit shame, embarrassment, and frustration on its object, not for the sake of something good beyond, but for the sake of this shame and embarrassment alone. It wants to induce absolute misery for misery's sake, and to fix it forever in its object. What it purposes, what it pursues as a final goal, what it centrally intends, is the utter hopelessness of the person against whom it is directed. It delights to involve him in the blackness of despair.

Can this disposition—which we call hate—in any sense be attributed to God? Yes, in one sense it can. God wants to destroy. He wants to destroy, negate, banish, and reduce to non-existence pride, injustice, cruelty, lying, in short, all wickedness and vice, all sin and evil. These things he hates with a native, essential, and everlasting hatred. He is against them absolutely. They elicit from him nothing but a determined and final No! It is because God hates these things with a resolute and enduring hatred that men can hope that virtue and righteousness shall at last prevail, and that the Kingdom of God will ultimately stand unthreatened and unvexed. Because at the center of the universe there is an almighty determination to fight and destroy sin, there is the possibility that men can escape sin's domination and enter into uninterrupted fellowship with God. Because God hates so passionately, therefore the purposes of love can be achieved and men can be made whole. And it is because God hates whatever is injurious to virtue, purity, and love, and hates these things with the full force and fervor of his being, that hate can in good men be a virtue. Men can in their hate be imitators of God, and indeed should be.

But can it be said that God hates *men?* Is the destruction of men the inner impulse of his being? Is it against men that the very structure of his Godhead is turned? Is his word against men an essential and unqualified No? Has he no desire to heal, to restore, to rescue them? Is he against them, as he is against evil, by the inner necessity of his eternal and exclusive divinity? Does he delight in men's destruction, and does he bend all his efforts to bring it about? Is he concerned to bring men unhappiness and to involve them in despair? Is an eternal determination to plunge them into blackness the motive and impulse of all his dealings with some men? Has he created some men for destruction and does he methodically plan their everlasting hurt?

To put these questions is to answer them. The Bible and the sensitized Christian conscience allow only one response, in this instance an indignant response: God hates no man! It is Satan and the demons who hate men, which is why the devil is called a murderer from the beginning. Hate of men is against the very law of love; hate of men is the very antithesis of the divine.

Let this then be said: God hates evil, but he does not hate the evil-doer. He hates wickedness, but not men, not even wicked men. Hate of evil is a divine necessity; hate of men is a divine impossibility.

There are honest and upright men who seem to find it hard to distinguish in this way between the sinner and the sin. God, they recognize, hates sin, but, they think, because sin exists nowhere but in the sinner, and because sin and the sinner are inextricably intertwined, God must hate the sinner when he hates the sin. For my own part, I find it hard to feel the force of this contention. I find it easy, even natural, to distinguish between the sinner and his sin.

It is true, of course, that an attack on sin is always painful to the sinner; at the very best it yields the pain incident to spiritual surgery. It is also true that when God in heaven, or a judge in our courts, punishes sin, he also punishes the sinner. In these respects the two cannot be severed. Nevertheless, it is not to cause pain that the divine surgeon cuts sin out of our life, but to produce spiritual health. And it is not hate of persons that causes the righteous judge, whether on earth or in heaven, to utter even the ultimate sentence of death upon the convicted criminal or the guilty sinner. It is only God's unmitigable hate of sin, and not his supposed hate of men, which explains his judicial sentences. Of course, the sinner who refuses to be separated from his sin does in the embrace of it experience, as it were "by accident," the divine No! which no sin can ever escape. But in this concretized No! God takes no delight, and this the sentenced man will eventually confess. He will know and proclaim that it was not from God's hate of him, but from his own intransigence, that his doom depended.

Those who have difficulty severing in thought the sin from the sinner, and consequently find it hard to take up different attitudes towards them, need only to contemplate themselves to find the way out of their trouble. All of us are sinners, even those of us who have by grace been incorporated into Christ. Now it is certain that God hates the sin that is in us, is out to destroy it, and is concerned to enlist us in the task of its destruction. But does he therefore hate us? Of course not! He loves us with an enduring and all-encompassing love. He loves us, but he hates our sin.

To appreciate the distinction we may also contemplate the crucifixion. Did the Father hate his only-begotten Son when he poured his hate on the sins the Savior bore, and when, in destroying sin, he plunged his Son-made-sin into hell? Of course not! Christ even on the cross remained the Father's well-beloved Son. But there is no finer symbol of God's hate for sin than the cross on which Christ died.

We may conclude, therefore, that it is both intelligible and proper to distinguish the sin from the sinner. And it is right and necessary that we take up contrary attitudes to each. The sin we must always hate, the sinner never. Remembering this we will be imitators of our heavenly Father who hates the transgression but never the transgressor.

But what then of Esau? Did God hate him? Not, surely, in any sense in which hatred is distinguishable from non-election and just judgment. In the passage in Malachi the primary reference is to two nations—Israel and Edom. The prophet shows how in the course of history the people of Israel have prospered under the blessing of God, and how, on the other hand, the evil fortunes of Edom have been in consonance with its national perverseness and misconduct. Back of these historical actualities of national prosperity and adversity lies the divine determination to convey his grace and revelation to the world through the agency of one people only, a people elected, not because it was any better suited to this purpose than any other, or more deserving of this honor, but simply because God freely chose it to be the eventual vehicle of his disclosures to all the world.

In order to grasp this grand divine design it is not necessary to ascribe to God a misanthropic disposition. This is to say that in order to account for election and reprobation it is not necessary, or even proper, to take recourse to the concept of hate-of-persons in God. God's procedures we may not be able wholly to understand, but then let us not pretend to understand them by referring them to a dispositional hate in God, the hate of persons which the love commandment of our Lord proscribed. If we do so refer it we are teetering on the brink of blasphemy. We are then planting at the center of the universe an arbitrary and essentially destructive negativity towards personal creatures which grossly contradicts the central affirmations of the Gospel.

As for me, I think that to ascribe hate of persons to God is to pervert the very thought of God. I believe that we are emphatically not permitted by the total witness of the Scriptures to say that God hates men in the ethico-spiritual meaning of that term. And I contend that every responsible theology is called upon to purge itself of the idea.